HG
4910
.R69
1982

Rosenberg, Jerry
Martin,

Inside the Wall
Street journal

Inside The Wall Street Journal

INSIDE
THE WALL STREET
JOURNAL

The History and the Power
of Dow Jones & Company
and America's
Most Influential Newspaper

JERRY M. ROSENBERG

MACMILLAN PUBLISHING CO., INC.
NEW YORK

COLLIER MACMILLAN PUBLISHERS
LONDON

Macmillan Publishing Co., Inc.
866 Third Avenue, New York, N.Y. 10022
Collier Macmillan Canada, Inc.

Library of Congress Cataloging in Publication Data

Rosenberg, Jerry Martin.
    Inside the Wall Street journal.

    Includes index.
        1. Dow, Jones & Co.—History.   2. Wall Street
journal—History.   I. Title.
    HG4910.R69   1982   071'.47'1   82-13005
    ISBN 0-02-604860-4

        10   9   8   7   6   5   4   3   2   1

Printed in the United States of America

Freedom for what.

Freedom to be.

Freedom to love.

FOR ELLEN

Contents

Contents

Acknowledgments

IN ADDITION TO the numerous *Journal* reporters, editors, technicians, bureau chiefs, and other Dow Jones staff that were interviewed, special gratitude is given to the following senior executives who spent time with me:

Warren H. Phillips, chairman of the board and chief executive officer, Dow Jones & Company

Ray Shaw, president and chief operating officer, Dow Jones & Company

Don Macdonald, vice chairman, Dow Jones & Company; and president, magazine and international group

Peter Kann, associate publisher, *The Wall Street Journal;* and vice president, Dow Jones & Company

Fred Taylor, executive editor, *The Wall Street Journal*

Robert Bartley, editor, *The Wall Street Journal*

Robert Bleiberg, editorial director-publisher, *Barron's;* and vice president/magazine group, Dow Jones & Company

Alan Abelson, editor, *Barron's*

Betty Duval, vice president/staff development, Dow Jones & Company

William Dunn, president, operating services group; president/publisher, information services group; and vice president/general manager, Dow Jones & Company

George Flynn, president/affiliated companies group; and senior vice president, Dow Jones & Company

Edward Cony, vice president/news, Dow Jones & Company

Paula Jameson, assistant to the chairman, Dow Jones & Company

Thanks also to Everett Groseclose (now managing editor of Dow Jones News Service), who was my initial contact at Dow Jones and who helped me launch this project several years ago when he was director of corporate affairs; and to Lawrence A. Armour, presently corporate relations director; both supplied me with encouragement, open contact with anyone I wished to see at Dow Jones, and a shared belief in the wonderful mesh that can exist between the free-enterprise system and the tenants of a free press.

Staff members at Dow Jones's library and archives unit were supportive and constantly seeking ways to assist me in studying old files.

Other than checking for accuracy of fact, no one at Dow Jones & Company influenced, controlled, or manipulated my writing. Together, members of the firm and I attempted, and I believe successfully, to demonstrate how the truth need not be embellished with mystique or disguise.

I appreciate the permission given to quote from the following sources:

Dow Jones & Company, from publications and releases.

William Kerby, *A Proud Profession,* Homewood, Ill.: Dow Jones-Irwin, 1981.

Winthrop and Frances Neilson, *What's News-Dow Jones,* Philadelphia: Chilton Book Company, 1973.

Kathryn L. Shadoan, Master's Thesis on *The Wall Street Journal,* (School of Journalism, The Pennsylvania State University, 1970).

Martin D. Sommerness, Master's Thesis on *The Traverse City Record-Eagle* and Ottaway Newspapers (School of Journalism, Michigan State University, 1979).

At Macmillan Publishing Company, editor-in-chief George Walsh gave this project unwavering support from beginning to end.

And at home, my love reaches out to Ellen, my wife, and to my daughters Lauren and Elizabeth, for their understanding, cooperation, and belief in my task.

—J.M.R.

Preface

SURVIVING TO THE AGE OF 100 is a corporate rarity. Starting at the bottom and climbing to the very top is also a remarkable achievement. The story of Dow Jones & Company, which has done both, has intrigued me and, I suspect, others for years.

The Wall Street Journal currently has the largest circulation of any newspaper in the United States. Many people consider it the nation's most influential newspaper as well. The corridors of power have long fascinated me, and after a brief meeting with a Dow Jones senior executive on a totally separate matter, I found myself stimulated by, and eventually deeply involved in, some interesting questions.

How did Dow Jones & Company come about? How has *The Wall Street Journal* earned the respect of so many readers? Does Dow Jones attempt to influence the destiny of corporations? Can a publishing empire with the power to affect the country's economy remain free of corruption and conflicts of interest? Most important, would the company live up to its acknowledged belief in a free press and permit an outsider to scrutinize its operations and delve into its seldom-seen archives?

An affirmative answer to that final question led me to undertake this task. I made the decision over a complimentary cup of coffee at 22 Cortlandt Street. I was sitting in the office of Everett Groseclose, who at that time was director of public affairs at Dow Jones. Groseclose looked me in the eye.

"Jerry," he said, "other than cooperating with you, we will provide no special treatment or favor, and likewise you will have no obligation to us."

That was my last free cup of coffee at Dow Jones. Ev and I shook hands, and I left for the library to commence my research.

Inside The Wall Street Journal

The New England Baptist and the Connecticut Yankee

Nobody who plants corn digs up the kernels in a day or two to see if the corn has sprouted, but in stocks most people want to open an account at noon and get their profit before night.

CHARLES HENRY DOW

DOW JONES & COMPANY is one of the few Wall Street partnerships that has not changed either its name or its aim in the past hundred years. Organized in 1882, the company is still dedicated to its original purpose: gathering news about and affecting the world of business and reporting that news in a lucid, lively, and levelheaded style.

Dow Jones's founders, Charles Dow and Edward Jones, were not the first to perceive the need for news about commercial matters. In 1795, three years after a group of merchants gathered under a buttonwood tree on Wall Street and agreed to form the New York Stock Exchange, James Oram, a printer with offices at 35 Liberty Street, launched the country's first financial publication.

Oram called his paper *The Shipping and Commercial List and New York Prices Current.* Its contents were as matter of fact as its title. There were no news stories, political commentaries, or social notes. The *List* was devoted exclusively to matters of commerce, finance, and shipping.

For over two decades shippers and traders depended on this unique paper for the latest and most reliable news about business in and around the port of New York. When James Oram died, the *Shipping and Commercial List* was taken over by the *Commercial Advertiser*. In 1827 both papers were absorbed by the *Journal of Commerce*, which is still published and has the distinction of being the oldest newspaper of its kind in the country.

With the opening of the Erie Canal in 1825, New York City was firmly established as the nation's financial capital. Wall Street and its environs rapidly became the headquarters for most of the country's banks, brokerage houses, insurance companies, and commodities exchanges. In time they were joined by steamship, railroad, and telegraph companies plus leading industrial corporations.

The need for business news was more acute than ever. What cargoes were arriving in the harbor? Where was the latest rail line going to be built? What new invention was about to become the cornerstone of a multimillion-dollar company?

Speculators paid dearly for the latest information, any piece of news that might guarantee a profit or protect against a loss. More often than not the man who could put over the best deal was the man who knew what was happening before his rivals did.

Unfortunately, there was little in the way of reliable reporting. Gossip and rumors abounded and stock market manipulators like Daniel Drew, Cornelius Vanderbilt, and Jay Gould found it easy to spread the kind of stories that would drive the market up or down as they saw fit.

The first person to see the need for a faster and more trustworthy means of delivering business news was John J. Kiernan. Born in Brooklyn, New York, in 1845, the son of Irish immigrants, Kiernan landed his first job—as a Western Union delivery boy—straight out of grammar school. He worked at an office near Wall Street, and it did not take him long to see what an important service he performed. Businessmen rushed to read the news dispatches he delivered to them. More than a few offered him money to tell them what else had come over the wires that might affect their companies.

Kiernan decided to capitalize on this passion for the latest information. Shortly after the Civil War the former messenger used his own savings and money borrowed from his family and friends to form the Kiernan News Agency with an office on Wall Street. He offered his subscribers up-to-the-minute news about shipping, foreign financial developments, and corporate earnings and dividends. The service cost $300 a month, and bulletins were delivered by messenger several times a day.

Until the Atlantic Cable was completed in 1866, Kiernan got his overseas news by rowing out to meet incoming vessels. He would buy any foreign newspapers they carried and pay sailors, and occasionally passengers, for last-minute information they might have picked up before sailing. Rushing back to his office, Kiernan would write up the news he had collected on short white sheets of paper and send his team of fleet-footed messenger boys dashing around Wall Street to drop off their bulletins at each subscriber's desk.

After 1867, when the first stock market ticker was invented by E. A. Calahan, more and more firms began installing telegraph tickers for the instant transmittal of stock prices. Julius Reuter had already discovered the virtues of sending news around the world by telegraph. Now John Kiernan decided to use the newly installed stock tickers for sending news around Wall Street. Subscribers who could not afford the latest technology, however, could still get their bulletins delivered by hand.

"Kiernan's Corner" on the southwest side of Wall and Broad Streets, site of the present New York Stock Exchange, was the city's center for financial news. It was hardly surprising that Charles Henry Dow, a New England journalist who had arrived in New York with the express purpose of becoming a financial reporter, eventually found work there.

Dow was born on November 5, 1851, on his family's farm in Sterling, Connecticut, a sleepy hollow of rolling hills in the eastern part of the state, not far from the Rhode Island line. Realizing early in life that he had no interest in tilling fields and tending cows, Dow decided on a career in journalism. He got his first job at the age of twenty-one on the *Springfield* (Mass.) *Daily Republican*. Although he had little in the way of education or training, the young man's

3

talents were soon recognized. He moved up the ladder from cub reporter and eventually found himself behind the editor's desk.

Charles Dow later emigrated from Massachusetts to Rhode Island and took a new job on the *Providence Journal*. It meant a return to reporting and at the same time a chance to write about a subject that was beginning to fascinate him—money.

The panic of 1873 had thrown the country into a severe depression; money was on everybody's mind. Debt-ridden farmers were beseeching Congress to increase the supply of greenbacks, as government notes were called, and give them full status as legal tender. Other groups were pushing for the unlimited coinage of silver, which had long been regarded as the currency of the common people. On Wall Street the nation's financial wizards remained convinced that gold was the only acceptable medium of exchange.

Charles Dow followed all of these arguments with avid interest and soon became an expert on money matters. His first inkling that his expertise could have important implications for his future came when he was assigned to accompany a group of eastern businessmen who were traveling to Leadville, Colorado, to get a firsthand look at its booming silver industry.

The tall, bearded young newsman spent a good part of the journey in the train's "hotel car." He conversed with and interviewed some of the country's most successful financiers, including Brayton Ives, president of the New York Stock Exchange, and Charles Dodge, the former Civil War general who was now a partner in a leading copper company, Phelps, Dodge.

If Dow was impressed with his traveling companions, they were equally impressed with him. Said one biographer, "The men of the Street soon learned that this reticent quiet-speaking man who took shorthand notes on his cuffs could be relied on to quote them absolutely and without embellishment and moreover, that it was safe to tell him news in confidence."

The lengthy trip gave Charles Dow ample time to compose a series of "letters" that were subsequently published in the *Providence Journal*. His first article vividly described the men on board the elegantly appointed train. Their combined wealth, he estimated, came to about

$90 million. Later columns discussed the profits and risks involved in the mining business and the gradual disappearance of individual mine owners as financiers underwrote shares in large mining consortiums.

When he arrived in Leadville, Dow turned his attention to the miners, prospectors, and speculators: He wrote about their backgrounds, how they lived, their capacity for hard work, their mining techniques, and the fiercely protective attitude they had toward their claims. The most important outcome of Charles Dow's trip to Colorado, however, was the realization that if he was going to write about business and finance, the best place to do it was in New York.

Arriving in the city in 1880, the twenty-nine-year-old reporter had no trouble finding a job on one of New York's many newspapers. He had even less trouble gaining access to the city's financial leaders. Many of them had already been won over by his honesty and his ability to keep a secret. Now, as he met with them in their boardrooms and private clubs, the Wall Streeters began to appreciate the fact that this solemn-faced, plainly dressed New Englander also had a keen mind and a quick sense of humor.

Charles Dow's stories soon caught the eye of John J. Kiernan, and he was invited to join what was now called the Kiernan Wall Street Financial News Bureau. A few months later Kiernan asked Dow to hire another reporter to work with him, and Dow got in touch with his friend, Edward Davis Jones.

A lanky redhead five years Dow's junior, Jones was born on October 7, 1856, in Worcester, Massachusetts. He went to Brown University but dropped out in the middle of his junior year to become a reporter for the *Providence Evening Press*. Although by the time of Dow's offer Jones had become editor of the more prestigious *Sunday Dispatch*, a job in New York sounded much more appealing, and he wired his acceptance.

The two proved to be an excellent team. Dow was an idea man, while Jones could dissect and analyze a financial report "with the speed and accuracy of a skilled surgeon." Equally important, they were determined to write about Wall Street without fear or favor. This in itself was rare. Dishonesty was rampant in the business-news

5

agencies of the day. It was not uncommon for a corporate president, anxious to raise the price of his company's stock, to bribe reporters to print imaginative distortions of its value.

Dow and Jones refused to participate in this practice, but they were in no position to stop it. It was an accepted way of life on Wall Street. Stock manipulation was all part of the "game," and the unprotected public was always the loser. Some years later, writing for his own paper on the ethics of investment, Dow said:

The manipulator is all-powerful for a time. He can mark prices up or down. He can mislead investors inducing them to buy when he wishes to sell, and to sell when he wishes to buy; but manipulation in a stock cannot be permanent and, in the end, the investor learns the approximate truth. His decision to keep his stock or sell it then makes a price independent of speculation and, in a large sense, indicative of true value.

The New England Baptist and the Connecticut Yankee, as Edward Jones called himself and his colleague, were convinced that there was plenty of room on Wall Street for another news bureau. John Kiernan's business was thriving despite the fact that its owner was too busy dabbling in Democratic politics to take an active role in its operations. If Kiernan, a newly elected state senator, could run a successful news bureau with his left hand, a pair of younger men, willing to work full time, could certainly make a go of one.

On that assumption the thirty-one-year-old Connecticut Yankee and the twenty-six-year-old New England Baptist said goodbye to "Kiernan's Corner" and in November, 1882, opened their own financial news agency, Dow, Jones & Company, Inc. (Some sixty-six years later the comma separating the two names mysteriously disappeared. It was in the copyright line of a new edition of *The Wall Street Journal* published in Dallas, Texas, on May 3, 1948, but by the time the Mid-West Edition came off the presses of the newly acquired *Chicago Journal of Commerce,* on January 2, 1951, the comma was no longer to be found.)

Dow, Jones's original headquarters were in a small back room in the basement of Henry Danielson's candy store on Wall Street. There was no direct entrance; employees and visitors alike had to march past a soda fountain and clamber down the stairs. The new company started with six employees, including its owners. The workload proved to be so heavy, however, that Dow and Jones recruited another Kiernan staffer, twenty-four-year-old Charles M. Bergstresser, to join them.

The stocky, imperturbable Pennsylvania Dutchman hesitated; if he was going to give up a secure job, he felt he should at least be given a share in the new venture. Dow and Jones agreed. After a brief trial period, in which he proved to be a valuable addition to the team, Bergstresser was asked to become a full-fledged partner.

His main talent was interviewing. Edward Jones once remarked that Bergstresser could not only make a wooden Indian talk, he could make him tell the truth. These persuasive powers were essential in the financial news world of that era. Many years later Oliver Gingold, a sixty-seven-year veteran of the company, recalled the difficulties of those early days:

Gathering news also was a bare-knuckle business in this era, long before SEC regulations had been dreamed of and before the advent of the public relations man and the press release handout. Many companies refused to issue annual reports even to their own stockholders, and stories on their financial condition had to be put together in bits and pieces from brokerage firm rumors and occasional comments from key officials.

But usually the news came much harder than that, with long hours of waiting outside directors' rooms or corporate offices for a chance at buttonholing an "insider."

Bergstresser's addition to the partnership seemed to require a change in the company's name. Dow, Jones and Bergstresser sounded clumsy, and another suggestion—shortening Bergstresser's name and calling themselves Berger, Dow and Jones—was vetoed by the new partner. Unable to settle the matter to everyone's satisfaction, the three men agreed to stick with their original title, Dow, Jones & Company.

The fledgling news agency scored its first beat with a story on the Standard Oil Trust, a company that was notorious for staying out of the public eye. Trustee Henry H. Rogers, testifying at a congressional hearing, characterized Standard Oil as having "two purposes; two principles: making money and making no noise about it." The nation's newspapers cooperated with that purpose by printing virtually nothing about the trust's operations. Only Dow, Jones persisted in trying to find out what John D. Rockefeller and his associates were up to.

The Wall Street of that era was a much smaller community than it is today. Inevitably Edward Jones encountered William Rockefeller, John D.'s brother and New York representative. To Jones's amazement the younger Rockefeller said to him, "Why don't you send your bulletins down to Eighteen Broadway?" (Standard Oil's headquarters at the time.) Even more amazing was Rockefeller's next question: "Would it mean anything in particular to you to get a little advance Standard Oil news?"

"Kind sir," beamed the delighted Jones, "would you dare to say that again?"

Rockefeller responded by handing Jones a memo. "Here's something I've jotted down for you, if you care to use it," he said. "Only, please, keep your authority confidential."

The memo contained the news that an increase in the capitalization of Standard Oil was being authorized. The new stock would be issued in stages as the company expanded. "You may say, too," Rockefeller added, "that Standard Oil dividends are to be raised to six dollars. Only mind you, keep your authority confidential."

Jones promptly reported, without naming his source, that William Rockefeller was en route to Cleveland to join his brother John at a company meeting where the new stock issue would be authorized and the increased dividend declared. By the end of the week Standard Oil stock had shot up 100 points! Investors had even more to cheer about when Standard Oil's dividend disbursements jumped from $3 million to $47 million a year.

In the beginning Dow, Jones's operations relied entirely on manpower. Reporters toured the brokerage houses, banks, and company offices, listening, asking questions, taking notes. Each man was accompanied by a messenger, who ran his stories back to the office. There they were dictated to a group of manifold writers, who copied them onto short white sheets of tissue paper separated by carbons. These men wrote with ivory-tipped styluses that could penetrate as many as twenty-four copies. The slips—or flimsies, as the copies were called—were then handed to waiting messengers, who dashed around Wall Street dropping them off to subscribers. The ritual was repeated at intervals throughout the day as new stories developed. No matter how much was going on, Dow, Jones could sum it all up in a sentence or two; a day's service rarely ran to more than 800 words.

A messenger who was paid $5 a week to deliver the Dow, Jones flimsies described the company's first office:

This was, indeed, a small dark room (lights on all day) without any attempt at painted walls or floor covering. On one side of the room a little space was walled off by a few plain pine boards which gave privacy of a sort to two desks—one for Mr. Dow and the other for his assistant, Mr. Henderson. Mr. Jones' desk was at the far end. If Mr. Bergstresser had a desk I never knew where it was. The center of the room was taken up by the copywriters. We boys—well, we were just there.

In November, 1883, Dow, Jones began issuing an afternoon summary of the news delivered during the day. The two-page *Customers' Afternoon Letter* soon had a circulation of over 1,000 and was regarded as a major source of news for financiers and investors.

Although the agency was thriving, its owners were aware that writing the flimsies by hand was slow and inefficient. On top of that they were not always easy to read. In 1885 the partners decided to invest in some modern equipment. The overworked manifold writers were relieved of their duties, and the bulletins were printed on a hand-operated press. The messenger service remained until halfway into the twentieth century. Dow, Jones did not completely discontinue its hand-delivered bulletins until 1948.

By 1889 Dow, Jones & Company had a staff of fifty people, including their first out-of-town reporter, Boston-based Clarence W. Barron. There was not enough room in the two-page, five-by-nine-inch *Customers' Afternoon Letter* to cover everything that was happening in financial circles. Bergstresser, Dow, and Jones agreed that it was time to think about publishing a regular newspaper. Jones, the expert on figures, did some homework and projected both the cost and the circulation possibilities; the prospects were promising. A Campbell flatbed press was purchased and put in place, and on the afternoon of July 8, 1889, *The Wall Street Journal* was born.

Priced at two cents per issue or $5 for a yearly subscription—with

9

a special discount for firms that bought multiple subscriptions—the four-page 15½-by-20¾-inch *Journal* was delivered by hand to a few hundred subscribers. It was printed every day except Sundays and Stock Exchange holidays and came off the press in the late afternoon. This enabled the paper to include a full roundup of the day's financial activities and allowed advertisers to purchase space on the day of publication.

Volume 1, No. 1, of *The Wall Street Journal* included financial briefs, a review of late news from other cities, a table of bond quotations, as well as ads for banks, brokerage houses, bond offerings, maps from Rand, McNally Company, and a notice of a Central Railroad dividend.

The paper also provided its readers with a no-nonsense statement of its policies:

Its object is to give fully and fairly the daily news attending the fluctuations in prices of stocks, bonds and some classes of commodities. It will aim steadily at being a paper of news and not a paper of opinions. It will give a good deal of news not found in other publications, and will present in its market article, its news, its tables and its advertisements a faithful picture of the rapidly shifting panorama of the Street.

The new publication was well received. No one commented on the typographical error that slipped through in the first edition. The story of the seventy-five-round prize fight between heavyweights Jake Kilrain and John L. Sullivan in Richburg, Mississippi, appeared under a Cincinnati dateline: "It is reported here from a reliable source that Sullivan and Kilrain were fighting at 11:45 a.m. The contest was a long one and Sullivan was having the best of it and was sure to won." . . . instead of *win*.

In its inaugural issue *The Wall Street Journal* boasted of its private wire to Boston, its telegraph connections to Washington, Philadelphia, and Chicago, and its correspondents in—among other places—Chicago, Washington, St. Louis, Pittsburgh, Philadelphia, Albany, Boston, and London. A month later the paper's man in Washington fell down on the job: "Our Washington correspondent sent us today that since October, 36 National Banks have gone into liquidation and two failed. We wired for the new banks authorized and he replies that there were 151.''

The second issue of *The Wall Street Journal* included statements from other New York papers about the newest member of their fraternity. Calling the paper unique because it intended to print news, not opinions, the *New York Star* also noted that it presented ''varied statistical and financial intelligence, not found in any other daily publication.''

None of the dailies pointed out that *The Wall Street Journal* was unique in another way. Its motto was ''The truth in its proper use,'' and its editors had vowed to ''print a daily journal that could not be controlled by any advertiser or combination of advertisers or by any speculative or promotion interests.''

Charles Dow repeatedly warned his reporters against trading slanted stories for inside tips on stocks. This type of mutual back scratching regularly lined the pockets of newsmen and financiers. Then as now, a story—even a hint or a rumor—could send the price of a stock up or down, and vast sums of money were made or lost accordingly.

Staffers were also admonished to steer clear of any offer to put stocks in their names at no cost or risk. The company followed the same policy. Occasionally a financial house would offer to purchase or carry securities for Dow, Jones without margin or personal risk. The partners' response was always: ''Thank you. We can invest our own money when we have any. When we elect to speculate we will do so at our own risk.''

With the appearance of *The Wall Street Journal,* the practice of printing fly-by-night news sheets touting dubious investments declined sharply. It was hard to conceal the fact that they were sponsored by self-interested speculators when the *Journal* could so promptly refute their lies.

As part of its crusade for honesty in business reporting, the paper never hesitated to publish the names of companies that were slow in providing information about their profits and losses. Because of its determination to win respect instead of friends, *The Wall Street Journal* had power that was acknowledged from the outset, and the paper was read with confidence as well as interest.

On April 18, 1893, Dow, Jones moved to a new address, the basement at 44 Broad Street. Formerly the headquarters of the Edison Company, the building had been the first in the city to be equipped with electrical wiring. Newspaper copy no longer had to be written and edited by the light of inadequate gaslamps. The new premises proved to be quite suitable.

In the early 1880s railroads were by far the nation's biggest growth industry. The thousands of miles of steel tracks that were being laid across the country served the double function of uniting east to west and robber baron to fortune. Most of the *Journal*'s columns carried stories about railroad rates, problems, earnings, and stock market fluctuations. The paper also printed the annual reports of every railroad in the country, and for a long while its list of active stocks included nothing but rail offerings.

Eventually other industries began to come to the fore, and the list of stocks was expanded to include a variety of companies. They were presented alphabetically in categories—rails, telegraph and telephone, land, banks, mines, U.S. government securities, coal and iron, gas and electric, city railways—with rails still far and away the largest group. At first the stock exchange listings gave only the last sale price, the date, and the last bid and asked figures. Later the list was broken into time periods with all the stock sold between 10 and 10:25 A.M., for example, presented together alphabetically.

In the top left-hand column on page one *The Wall Street Journal* printed two or three paragraphs about the market's developments and general financial movement. The top of the second column was reserved for "The Market Today," which described the condition of the market at the opening bell and followed its movements until closing at 3 P.M. Another column, "Comments on the Market," contained brief market opinions by brokerage house partners and analysts.

The rest of the paper was equally business-oriented. There was news about recent mergers, tariffs, dividends, strikes, and increases of capital stock, reports on the nation's supply of gold coins, silver dollars, gold and silver certificates, and banknotes. Nor were the commodities markets ignored. Crop damage, sugar and grain production, and the activity on the cotton, coffee and produce exchanges always merited attention.

Charles Dow's and Edward Jones's decision to start a financial newspaper could not have been better timed. Almost 100 years later, Robert Feemster, former chairman of Dow Jones's executive committee, pointed out:

The 1880–1890 decade was one of remarkable national growth and expansion. Population jumped from 50 million to almost 63 million, with more than 5 million immigrants. More railroad mileage was built, 69,000 miles, than in any ten years before or since. There was a vast growth in the packing industries and in the production of iron ore, wheat and flour, lumber, steel, and coal. In a reviving South, cotton and other manufacturers were developing on a tremendous scale.

The United States was taking its place among the great nations of the world, and *The Wall Street Journal* reflected and reported on its progress every step of the way.

Charles Dow, who wrote most of the *Journal*'s editorials, was also the initiator of the Dow Jones stock average. It appeared in 1884 and was primarily a transportation average, being made up of nine railroads, one steamship line, and Western Union.

The Dow Jones Industrial Average was compiled from the closing prices of a dozen leading stocks. The first one appeared on May 26, 1896. On January 2, 1897, Dow, Jones began publishing another average for railroad stocks.

A longtime student of financial cycles, Dow made observations that led him to devise an ingenious barometer of the relationship between stock market trends and general business activity. His concept, subsequently labeled the Dow theory, was based on the price action of the various stocks making up the Dow Jones averages. If the industrial average moved to a new high, or low, the rail average (known today as the transport index) would follow the same pattern, thereby confirming that a significant shift was taking place. Since these two averages represented two major areas of investment, it was Dow's belief that unless they both shifted in the same direction at the same time, the move could not be considered critical. It was probably reflecting some regional event and would have only a minor impact on the market.

Dow also theorized that both indexes hitting a new high signals investors that a bullish trend is under way. When both averages drop to a lower level, they are said to be "in gear," an indicator of a secondary bear market in a bull market or, in some cases, the beginning of a predominantly bear market.

Both the industrial average and the transport index have undergone major changes since the turn of the century. They no longer represent the same segments of the American economy that they once did. As a result the Dow theory has been largely replaced by new forecasting techniques. Nevertheless, a number of financial experts still swear by "the Dow," and some investment-advisory services continue to view it as an important indicator.

Ever since their inception the Dow Jones averages have been subject to misunderstanding, misuse, and misquotation. Charles Dow never intended his theory to be used as the sole predictor of economic ups and downs. He saw it simply as a tool, an instrument that could be helpful in providing sound guidance to an investor's overall business and market strategy.

In the partnership between Dow, Jones, and Bergstresser Charles Dow was the consistently dominant figure. He was the innovator, the decision-maker, the man whose suggestions were most likely to be put into action. Only one of those suggestions failed to work out as planned.

In 1892, not long after the company installed its first telephone, Dow insisted on hiring its first female employee. Her job: to answer the new phone and help with the typing. It was Dow's secret hope that a female presence in the office would cut down on his staff's swearing. However, although the woman fulfilled her responsibilities in every other respect, the level of unseemly language remained the same.

The telephone was not the only innovation in that decade. Some years earlier John Kiernan had started sending his financial news out on a telegraph ticker. Now a new type of ticker had been developed that could print out an entire page. In 1897 Dow, Jones leased some of the new page-printing tickers and formed the Dow, Jones News Service to oversee their operations.

The February 26, 1897, edition of the paper described the ticker as a cumbersome machine that had to be wound by hand every half-hour. This raised the ninety-six-pound weight, enclosed in a tall wooden case, that operated the machine. The machine stopped when the weight reached the bottom, so it was essential to wind it on schedule. This contraption was eventually replaced by a ticker that was powered by a four-volt battery. In 1926 a motor-driven model was installed.

In 1898 *The Wall Street Journal* published its first morning edition. By now the paper had extended its coverage well beyond financial news. Anything that could have the slightest impact on the economy was considered worthy of being included in its columns.

The paper was quick to report the sinking of the battleship *U.S.S. Maine* in the Havana, Cuba, harbor on February 16, 1898, and the disclosure of a letter from the Spanish minister in Washington to a Cuban friend attacking President William McKinley for "his weakness."

The *Journal*'s editors kept their eyes on the financial implications of the strain in U.S.-Spanish relations. In reporting the explosion on the *Maine,* which killed 200 of her 350-man crew, the *Journal* coolly noted: "The market responded closely to the news. It opened down on the catastrophe, rallied on belief that it was accidental and declined heavily on indications of intention and apprehension for the future."

When the Spanish-American War was finally declared on April 25, 1898, Joseph Pulitzer's *World* and William Randolph Hearst's *Journal* were quick to blast the enemy in their columns. *The Wall Street Journal* took no position, preferring to study the impact of hostilities on future securities prices. Trading, they felt, would be heavily influenced by the war's progress; in all likelihood the market would be bullish on U.S. victories and bearish on defeats.

Within days after the declaration of war, trading on the New York Stock Exchange plummeted from 145,162 shares traded on April 25 to 81,630 on the 27—"about the amount of business," the *Journal* noted, "which was being done per hour a few weeks ago." In the editors' opinion investors were reluctant to make commitments because the future was too uncertain.

Two columns of the paper were regularly devoted to war news. This often consisted of interviews with on-the-spot observers in Cuba or Manila. Unlike New York's other dailies, the *Journal* never resorted to patriotic rhetoric or anti-Spanish propaganda. Its mission, pursued to this day, was to inform, not to inflame.

As the new century approached, Charles Dow began an editorial column, "Review and Outlook," that is still a regular feature of the *Journal*. Another column, "Answers to Inquirers," responded to readers' questions about their personal investments. Typical queries included "Should I buy New York, Ontario and Western Railroad Company Mortgage Bonds?" and "In what should I invest with my limited amount of insurance money?"

In the summer of 1899 Edward Jones decided to retire from Dow, Jones. Bergstresser and Dow stayed on the job, working harder than ever to keep the company in the forefront of financial news reporting. It was about this time that Charles Dow produced some of his finest editorials, focusing in particular on the role and impact of the government on American business.

In the 1900 presidential campaign the *Journal* established a precedent for endorsing political candidates. It supported President William McKinley, criticizing his Democratic opponent, William Jennings Bryan, for his stand on free silver. Attempting as always to interpret events in the light of the market, Charles Dow and his editors spelled out what might happen if Bryan was elected:

In the first place, there would be a great shock to whoever has any property, outside of silver mines, all over the country. . . . The effect of locking up the available gold legal tenders and Treasury notes would be an immediate and enormous contraction of the currency, leading to the liquidation of loans, the withdrawal of deposits, and the enforced sale of securities. . . .

If Mr. Bryan should be elected president, he would wish to see his administration successful. If he should see it begin with panic and disaster over the country he would endeavor to allay alarm. But what could he do? . . . We think it fortunate that election probabilities continue to be strongly in favor of McKinley.

When the President was reelected Dow wrote in "Review and Outlook":

The election proved to be a victory for sound money, for business stability and for the policy of expansion. There are those who will regard its magnitude as further evidence of what has seemed to be a leading and protecting power in the affairs of this country in the last few years. Others will regard it as further proof of the sober sense of the common people.

. . . In short, those measures which are on the whole sound and wise will prevail and . . . the country will not suffer the comprehensive evils embraced in the term "Bryanism."

As preparations were under way for McKinley's inauguration in Washington, there was an interesting turn of events on Wall Street. J. P. Morgan and Andrew Carnegie issued an announcement to the stockholders of seven of the nation's steel firms that the companies would be merged into the United States Steel Corporation.

Charles Dow found little cause for alarm in the steel trust, which would also create the first billion-dollar corporation in the world. The *Journal* informed its readers that Carnegie, had he chosen to, could have started a steel price war at little risk to himself. The merger, which would eliminate competition and result in uniform prices, would cause fewer disruptions in the national economy.

Several days prior to the formal public announcement of the new company Dow discovered that its stock had been inflated by some clever manipulations of J. P. Morgan. As underwriter for the issue Morgan had watered the stock. He had ordered the printing of certificates bearing par value of more than $1 billion. A congressional investigation later revealed that this was $726,846,000 above the visible property value of the newly established steel firm.

As one writer put it, Morgan "had far outdone all the other promoters in capitalizing the future." His firm put up $25 million to finance the merger and realized a commission of 50 percent. In addition to walking off with a tremendous hunk of U.S. Steel's stock, the financier earned a profit of $12 million for J. P. Morgan and Company.

It is more than probable that Dow did not know the full scope of Morgan's stock watering when he wrote on February 26, 1901:

We regard it as unfortunate that the new steel company should have carried the tendency toward over-capitalization further . . . [as] consumers of iron and steel are to be asked to pay dividends on watered stock and this will have its effect, first in promoting competition, and second in the agitation of tariff legislation intended to deprive the United States Steel Company of protection as far as other countries are concerned.

No mention was made of the significant losses to investors in U.S. Steel. Moreover, the newspaper seemed content to take the word of the trust's creators, who assured lawmakers, worried about violations of the antitrust act, that "the new company will be an aggregation in name more than in fact."

It might be argued that Charles Dow had failed as a responsible journalist and that *The Wall Street Journal* had compromised its pledge to protect the public. The *Journal,* however, had always been a firm supporter of big business. Condemning corporate expansion would have been a contradiction of its basic philosophy and purpose. Dow himself felt that his position was vindicated by the fact that the revelation of J. P. Morgan's deception produced no outpouring of public mistrust and no wide-scale demands for government regulation of industry.

Dow's tender handling of J. P. Morgan is in sharp contrast to his negative statements about Theodore Roosevelt. The entire country was shaken by the shooting of President William McKinley on September 6, 1901. The *Journal* abandoned its usual one-column headlines for a banner announcing "Attempt to Kill the President." When McKinley died on September 14, businessmen were not only distressed at the loss of a staunch ally, they were concerned about what his young and impulsive successor might do.

There seemed little question that Roosevelt would be far less supportive of big business. In fact, the *Journal* quoted the Republican boss Mark Hanna, a Wall Street favorite, as saying, "I told William McKinley it was a mistake to nominate that wild man. . . . now look, that damned cowboy is President of the United States!"

Charles Dow lost no time in contacting the new President's advisors to find out what was happening in Washington. The advisors reported that they had urged Roosevelt not to do anything that might disturb the equilibrium of Wall Street. The President, already aware that his arrival in the White House could cause a slump in the stock market, heeded their advice and was extremely cautious for several months. Dow assured business leaders that the new President could be trusted, and for a while, at least, calm and stability returned to Wall Street.

Charles Dow's health was beginning to fail. He no longer felt up to the fast pace of Wall Street. Bergstresser, too, was ready to retire from the race. In February, 1902, the partners sold their shares of Dow, Jones & Company to Clarance W. Barron, an old friend and associate who had long been their Boston correspondent.

Dow wrote his final column and left the firm in April. He died the following December at the age of fifty-two. Edward Jones outlived him by eighteen years, dying of a cerebral hemorrhage at his New York residence on February 16, 1920. The third member of the triumvirate, Charles Bergstresser, died three years later.

Charles Dow had a keen eye for spotting events that would affect the financial scene. He also had a special flair for writing about the stock market. Here's how he described its workings:

In the game called the tug-of-war a score of men, an equal number being at each end of the rope, pull against each other to see which party is stronger. In the game called stock-market speculation, the speculators are at liberty to take sides, and the side which they join invariably wins because in stock-exchange parlance "everybody is stronger than anybody." When everybody takes hold on the bull side, the market goes up very easily, but, as it goes up, one after the other lets go until the advance halts. Meantime, those who have let go sometimes go around and take hold on the other side.

Dow was essentially a journalist who happened to specialize in business news. He had a gift for writing simply and still communicating both the essence and the excitement of his material. His flowing style made the most complex financial matters easier to comprehend. A later editor of *The Wall Street Journal,* Vermont Royster, said of his predecessor:

Dow himself always believed, and wrote, that business was something more than balance sheets and ticker tape and that information about it was not the private province of brokers and tycoons. In writing even about high finance Dow used homely analogy and the language of everyday life, although in his day *The Wall Street Journal* did not reach a wide audience. Neither as a writer nor as a person did he ever lose touch with Main Street.

As proof that he did not mindlessly reflect the views of big business, Charles Dow supported the anthracite coal strike of 1902. He wrote indignantly of the abuses long prevalent in the coal industry and sympathized with the miners' fight.

Shortly after Dow's death three representatives of the miners' union appeared at 44 Broad Street. They wanted the *Journal* to provide them with facts and figures to support the union's claims in a forthcoming inquiry by the anthracite coal commission. This acknowledgment by labor of the accuracy and reliability of *The Wall Street Journal* prompted its new editor, Thomas F. Woodlock, to declare, "No higher compliment was ever paid to the paper than was paid on that occasion."

CHAPTER

2

The Barron Years

The Wall Street Journal must stand for the best that is in Wall Street and reflect that which is best in United States finance.
Its motto is "The Truth in its proper use."

"My Creed," CLARENCE W. BARRON

CLARENCE WALKER BARRON bought Dow, Jones & Company in February, 1902. For the next twenty-six years he was the dynamic force in the life of the *The Wall Street Journal*.

One of Barron's step-granddaughters described him as "a Santa Claus-like figure." Indeed he must have been. Five feet, six inches tall, he weighed about 300 pounds and sported a patriarchal white beard. Instead of a red suit, however, he favored braid-edged morning coats, white-piped waistcoats, and jaunty silk ties.

In the autobiography he started at the age of seventy-two Barron described his early years:

I was born July 2, 1855 (the oldest of 13 children) in the north end of Boston on Cross Street, in a stone house whose front was covered with a green vine growing from the smallest kind of a front garden, and whose rear was marked by a spacious yard surrounded, as I remember, by a low structure topped by terraces, for clothes line work, and largely occupied by several large cats. . . .

Young Clarence attended Boston's English High School, which, coincidentally, was J. P. Morgan's alma mater. When Barron graduated (nineteen years after Morgan) in 1873, he had long since decided on his future career. "I was not fifteen years of age before I determined I would be a newspaperman," he wrote. There was no question of his talent; he had won two prizes for journalistic compositions while still in school. He had also taught himself stenography. In addition to learning the standard symbols he invented a few of his own that he continued to use throughout his life:

I believe it is a great mistake to give the shorthand field over to the girls. I think it is the best training for young men in practical life, far ahead of Greek or Latin. . . . I have followed the practice in my different offices of employing the best stenographers available and developing them into newspapermen. Many of them have graduated or fallen into banking fields and the way of wealth.

Barron's stenographic skills won him a job at the *Boston Daily News*. He stayed longed enough to find out how a newspaper was run. Then he was off knocking on the door of the *Boston Evening Transcript*, telling its editors how he could start a financial page by covering the news from State Street, Boston's financial hub. The editors liked his idea and hired him to go ahead and try it.

"How did I get into the financial field?" Barron asked himself in a self-interview some years later.

I used to write up commercial features for *The Transcript*, finding my own problem and solving it. . . . One day I reported to my superiors that it was absurd to give the quotations of Boston securities and every transaction, yet never give the news under the fluctuations; that I believed there was a news item every day in State Street that might be picked up. I was asked to annex that to my daily duties. I said, "Give me my whole time." My request was granted.

Barron soon learned everything there was to know about the history and operations of the country's leading corporations. Many of them had their roots in New England. He was at the birth of the American Telephone and Telegraph Company and wrote up the first Telephone Exchange in Boston; it was used by merchants to notify a local express company when to call for goods. The president of the telephone company later declared that Clarence Barron understood its operations better than anyone on the board of directors.

Barron was also in on the beginnings of the General Electric Company. He witnessed the inauguration of electrically propelled street cars in Boston and persuaded the company to let him publish the first report of the costs of operating the horseless trolleys.

Railroads were another area of interest. The young reporter followed all the steps in the expansion of both the Chicago, Burlington and Quincy and the Atchison, Topeka and Santa Fe lines and held the confidence of their directors and managers. He also became a close friend of the pioneer rail builder, Thomas Nickerson, visiting him at his estate in Lakewood, New Jersey, and listening by the hour as Nickerson described his role in constructing the longest and most successful transportation system in the United States.

Clarence Barron's insistence on digging out all the facts in every story soon got him into trouble. In the course of reporting on the activities of the Northern Pacific Railroad president, Henry Villard, he made some harsh comments. Several of the tycoon's relatives protested to the *Transcript*'s publisher, and Barron was fired. Undaunted, he decided to become a publisher himself.

Borrowing an idea that was new to Boston but was already being practiced successfully by Dow, Jones in New York, Barron organized the Boston News Bureau. He hired a few messenger boys, found a printer with a small press, and immediately realized that he had stumbled on a much-needed service. Barron charged his clients a dollar a day for information that was distributed on flimsies similar to those used by Dow, Jones & Company. Working from 8:00 A.M. to 8:00 P.M. he issued twenty-five to thirty bulletins a day.

Soon after the opening of the Boston News Bureau Charles Dow and Edward Jones learned of its existence and enlisted its founder to become their Boston correspondent. The job consisted of telegraphing regular reports to New York of everything that was happening on State Street.

Dow, Jones's newly established link between two of the country's key financial centers was almost buried by the blizzard of 1888. Clarence Barron saved the day and proved his ingenuity by forming what was later called the Great Triangle. The storm had knocked down the wires between Boston and New York. Aware that his reputation for delivering up-to-the-minute news was in jeopardy, Barron came up with a simple but effective solution. The cables between Boston and London and New York and London were still in operation, so he had the leading stock prices on the New York Exchange cabled to London and from there to Boston. Important news and prices on the Boston Exchange were sent via the same route in reverse.

With a steadily growing list of subscribers and an unquestioned reputation for reliability, Barron felt that the time had come to imitate Dow, Jones's example and publish a newspaper. His, like theirs, was made up of the day's bulletins run off on one large sheet. In 1896 he organized a similar operation in another financial center, Philadelphia.

With two news bureaus successfully launched Clarence Barron began looking for new fields to conquer. When Charles Dow and Charles Bergstresser let it be known that they were ready to sell Dow, Jones & Company, Barron was the most likely buyer. He raised some of the money within his own family, but the major part of the purchase price was paid in notes.

Clarence Barron was forty-six years old when he arrived in New York to take over Dow, Jones. He was also a newlywed, having been married two years before to Jessie M. Waldron, a widow with two daughters.

Barron had all sorts of plans for *The Wall Street Journal*. One of his first steps was to set up a training program for novice reporters, another was to establish ties with his Boston and Philadelphia News Bureaus. The *Journal* thus became the center of a small news network.

Unlike most publishers of his day Barron was less interested in expanding circulation than in maintaining a quality list of subscribers. He would have preferred to have the *Journal*'s readership remain at 10,000 with a sophisticated audience, but the potential for a business publication was far greater than he had anticipated. Within eight years after purchasing the newspaper Barron saw its circulation more than double—from 7,000 in 1902 to 18,750 in 1910.

Clarence Barron was no easy boss. It was part of his policy to "ride" his men until they were broken in to suit him. He considered this his duty toward them as well as toward his publishing properties and the public they served.

24

Barron was forever coming up with new ideas, new stories, new approaches. Many of them were spelled out in the hundreds of notes he dashed off daily to his staff, messages that were as likely to be dictated from a men's room or the bathtub as from behind his desk. Barron managed to work even when he was, theoretically, playing. An avid swimmer, he regularly arrived at the beach with a pair of secretaries in tow. "When he dove into the water," his step-granddaughter recalled, "it was rather like a pelican. His form was great, but the splash was immense."

More often Barron could be found standing upright in the water, his chest in full view, thanks to his "great tummy—dictating to his two male secretaries standing on the float."

Not two, but three, secretaries used to accompany Barron on his frequent trips to Europe. In Paris he once sat through a performance of the Folies Bergère dictating to the trio in strict rotation and paying not the slightest attention to the show. Said writer Lucius Beebe, "The management was torn between admiration and outrage."

Idiosyncrasies aside, Barron would concentrate his energies on money matters. The first major challenge came in 1901 when a fierce contest erupted between financier J. P. Morgan and railroad magnate E. H. Harriman for control of the Northern Pacific Railroad. The demand for common stock in the railroad sent its price soaring to $1,000 a share. A stock market panic ensued, and hundreds of small investors, unable to cover their purchases, were ruined. Many people blamed Morgan for their losses and for the panic's disastrous impact on the nation's economy; but when a reporter asked the financier if some statement was not due from him, Morgan's terse reply was, "I owe the public nothing."

Morgan and Harriman subsequently settled their differences by joining another Harriman rival, James J. Hill, in forming the Northern Securities Corporation, a holding company designed to prevent railroad competition.

In February, 1902, the very month in which Clarence Barron bought Dow, Jones & Company, President Theodore Roosevelt startled Wall Street by instructing his attorney general to file a suit for the dissolution of the Northern Securities Company under the Sherman Antitrust Act. The President's action came as a complete surprise. He did it without consulting his advisors, without fanfare or advance notice to the press. The current of fear that had run through Wall Street after McKinley's death and Roosevelt's accession to the presidency resurged.

Naturally, *The Wall Street Journal* covered Roosevelt's first "trust-busting" effort and the alarm it brought to the Street. The President had explained his action by saying that the Northern Securities Company posed a threat to the principle of free competition, endangering not only industry but the federal government as well. As an article in the *Journal* noted, the President was determined to show that Washington, not Wall Street, ran the country.

The *Journal* generally supported Roosevelt's actions against the trusts, acknowledging that it was his duty to enforce the nation's laws. With characteristic frankness the *Journal* also pointed out that part of Wall Street's distress at the President's plans to prosecute the trusts stemmed from the fact that big business was accustomed to having things its own way. The paper cautioned its readers that Wall Street "enjoys no prerogative of infallibility so far as the country is concerned even in matters of financial faith or economic moral."

Still the *Journal* refused to join Roosevelt and his allies in condemning the trusts. It struck the editors as naive to think that company directors would deliberately keep their prices low to preclude competition or that everyone, including the workingman, would gain from such a move. The paper also expressed the belief that "good" trusts would drive out bad ones. Editor Thomas Woodlock rather neatly split the profit issue from the campaign against the trusts:

Whether people make large fortunes out of their operation or whether they do not is a question that does not touch the main issue. . . . A thing that many people seem to forget is that the public's direct interest in the trust question centers in the terms upon which the trust product is sold. It is unfortunate that in the minds of most people the "anti-trust" question is confused with a general proposition that the possession of a million dollars is a criminal act.

Outside of Wall Street there were many who felt that the government should impose even tighter restrictions on big business. The *Journal* was firmly opposed to this idea. Fearful that tough antitrust legislation "which aimed at accomplishing too much would fail of its object and accomplish nothing," Woodlock insisted that "a plain measure of 'publicity' applied to corporations engaged in interstate commerce business [is] all the anti-trust legislation that [is] needed or desirable."

The *Journal* continued to see that Wall Street's financial maneuverings were discovered and reported on promptly. It was not an easy job. Standard Oil had become less secretive, and thanks to some prodding from Dow, Jones financiers like Harriman, Morgan, and Hill occasionally made themselves available for interviews with reporters. Generally speaking, however, the Wall Street moguls preferred to keep their activities out of the news. They avoided reporters' questions and provided as little information as possible on their various interests.

Unwilling to accept this state of affairs, Woodlock instructed his reporters to find out what was happening on their own. On August 11, 1902, the *Journal* explained:

From time to time *The Wall Street Journal* has published details of the transaction by which Morgan and Company have secured Louisville and Nashville stock by purchase and on options. In the absence of an official statement giving full details by those in interest, the news must be obtained by piecemeal from those who knew the details.

Few of the industrialists and financiers of that era were guilty of criminal acts, but there is little doubt that ethical wrongs were committed against millions of citizens. The public paid, either through higher prices or watered stock purchases or horrible working conditions, for the empires that were built by the men Roosevelt had denounced as "malefactors of great wealth."

The manipulations of J. P. Morgan, E. H. Harriman, and James J. Hill were regarded in money circles as sound—in fact, smart—business practices. Along with such robber barons as Andrew Carnegie and John D. Rockefeller, they forced out their competitors or bought them up, often pressing them into deals with tactics that smacked of Mafia-like persuasion, without the murders and the torture. The power of the magnates was boundless. This was made clear by an apologist for J. P. Morgan, who wrote, "It will be seen that Mr. Morgan is not only the financial ruler by virtue of what he already has—he is a monarch who can extend his kingdom to suit his ambition or need.''

The power of Morgan and his fellow moguls was considerably diminished on March 15, 1904, when the U.S. Supreme Court reversed an 1895 ruling that had curtailed the effectiveness of the Sherman Antitrust Act. By a five-to-four decision the justices ordered the dissolution of the Northern Securities Corporation for violation of the long-ignored law.

In the wake of the decision the financial community braced itself for further blows. While there were other suits, none attracted as much attention as the Northern Securities case, and there were no wholesale prosecutions. Overall the effect of the ruling was surprisingly mild; the interested parties restructured the railroad organization into a legal "community of interest" and continued to accomplish their aims. Several critics maintained that Roosevelt's battle against the trusts was not the all-out war he proclaimed it to be; the President countered by insisting that "corporation cunning has developed faster than the laws of the nation and state.''

The Supreme Court ruling against the Northern Securities Company was applauded by *The Wall Street Journal,* which said, "A time had come to put a stop to further attempts to evade the law." Although the paper drew a distinction between James J. Hill (who, as they saw it, was only furthering development of the Northwest) and other speculators, they made some dire predictions of what would have happened if the Hill-Morgan-Harriman plan had not been declared illegal: ". . . there would have been nothing to prevent its extension so as to include all the railroads of the United States and that would have been the first step toward government ownership and perhaps industrial socialism.''

No mention was made of the possibility of price-fixing or of the emergence of an unscrupulous corporate monopoly that could have put the nation at its mercy. Even when the *Journal* called on Congress to define the line between the legitimate and illegitimate suppression of competition and to pass a law banning the latter, the editors were not very concerned about eliminating the threat of manipulation and monopoly. Their overriding fear was that the government could take over industries.

Two days after the Northern Securities Company decision Clarence Barron reprinted some information from John Moody's *The Truth About the Trusts*. Moody estimated that $20 billion (or one-fifth of the nation's total wealth) was controlled by trusts. He listed industrial, franchise, and transportation trusts and cited seven that controlled 1,528 plants with an aggregate capitalization of $2.6 billion.

In another edition the *Journal* reprinted two large diagrams from Moody's book tracing the "Morgan-Rockefeller Family Tree" and the "Greater New York Public Utility Family Tree," indicating all the points at which their interests converged.

Moody's revelation horrified a large segment of the American public, but such power in a few hands did not dismay *The Wall Street Journal*. On the contrary, in the paper's opinion immense power contributed "to the stability and the power of American commerce." The editors saw "combination" as "another name for cooperation," though they were quick to stress that trusts should not violate people's liberties, evade the law, corrupt politics, destroy competition, or oppress the public by excessive rates and prices. There was hardly a trust that was not guilty of at least one of these charges, but the Northern Securities decision would serve as a warning to the others; the newspaper felt that the public would be "content for a while with the object lesson of their power."

In Clarence Barron's view unlimited competition was too often wasteful and unnecessary. His paper did not endorse 100-percent monopoly, but it was more than tolerant of the 60- or 70-percent monopoly that can be just as effective when it comes to cutting prices, lowering production costs, and squeezing out competitors through quiet, efficient financial attrition. To Clarence Barron reducing competition was analogous to states combining into a country to hold their own against other countries of the world.

Although Theodore Roosevelt generally received the credit (or, in some circles, the blame) for "trust-busting," the major part of the battle fell to his successor, President William Howard Taft. Roosevelt, said one historian, "stimulated and provoked, but the decisive measures of law, sweeping reforms from which he himself shrank, were to be enacted by others, thanks to the momentum he had helped to generate."

29

Roosevelt's administration saw suits filed against the packing and tobacco behemoths, but it was under Taft that suits against Standard Oil and American Tobacco resulted in the dissolution of those two large trusts; and the Clayton Act (which strengthened the Sherman Act) became law under Democrat Woodrow Wilson. Roosevelt "started only twenty-five proceedings leading to indictments under the Sherman Act, while Taft began forty-five. The significance of Roosevelt's corporation activities lay in what he said rather than what he did."

The first major financial calamity Barron faced after taking over *The Wall Street Journal* was the so-called Knickerbocker Trust panic of 1907. Barron began to suspect that the economy was in for some heavy weather when the Dow Jones averages, which had hovered around the mid-thirties in 1904, started climbing.

During this period of prosperity everyone was rushing to buy, borrow, or build. As a result there were severe strains in credit lines. Bank reserves and gold holdings started to dry up. Even when financial institutions raised their interest rates in an effort to curtail borrowing, the situation did not improve.

As early as January, 1906, Clarence Barron tried using his influence to force Wall Streeters to recognize what they were doing. The *Journal* quoted some remarks made by Jacob Schiff, head of Kuhn, Loeb and Company, to a group of bankers. "If the currency conditions of the country are not changed materially," Schiff had warned, "you will have such a panic in this country as will make all previous panics look like child's play."

Barron was sharply criticized for releasing Schiff's statement. Worse yet, the financier's admonition fell on deaf ears.

Money remained tight. A real estate boom put a further drain on credit, and the San Francisco earthquake in April, 1906, wreaked havoc of a different sort back east. Most of the claims for the damage were paid by New York insurance firms, which were then left with a great deal less cash to invest. Ironically, even after drawing $225 million from New York insurance companies, the city of San Francisco was unable to float a loan in New York.

In 1907, after the Dow Jones averages shot up to 75, the bottom began to drop out of the financial market. In October the Otto Heinze investment company failed, taking the Mercantile National Bank down with it. This led to rumors that the Knickerbocker Trust Company was about to go under, and on the morning of October 22 hundreds of nervous depositors queued up to withdraw their money.

The bank had opened its doors that morning with $8 million on hand. By midday the money was all gone. The Knickerbocker Trust Company was forced to suspend payments. *The Wall Street Journal*'s report of the incident provided details on what happened next:

A run was started in the Trust Company of America and its Colonial branch as soon as the doors opened, and continued up to the close of business. All depositors requesting their money were paid in full, and even after closing hours, the bank continued its payments to about three hundred depositors in line who were fortunate enough to be in the building when the doors were closed at the regular hour. This was regarded as one bright spot in the day's developments.

In reality the Knickerbocker Trust Company had been solvent, but the run had used up all of its available capital. The bank had to call on the New York Clearing House to step in with additional funds.

The *Journal* tried to calm the situation. Praising the Clearing House because it had "demonstrated (again) its power to deal with a grave situation effectively . . ." the paper proclaimed, "Now this is the best kind of business government, a government of business by business men without interference by the political authorities. This is the ideal."

The worst appeared to be over, but this was far from the case. The next morning *The Wall Street Journal* gave its readers the bad news all at once in its lead paragraph:

The temporary suspension of payments to depositors by the Knickerbocker Trust Company as a result of a run on the corporation, which followed the announcement that the National Bank of Commerce had declined to clear for it; a jump in the call money rates to 70 percent; stock demoralization which carried the prices of stock down to the lowest level since December, 1900; the failure of Mayer and Company, a Stock Exchange house, and disturbing rumors bearing upon the standing of other institutions, were the developments Tuesday which shook Wall Street to its foundations.

In the wake of these traumatic developments, call money (currency lent by banks for which payment can be demanded at any time) on the New York Stock Exchange shot from the previously mentioned high of 70 percent to a record 96 percent. Stocks fell to new lows, exchanges across the country closed, and banks sought in vain to assure depositors of their soundness. Money became so scarce that the vaunted New York Clearing House advertised its desperate state by issuing $100 million in certificates rather than currency.

Secretary of the Treasury George Cortelyou did what he could to stem the tide. The Treasury in Washington rushed $10 million to the Sub-Treasury in New York for use in paying depositors. The *Journal* sounded a hopeful note: "At noon Secretary Cortelyou (Treasury Department) said that the situation was much clearer. A large amount of United States deposits was placed in banks during the day and Secretary Cortelyou has promised to remain in New York to do all in his power to strengthen public confidence."

As it turned out, another $15 million in government money had to be rushed to the rescue of New York's banks. It soon became obvious that even this stupendous amount would not be enough. It was then that the mighty J. P. Morgan stepped into the picture. His giant U.S. Steel Corporation offered to buy the Tennessee Coal and Iron Company from the tottering Moore and Schley investment house to keep it solvent.

The aging financier subsequently poured millions of dollars into the Trust Company of America and the Lincoln Trust, saving them from collapse. Morgan eventually wound up matching the U.S. Treasury's $25 million loan with $25 million of his own. (This method of mobilizing bank reserves was the forerunner of the Federal Reserve System.)

Although J. P. Morgan saved the country's financial neck, it was, as usual, not without benefit to himself. As the *Journal* pointed out, "Morgan could have easily loaned Moore and Schley enough money to save the firm; a short term transfer of $5 million would have done it. But this would not have gained the Tennessee Coal and Iron shares for U.S. Steel."

Elsewhere there was speculation that Morgan's true motive for helping to curb the panic was to get President Theodore Roosevelt to back off from any trust-busting efforts against Morgan's pride and joy, U.S. Steel.

Although the *Journal* was not above questioning some of Morgan's motives, its attitude on the whole was decidedly uncritical. In assessing the impact of the panic the paper declared:

Scarcely less impressive than this was the spectacle of J. Pierpont Morgan in his office directly opposite from the Sub-Treasury representing the power of private capital directed for the relief of the financial situation. Mr. Morgan represented confidence. It is significant how in this time of strain Wall Street has turned to Mr. Morgan as to the only individual in private life who seemed to have the prestige and the ability to lead it out of danger, and in this connection it is noteworthy that Mr. Morgan has come out of the stress and storm of the past two years without any cloud upon his fame as a financial leader.

The following day the *Journal* reflected on the events flowing from the panic, and Morgan was again hailed as a hero.

That the situation has been saved thus far is, as everyone knows, due first to the support of the United States Treasury, and second to the heroic leadership of Mr. Morgan. Mr. Morgan has shown his old-time courage and aggressiveness. He has not hesitated to call the other members of the financial group to order, he has sternly repressed their animosities and differences and compelled them to come together for mutual protection.

The *Journal* was much less kind to President Theodore Roosevelt. His reaction to the crisis was to lash out at the "ruthless and determined men" whom he considered responsible for it. The *Journal* accused the President of "getting hysterical" instead of exerting his leadership and allaying the nation's fears.

In the aftermath of the Panic of 1907 Clarence Barron used the editorial pages of the *Journal* to urge a number of banking and currency reforms. They included the creation of an association of New York banks and trust companies that would provide members with regulations, safeguards, and cash reserves against panics; issuance of bank statements by all institutions to provide out-of-town businessmen and investors with accurate information; removal of the call money market from the stock exchange, or regulation of rates; and abolition of financial chains of banks owning other banks.

Since J. P. Morgan had "stood between the business of the country and disaster," the *Journal* felt that he should be called on to lead the reform movement. This was typical of the *Journal*'s attitude toward the problem. It did not deny that reform was needed, but it believed that Wall Street should put its own house in order. J. P. Morgan—not Theodore Roosevelt, not George Cortelyou, not Congress—was the man to do the job.

In 1910, the General Electric Company, which had succeeded the Edison Company, moved out of 44 Broad Street. The building was scheduled to be sold, and there was a good chance that its new owners would evict Dow, Jones.

Clarence Barron was perturbed at the prospect. It was crucial for the company to have its printing and electrical facilities in the heart of Wall Street. To be of any value, financial news had to be gathered and transmitted without delay. Barron soon concluded that the only thing to do was to buy the building himself.

The cost of acquiring, maintaining, and operating 44 Broad Street, to say nothing of interest charges and improvements, was more than the entire net earnings of Dow, Jones & Company, but Clarence Barron was undeterred. He put every cent he had or could borrow into the venture. The former Edison Company headquarters became the property of Dow, Jones and was officially rechristened The Wall Street Journal Building.

Of the many valuable contributions Clarence Barron made to Dow, Jones & Company, the most significant was his attempt to broaden *The Wall Street Journal*'s geographic reach. Linking the New York paper with his Boston and Philadelphia papers was admittedly a small step, but it led the way for the *Journal*'s eventual emergence as a national business daily.

Clarence Barron was as fiercely protective of *The Wall Street Journal* as its founders had been—perhaps even more so. Like Dow, Jones, and Bergstresser he considered accuracy one of the bulwarks of his paper's reputation. Realizing that the *Journal* exerted a strong influence when it mentioned a certain security or bond, Barron was careful about the type of firms that got space. This was double protection—for the reader as well as for the *Journal*.

On one occasion a minor industrialist of questionable intent pleaded with Barron to mention his company. The publisher reminded the man that his company's stock, which was worth $15 a share, had been palmed off on the public for $31 a share, before being quoted at a more honest price of $16. Barron informed the man that the future of his business, the very life of Dow, Jones, depended on not promoting dubious companies. He wrote:

There are good things that we know nothing about, but we propose to know the facts of the things that we elect to talk about. . . . But I don't make or unmake enterprises. I only decide what enterprises we will give a chance to unmake Dow, Jones & Company and *The Wall Street Journal,* for if we call investment attention to enterprises that do not make good or go wrong, five years afterwards we are the sufferers.

Not all of the companies and trusts that were mentioned in the *Journal* were above reproach. Many were rife with manipulators and robber barons. J. P. Morgan is one of any number of notable examples. Barron tended to go easy on these men and their firms. Perhaps it was because they had long since achieved respectability and profits and had made a great deal of money for their investors. Or perhaps he saw little chance of righting the wrongs they had done. Barron may have been trying to prevent further abuses when he slapped down the smaller upstarts who fancied themselves latter-day J. P. Morgans and undertook to imitate his tactics.

Barron was not above criticizing larger corporations when he thought it necessary. Always on the lookout for greedy companies trying to take advantage of the public, he had no qualms about dropping a well-known name from the *Journal*'s columns without warning if he thought the firm had overstated its claim about the value of its stock. He once showed his displeasure with the statements issued by Sinclair Oil by refusing to list the company's stock in either the *Journal* or on the Dow, Jones ticker.

Few Americans paid much attention to the dispute that had erupted between Austria-Hungary and Serbia as a result of the shooting of Austria's Archduke Francis Ferdinand by Serbian nationalists on June 28, 1914. The Balkans had always been a trouble spot, and the exchange of angry notes, the ultimatums, the mobilization of troops

35

that began after the assassination seemed like more of the same.

On July 28, one month to the day later, Austria-Hungary declared war on Serbia, and the nations of Europe began choosing up sides. There are few world events that do not affect economic conditions. The beginning of World War I is a particularly dramatic example. On July 31 a series of early-morning cables arrived in New York announcing that the London Stock Exchange would close indefinitely because of the outbreak of hostilities. Every other important stock exchange in the world promptly followed suit. Only the New York exchange remained open.

The outbreak of war in Europe posed a serious threat to the U.S. economy. European countries owned approximately $6 billion in American securities. International firms were already being swamped with sell orders, and the nation's supply of gold was declining at an alarming rate as foreign investors rushed to convert their assets into hard currency.

The news from London prompted a series of hastily called meetings on Wall Street. Should the New York stock market—the only one still open in the entire world—be shut down?

The decision was no, and the market opened as usual at 9:00 A.M. The chaos was incredible. Sell orders continued to pour in. In a matter of minutes every major stock had dropped at least twenty points. If the trend continued, the nation's banks would be overwhelmed by the demand for cash. That settled the matter. At 10:00 A.M. the New York exchange suspended all trading "until further notice." At 7:00 P.M. Berlin time that same day, Germany declared war on Russia, and within a few days Europe was in the throes of World War I.

The stock exchange did not reopen until November 28, and then only for bond trading. Stock trading resumed on December 12, but all sales had to be for cash. Unrestricted trading was not resumed until April 1, 1915.

Even with stock trading at a standstill, there was little panic in the financial community. *The Wall Street Journal* printed exchange rates, and the public was convinced that the dollar remained the strongest and safest of the world's currencies. In addition the Glass-Owen Act, which created the Federal Reserve system, had been signed into law on December 23, 1913. The act, originally resented by bankers, made emergency funds available, pouring nearly $400 million into cash-short banks. By the fall of 1914 it was obvious that the economy was safe; the banking bubble was not going to burst.

As a number of *Wall Street Journal* editorials stressed, however, overseas obligations could not legally be paid from emergency currencies. As more foreign loans approached maturity, bankers feared a surge in demands for payment of principal with gold. Miraculously this did not occur. To the surprise—and relief—of U.S. bankers, European banks did not press for repayment of bonds.

Instead of flowing out of the country, gold began to return. Thanks to European gold deposits hidden away in U.S. bank vaults, the dollar remained safe. Rather than destroying the economy, as many had feared, the war in Europe served as a catalyst for the expansion of business and industry, and soon New York replaced London as the financial capital of the world.

Clarence Barron was always happy to see the country prospering. He was also firmly behind President Woodrow Wilson when, in 1917, he led the United States into war on the side of the Allies. Like the vast majority of Americans Barron felt that Germany had to be stopped.

The war brought even greater wealth to America. There was a steady output of munitions, ships, and tanks and a vast increase in exports of all kinds—food, supplies, equipment—to our European allies.

After the war America found itself a creditor nation for the first time in history, but the booming economy suffered a serious blow in 1920, when cutbacks in war production and construction, a fall-off of agricultural prices, and the growing fear of Bolshevik infiltration combined to produce a serious recession. The election of Republican President, Warren G. Harding, did not immediately stop the decline, but within the year Congress, acting on the recommendation of Secretary of the Treasury Andrew Mellon, sharply reduced taxes. Mellon also moved to pay off the public debt. These measures, along with the lowering of the rediscount rate, served to bolster the economy, and business gradually got back on its feet.

As the strikes and recession subsided, Americans in the twenties found themselves ascending a ladder of staggering prosperity. There seemed to be no place to go but up.

The "seven fat years" began in the fall of 1922. Wall Street gave much of the credit for the boom to multimillionaire Andrew Mellon, champion of the Street, friend of financiers and secretary of the treasury under three presidents—Harding, Coolidge, and Hoover. Needless to say, *The Wall Street Journal* was among Mellon's chief admirers. They quoted him regularly and regarded him as a vital link between government and big business, the man who knew better than anyone else what was good for the country. Both Mellon and Wall Street agreed that it was a minimum of government interference in the bailiwicks of economics and commerce.

This is precisely what happened during the 1920s, as the government adopted a hands-off policy toward big business. No one in Washington would have dared suggest, as Democrat Woodrow Wilson had done, raising corporate taxes, imposing a stock-transfer tax, or adopting a federal income tax. The antitrust laws were not very vigorously enforced, and new legislation, such as amendments to the Delaware incorporation laws, resulted in greater freedom for profit-oriented Wall Streeters.

Huge corporations grew still larger. Bank mergers became fashionable until, of the approximately 25,000 banks in the country, a mere 250 controlled 46 percent of the total resources. It was a golden age of prosperity for America's money men. The presidents' cabinets were dominated by their cronies. Best of all, the rest of the country was obviously content with its newfound wealth. A wild bull market caught the imagination of everyone; people who had never bought stocks before rushed to find brokers. *The Wall Street Journal* printed column after column of joyous statistics. In 1922 annual trading averaged 260 million shares. By 1927 it reached 576 million. The following year the volume hit a whopping 920 million, and in 1929 an all-time record of 1.124 billion shares traded was set.

Another set of figures told the other side of the story. In 1922 loans to brokers to carry customers' accounts were less than $2 billion. By 1926 they were nearly $3 billion. They jumped to $6.5 billion in 1928, and by September of 1929 they reached a staggering $8.5 billion. All told, there were more than a million people speculating on margin.

No one seemed bothered by this phenomenon. Most investors were making too much money. Even the experts who conceded that the market would eventually go into a stall saw no need to panic at the prospect. The general belief was that only a few people would be hurt by the shakeout; the overall damage would be negligible.

The booming twenties brought new banks, brokerage houses, and corporate offices to Wall Street. Dow, Jones was by no means immune to the general expansion. On May 9, 1921, the company introduced *Barron's,* a national financial weekly newspaper. A few years later their news ticker service was extended beyond New York City: In 1925 it became available in Chicago, St. Louis, and Detroit; in 1927 in Boston, Washington, and Richmond. San Francisco and Los Angeles were added in 1928, along with several cities in Pennsylvania, New York, and Ohio.

Although Clarence Barron left most of the editing of *The Wall Street Journal* to his staff, he could not resist compiling a set of "news rules" for them. Stressing that they were to be regarded as "suggestions rather than rules," he went on to offer a wealth of shrewd and helpful advice for covering the complicated world of finance.

Barron's first suggestion read in part:

The soul of all writing, and that which makes its force, use and beauty, is the animation of the writer to serve the reader. Never write from the standpoint of yourself, but always from the standpoint of the reader. Economize his time and crowd the most important facts and determining factors into the smallest possible compass that will carry the truth into his brain, remembering that the frame is always part of the picture.

Barron often remarked on John D. Rockefeller's abhorrence of a wasted dime or dollar; he had the same detestation of the wasted word. "The truth and the picture are most vitally improved by every word that can properly be eliminated. It is wonderful how much language can be cut away from around fact."

Barron proved his point by condensing a two-page weather report into: Chicago—Snowing. That one word "snowing," however, would also mean to him railroad and traction expenses, fire losses, municipal costs, dividend effects, future floods, and possibly some agricultural wealth.

There was no question that Clarence Barron's views were reflected in every article that appeared in *The Wall Street Journal*. Unlike Charles Dow, however, who was first and foremost a journalist, Barron devoted himself almost exclusively to a managerial role. The writing of editorials and the day-to-day operations of the paper were left to its editor, Thomas Woodlock. Woodlock had joined the paper as a twenty-six-year-old general reporter in 1892. A recent immigrant, he had come to the United States from Dublin by way of London. Woodlock and *The Wall Street Journal* seemed to suit each other perfectly. He was soon considered the outstanding man on the staff and the logical successor to Charles Dow. The former Dubliner moved into the editor's office when Dow retired in 1902, and his editorial influence proved to be second only to his predecessor's.

In 1903 Barron hired Sereno Pratt away from the New York office of the *Philadelphia Ledger*. Barron, who had been impressed by Pratt's bestselling book, *The Work of Wall Street,* made him assistant to Thomas Woodlock and his aide in writing *Journal* editorials. In 1905 Pratt was named editor, a job he held for another three years until he resigned to become secretary of the New York State Chamber of Commerce.

Sereno Pratt's departure made room for William Peter Hamilton, who took over the editor's chair on January 1, 1908. An English-reared Scotsman, Bill Hamilton came to the *Journal* from the *Pall Mall Gazette* in London, where he and Thomas Woodlock had become friends. Hamilton had also been a war correspondent in the 1893 Matabele, South Africa, campaign and had worked on the *Johannesburg Critic,* a weekly financial paper. At the beginning of the Boer War in 1899 Thomas Woodlock invited his old friend to come to New York and write about the war and its importance to the securities market.

In his spare time Hamilton also turned out short paragraphs about stock market price fluctuations. He was one of any number of experts who were working to develop the proposition that there were definite reasons for market movement, reasons that could be predicted fairly accurately. Reflecting on those early days when he struggled to find out what prompted the swings, Hamilton admitted he was ". . . still humbled by the crudity of some of the reasons I had to give, especially as I was evolving a method. But, at last, it was genuine news collecting and not guessing."

Although explaining the world of finance had never been an easy task, Hamilton felt that *The Wall Street Journal* should definitely eschew the "quackery and mystery" that so often prevailed:

. . . the man on the desk must know as much and more about the news he handles as the reporters who write it . . . it is the aim of the paper to make its news staff not second-rate specialists who might be able to explain a matter to someone already acquainted with the subject, but first-rate specialists who know the subject so well that they can make any portion of it clear to a school boy.

Hamilton also had some strong opinions about editorial writing. Damning the majority of newspaper editorials as mere "fillers," he said that just one thought should be left in a reader's mind, not a jumble of ideas. He suggested following a syllogism in editorials, ". . . with a major premise founded upon a truth, a minor premise based upon the news of the day, and a conclusion which is the logical deduction."

Bill Hamilton and Clarence Barron maintained an extremely close working relationship. Hamilton's recollections of *The Wall Street Journal*'s publisher demonstrated both Barron's zest for action and his ideas on how a financial newspaper should be run:

He was the most astonishing worker I ever saw. He would begin a conversation with me while carrying on business with two secretaries and attending to two telephones. He would never get one of these threads of interest entangled with the others. He would put down one subject and resume his discussion with me exactly at the point he had left it a few minutes before. In the gathering of news he was utterly indifferent to the criticisms of others, and for that reason no one was big enough to snub him.

It was useless to tell Mr. Barron that he was working too hard and that he should reduce his allotted six men's work to about two. . . . He knew that I loved him not merely for his qualities but for his faults as well, and he took advantage of it in a way which makes me smile sadly, now.

He interfered little, if at all, in the conduct of the editorial page. From

1919 to his death I doubt if he saw an editorial before it appeared in type. We worked out between us a theory of editorial-writing which has stood the test of time and experience. We were agreed that opinion was utterly out of place in news. The reporter, always a specialist in our case, must state the facts fully, clearly, and with an accuracy not commonly expected on a general newspaper. We considered that an editorial should be an expression of opinion after bringing out what was implicit in the news but not expressed in the news story. Barron thought that an editorial which did not tell something the reader had not known was poor stuff. When it was apparent we were not seeing eye to eye, I would thresh things out with him at his house on Beacon Street or on the porch of his country residence at Cohasset, looking out into that lovely little harbor. Sometimes he would work by a process of exhaustion. We would talk about everything . . . frequently until four in the morning, when I felt like propping my eyes open with spent matches. Then he would come to the point. He never fought on the other fellow's ground, and he clearly appreciated the advantage of a tired opponent.

Clarence Barron was well known on both sides of the Atlantic. He traveled to Europe frequently and conferred with Kaiser Wilhelm on the world money situation and Czar Nicholas II on the stabilization of Russian currency. At home he regularly hobnobbed with the rich and powerful. A close friend of President William Howard Taft, he was frequently called to Washington to confer with Treasury officials. He was, for a while, a critic of Henry Ford, but Barron and the millionaire automobile maker eventually settled their differences and became mutual admirers.

Barron had seen the United States grow from a nation that had once been obliged to go hat in hand to the European money centers for financial resources to one that was now in the superior financial position. The U.S. had become the owner of many properties around the world formerly held by Europeans and the lender to Europe of approximately $10 billion. Barron applauded the nation's progress. He was well aware of the disagreements and vicissitudes encountered along the way. He had taken sides in all of them, but in the main his attitude was governed by an abiding belief in the country's financial strength and a strong partiality for any business undertaking based on such a belief.

Normally Barron was strongly on the side of big business, but he occasionally took an iconoclastic position. One stand that ran contrary to the opinion of both honest investors and manipulators was Barron's endorsement of a stock exchange limit on the short sellling of standard securities. "The person who sells short is selling stock he has only borrowed and expects to buy back at a lower price before the date of delivery as contracted. If the market goes up, instead of down as the borrower expects, the financial squeeze sets in."

Since Barron was invariably opposed to business restrictions of any sort, his position seemed inconsistent, but as a biographer noted, ". . . it reflected not only a congenital optimism, but also his growing conviction that the investing public of America, now become the chief investment block in the world, needed protection from the buccaneers of Wall Street."

Clarence Barron spent as much time as he could in his native New England. He owned a number of farms in Cohasset and Hingham, south of Boston, and was one of the foremost breeders of registered Guernsey stock in the United States. He liked to call himself a farmer first, a publisher second. He was rarely idle in either role. One of Barron's step-granddaughters and a former director of Dow Jones, Jessie Bancroft Cox, recalled him as plunging

. . . wholeheartedly into whatever he did, whether it be establishing a prize herd of Guernsey cows to give milk for the underprivileged . . . with an enthusiasm which nearly killed the foreman; or yelling to people in nearby boats to "watch out and not go onto a rock," whereupon he would himself crash onto one; or playing bridge. . . . He played his cards . . . all of them . . . beautifully, throughout his unique lifetime.

Clarence Barron had fought a lifelong battle against obesity. One stop on his busy itinerary was Battle Creek, Michigan, where he periodically checked into Dr. Kellogg's famous sanatorium to launch an all-out attack on his waistline. Never a scale-watcher, the publisher kept a wardrobe in six progressively larger sizes. When he could only squeeze into the largest, he knew he had gained fifty pounds above his normal 300; and it was time for another trip to Michigan.

In 1928, in the course of one of his visits to Kellogg's sanatorium, Barron came down with pneumonia. As he lay bedridden, he was

43

visited by Kenneth C. Hogate, the *Journal*'s editor at the time. Still following everything that was going on at Dow, Jones, Barron instructed Hogate to send a new staff member out to visit him with his wife, whom he had never met. It was his contention, Hogate later reported, "that a good wife was the inspiration for all good work."

Soon after that Barron took a turn for the worse. He died on October 2, uttering one brief phrase that summed up his entire career: "What's the news?"

3

The Depression Years

With the sale of 16,410,000 shares, the stock market passed through its record day of business on Tuesday as the general level of prices reached new lows. The drastic declines carried industrials used in the Dow-Jones averages to a new low ground for the year at 260.64, a decline of 120 points from the record high established September 3.

The Wall Street Journal, October 3, 1929

CLARENCE BARRON'S ONLY SURVIVORS, his stepdaughters, inherited Dow, Jones & Company at his death. Both women had married New Englanders, but Martha and her husband, Wendell Endicott, remained in Boston while Jane and her husband, Hugh Bancroft, settled in New York.

Bancroft had graduated from Harvard at the age of seventeen and gone on to earn a degree at Harvard Law School. He was more than familiar with Dow, Jones's operations, having served as his father-in-law's trusted lieutenant for a number of years. Bancroft had been instrumental in launching *Barron's National Business and Financial Weekly* in 1921 and had been its first editor-publisher. With the death of Clarence Barron, he became president of Dow, Jones & Company, the Boston News Bureau, and Dow, Jones, Ltd. of Canada, as well as publisher of the *Philadelphia Financial Journal* and *Barron's*.

One of Hugh Bancroft's first moves as president was to issue a statement that "Dow, Jones and *The Wall Street Journal* will continue their policy of national aggressiveness and independence under the same ownership and practically the same management as before.''

By the summer of 1929 *The Wall Street Journal*'s circulation had risen to nearly 50,000. Dow, Jones's other properties were also prospering; *Barron's Financial Weekly* continued to expand, and the backbone of the company—its News Service, popularly referred to as ''the ticker''—busily reflected the optimistic mood on Wall Street. The future of Dow, Jones, of Hugh and Jane Bancroft, and of the financial world in general seemed extremely rosy.

Only a handful of shrewd investors foresaw the stock market crash of October 29, 1929, but the telltale signs had begun to appear the summer before. A series of declines occurred in August, but they were quickly concealed with bull rallies.

The August 13 issue of the *Journal* was optimistic:

The first pages of the Friday morning and Saturday morning newspapers brimmed over with the bear market. The first pages of the Saturday afternoon and Sunday morning papers brimmed over with the bull market. . . . After the break Friday and the recovery Saturday, experienced traders expressed the opinion that the market is still ''all right.'' If conditions had not been sound fundamentally the market would not have acted the way it did.

Giants in industry took a positive view of the situation. The *Journal* was quick in spreading assurances from John D. Rockefeller, among others, that all was in order; the rocky past would have little relationship to the coming boom. Transactions were executed on the thinnest of margins; investors continued to cherish their fantasies of amassing fortunes in a single day. Warnings against such unrealistic expectations were dismissed as un-American, a dismal denial of the promised dream. The generally conservative *Wall Street Journal* shared in the wholesale optimism and served to perpetuate the myth of economic immortality. On August 21 the *Journal* declared:

Stocks derived further powerful impetus on the up side yesterday from the establishment of simultaneous new highs in the Dow-Jones industrial and railroad averages at Monday's close. According to the Dow Theory, this development re-established the major upward trend. . . . The outlook for the fall months seems brighter than at any time in recent years.

Hugh Bancroft and his staff retained their confidence despite some market setbacks. The September 5 issue claimed:

Substantial recessions took place in the principal trading stocks yesterday representing the first technical correction of importance. Many commission house observers had been expecting such a development, and advices to take profits gave impetus to the selling movement throughout the morning.

There were warnings nevertheless. "Abreast of the Market," the *Journal*'s commentary on the day's business, informed readers that the prevailing sentiment was caution and suggested reducing stock-holdings because a "correction" was expected. There and elsewhere the paper increasingly used words like "acute weakness," "convulsive declines," "unsteady," and "tension" to describe the action on the New York Stock Exchange.

The terms mirrored an economic structure made rickety by a combination of factors—the holding company mania (which still prevailed, though shrouded in euphemism), the Florida land boom, frenzied speculation by the man in the street, and virtually unrestricted credit—which meant that "if values fell, bank after bank, and company after company—and their depositors and employees—would be hard hit."

Bancroft and his senior staff, like everyone else, wore blinders. In retrospect the signs of an impending collapse were everywhere, but the financial experts insisted that such shifts were merely corrections necessitated by dramatic swings in the economy. Downward slides were dismissed lightly; there was no point in encouraging negative thinking. The demand for a positive approach was allowed to distort the truth, and more out of ignorance than deception, the *Journal* continued to exude confidence.

Hugh Bancroft would stand at the ticker day after day, watching the stock prices of numerous American corporations begin to plummet. As the declines became more widespread, the *Journal* noted on September 25:

Stocks broke badly under a heavy selling movement in yesterday's late trading on the Stock Exchange. Signs of a temporary oversold condition were shown in the early dealings, and rallying tendencies developed in the principal trading issues.

47

Every crisis in the stock market had resulted in an upsurge of interest in financial news, and 1929 was no exception. All during the month of October, Dow, Jones & Company worked overtime to keep up with the growing demand for copies of *The Wall Street Journal*. It did not seem foolish to assume that things would continue to go well.

New York City had housed the sole printing and operating facility of the newspaper for nearly forty years, but with commercial expansion shifting westward and California fast becoming home to all sorts of multimillion-dollar industries, the company decided to launch a Pacific Coast edition of the *Journal*. The paper would be separately edited but would draw some of its basic news from the East Coast.

October 21 was an exciting day for the Bancroft family. With the advent of its Pacific Coast edition, *The Wall Street Journal* became the first daily to be published on both the East and West coasts. To celebrate the occasion a large party was held in their West Coast headquarters, a remodeled building in San Francisco that had once housed the Poodle Dog Café, a favorite haunt of Barbary Coast brigands.

The dumbwaiters of the old café were put to use lowering hot lead plates into the basement pressroom. "If the dumbwaiter rope didn't break and send the plates crashing into the basement," said a former circulation staffer, "then we'd get our paper out on time."

The paper itself bore little resemblance to its New York counterpart. The format was different, and only a few of the East Coast news items were repeated. In its early days the Pacific Coast edition was almost a local newspaper, partly by intent and partly because of the relatively primitive state of communications in those days. As a veteran staffer recalled, "We had one Western Union wire that worked only about half the time from New York to San Francisco, and even then, we got very little from it. We received some stories and our editorials from New York by mail."

The papers were usually off the San Francisco press by 8:00 P.M. Reliable air cargo service was not yet available, so the copies for distribution in Los Angeles, 450 miles away, had to be transported by truck that same night. Subscribers elsewhere on the West Coast received their copies by mail.

Back in New York the *Journal* was still confidently expecting an upturn in the market. It didn't occur. Even before the empty bottles of champagne from the celebration of the Pacific Coast edition could be discarded, six million shares of stock changed hands in one day, as the downward slide continued.

The following week was more frantic than ever for Dow, Jones. The market was moving at a dizzying pace. News stories had to be prepared and put to bed for the New York edition, while the same information was simultaneously transmitted to the West Coast. Telephone and telegraph wires crackled with news of financial turbulence. Panic—the very word was as dreaded as the plague—began to creep into conversations on the Street. Gloomy faces became common among market watchers. Even Hugh Bancroft and his editors were beginning to lose a bit of their confidence. Their October 22 issue conceded:

The market has had a very bad break, the most severe in a number of years. There may be some stocks that are still selling too high on a basis of selling price times earnings, but on the other hand, there are a number of stocks that are now selling at attractive levels. . . . There is a vast amount of money awaiting investment.

The stock market may have been having problems, but *The Wall Street Journal* was thriving. Both the East and West Coast editions showed dramatic surges in circulation. One reason may have been that more people wanted to find out whether the convulsions the stock market had been having for the past few weeks were a sign of serious trouble.

Thursday, October 24, was the worst day yet. By 11:30 A.M. everyone was rushing to sell. Prices shot downward, and the floor of the New York Stock Exchange was a wild melee. In a frantic effort to stave off disaster Richard F. Whitney, vice-president of the Exchange, strode onto the floor and bought $30 million worth of shares. The money had been contributed by a group of Wall Street bankers under the leadership of Thomas W. Lamont, a senior partner at J. P. Morgan and Company. By 3:00 P.M., when the closing bell clanged, things were looking up. All but $3 billion of the day's losses had been recovered.

The following day the *Journal*'s editor. Bill Hamilton, published

49

one of his best-known editorials. He called it "The Turn of the Tide," and in it he projected sobering possibilities for the price index. "The 20 railroad stocks on Wednesday, October 23, confirmed a bearish indication given by the industrial two days before. Together the averages gave the signal for a bear market in stocks after a major bull market with the unprecedented duration of almost six years."

Although Hamilton felt it was too early to make any firm predictions, he was disturbed by the fact that each of the recent market rallies had been weaker than its predecessor. He noted laconically that Charles Dow would have been unhappy about the situation.

The market had moved downward eighty points from its previous high before the Dow indexes predicted trouble. This was still 150 points above the ultimate low—a remarkable achievement for a theory that was by then over thirty years old and had been propounded without benefit of a computer to calculate probabilities.

Despite the ominous dip the *Journal* evinced strong faith that the market could take care of itself without "financial catastrophe." On October 26 the paper noted:

Beyond indicating the trend there is no idea here of prediction. Conditions do not seem to foreshadow anything more formidable than an arrest of stock activity and business prosperity like that in 1923.

"Black Tuesday" was only three days away, but of course hindsight is always better than foresight. Just one day before the Crash *The Wall Street Journal* told its readers:

The recent break was due to the position of the market itself. It came when money was 5%, with a plethora of funds available for lending purposes, normal inventories, corporations flush with surplus money, sound industrial conditions and so on.

It is because of the fact that the slump was due to the market itself that the storm has left no wreckage except marginal traders forced to sell at a loss.

But the storm was far from over. The next day, October 29, 1929, was the grimmest in Wall Street's history. Over 16 million shares changed hands—three times the volume of what a year earlier had been thought an extremely busy day. Allied Chemical was off by 35 points; American Telephone and Telegraph by 28, DuPont by 34½.

The ticker tape was unable to keep up with the action—by the close of trading it was two and a half hours behind. "Black Tuesday" marked the beginning of a debacle that did not hit bottom until July 8, 1932.

There was little room for optimism on Wall Street, but the *Journal* did its best, pointing out that "Bargain Days" in the stock market were approaching. Still, the dominant mood was confusion. On October 30 a page-one headline quoted a banker who said, "Hysteria is passing," while "Abreast of the Market" on page fourteen declared, "It is impossible to get a prediction on the market. All observers admit that one guess is as good as another under the prevailing circumstances."

The general hope was for a return to stability, and the *Journal* clutched at any sign that things were moving in that direction. Editorially the paper stated that "uncontrollable liquidation" had passed and "stocks will take on a more orderly and even humdrum character from now forward." One could almost hear the editors whistling in the dark.

Profits increased for *The Wall Street Journal,* if not for anyone else. That may have explained why, in the days after the crash, the newspaper was able to transcend the prevailing gloom. The editors' renewed—if naive—optimism was apparent in the following item, which appeared on November 1:

The sun is shining again, and we will go on record as saying some good stocks are cheap. We say good stocks are cheap because John D. Rockefeller said it first. Only the foolish will combat John D.'s judgment. . . . Having had 70 years experience in business, and having accumulated the greatest fortune of any individual in the world, the elder Rockefeller should have an opinion worth something, particularly when he backs what he says with millions of dollars.

Hugh Bancroft and the *Journal*'s editors misread the unfolding disaster for two reasons. One was that they undoubtedly wanted to believe the best. The other was that never before had there been such a severe financial crash, so it was hard for them to grasp its dimensions. Business and industry had greatly expanded, and thus many more stocks—and stockholders—were affected.

51

Bancroft attempted a new strategy, one that he felt would be a major contribution toward pulling the nation out of its dilemma. Earlier in its history, the *Journal* had stated that publicity was the best remedy for illegal business practices. Now the paper did an about face and plaintively called for less attention from the nation's press until the market had a chance to recover. "What the stock market really needs," said the paper, "is better critics, fewer well-meaning but ill-informed friends, and a quiet corner on the inside pages of the newspapers."

The stock market crash caused a gradual change in people's living and spending habits. The sales of luxury goods were down. Construction tapered off. Few people had any spare cash; those who did were not rushing to buy stocks. Investment houses and bankers took ads to calm the public's anxiety and entice investors back to the exchange, but they did no good.

In the beginning the *Journal* referred to the nation's financial troubles as a recession, but as the slump not only continued but got worse, the newspaper faced up to the dismal truth and started using the word "depression."

In 1930 the circulation of the *Journal* rose to 52,000 with another 3,000 subscribers to its Pacific Coast edition. The following year told a different story. Advertising in the *Journal* all but disappeared. The only survivors were a small group of hotels and restaurants. It may have seemed incongruous that they of all places would have the wherewithal to buy advertising space, but Hugh Bancroft had a carefully worked out plan. None of these ads were paid for in cash; they were inserted, as one old-timer explained it, "on a 'due-bill' basis."

. . . receipts were issued which could be used for rooms, food and drink. These due bills were parceled out to deserving staff members in lieu of pay increases. They financed many a vacation trip, including at least two honeymoons. . . . Now and again, they provided very welcome free dinners for members of the staff required to work at night.

On one occasion vice president Kenneth C. Hogate notified the *Journal*'s Washington bureau that a sizable due bill on the Willard Hotel was on the verge of expiring. A reporter who was on the scene described what happened next: "For a week the Washington staff gorged themselves in the hotel's gourmet dining room. No coffee shop for us! And at dinner, always the best French wines.''

Misery was everywhere. Hugh Bancroft and his editors watched the economy shrink and their circulation with it. The government considered an assortment of relief plans including a dole for victims of the drought that was turning the Southwest into a wasteland. President Herbert Hoover rejected the dole on the grounds that it would set a bad precedent. *The Wall Street Journal* agreed.

In the two-year period between 1929 and 1931 stock losses totaled $50 billion. Perplexed by the market conditions, Hoover called a conference of business leaders to see what could be done to right things. When their advice—to rely on the market's so-called self-correcting processes—did not work, Hoover resorted to an international debt moratorium. Still, the Depression held the nation in its grip.

The *Journal* remained behind the President. The editors supported his call for the revival of the War Finance Corporation, an increase in the capital of the Federal Land Banks, and a widening of the Federal Reserve eligibility provisions. But Hugh Bancroft and his staff were keenly aware that the President's programs were long overdue. Hoover's strategies meant little to the man who had been unemployed for two years.

The Republicans needed a miracle to make the Hoover administration a success. Instead they received more dismaying statistics. The Dow Jones industrial and rail averages sank to new lows. The rediscount rates in Boston, New York, and Philadelphia suffered their eighth successive drop in two years—this one moved the rate to the lowest on record.

On January 15, 1932, Hugh Bancroft attempted to bolster Hoover's sagging image. One full page of *The Wall Street Journal* was devoted to a letter "From an Old Fashioned Father to His Son." In it the editors warned that criticizing Hoover was counterproductive; it would sabotage whatever plans he had for reviving the nation. "God himself might propound such a plan," the letter went on, "but if He were either a Republican or Democrat the other side would viciously oppose Him."

Dow, Jones staffers were behind President Hoover to the end. They admired his policy of keeping government out of business and his determination not to let the nation go off the gold standard. But the suggestions for counteracting the Depression that were being put forth from other quarters met with stern disapproval from *The Wall Street Journal*. Hugh Bancroft and his editors opposed a proposal to boost the $2,500 ceiling on postal savings deposits, arguing that this would put the government in competition with the banks. They also attacked what was to become the Federal Deposit Insurance Corporation. They considered it an unfair means of compelling strong banks to pay for the financial ineptitude of weaker ones. The *Journal* felt that no member of any business group should have to answer for his brothers. No mention was made of the hapless depositors who might be spared losing their life savings.

On the positive side editor Thomas Woodlock did approve of the higher taxes that were imposed in an effort to get capital flowing again, if only through the government. But when Congress discussed raising estate taxes and taxes on people with high incomes as an alternative to a manufacturer's sales tax that would hurt the little man, the *Journal* howled. To tax the wealthy, it said, would "drain out of industry and commerce the working capital . . . to expand employment."

Thomas Woodlock saw unrestrained and unintelligent competition as the reasons for lowered profits. In his view a fall-off in profits developed from a "failure to coordinate production to demand with a consequent destruction of profit in production leading in turn to unemployment and shrunken demand."

Woodlock also upheld Clarence Barron's tenet that government should keep hands off the financial world; in the editor's own colorful words, "It is necessary to keep the clumsy fingers of incompetent bureaucracy out of the machinery."

The Great Depression showed no sign of ending, but Hugh Bancroft felt optimistic enough about Dow, Jones's future to undertake the construction of a brand-new building. On an August weekend in 1931, 44 Broad Street was abandoned, and temporary quarters were set up at 130 Cedar Street. The Wall Street Journal Building was scheduled to be torn down and a bigger and better headquarters erected in its place.

Because of the tremendous number of wires connecting Dow, Jones to all parts of the United States and Canada, the move was a complex and delicate operation. Bancroft had arranged to have all the ticker service equipment transferred the weekend before. Several hundred circuits were cut over to the new location, but only two tickers were out of action—and those only briefly—as a result of the move. Bancroft set up a timetable that would avoid disruption in any department. The newsroom was the last to be shifted, after the wires to the Pacific Coast edition had closed on Saturday night.

The opening of the new Dow, Jones & Company plant in 1932 marked the fiftieth anniversary of the organization. Even in that dark time it was a day for rejoicing. Hugh Bancroft and his staff were delighted to celebrate a half-century of financial reporting in one of the most modern newspaper plants in the world.

When the party in New York was over, Bancroft turned his attention to San Francisco. The Pacific Coast edition of the *Journal* was in serious straits. At the end of 1930 its circulation in the states of California, Nevada, Washington, and Oregon stood at 2,848. The following year it rose to 3,419, but in 1932 the Depression started taking its toll. In December of that year advertising lineage in the West Coast paper dropped to its lowest point.

The revenue from sales was equally disheartening. Years later Bob Bottorff, who had joined the *Journal* staff about this time, recalled, "We may have been distributing three thousand copies of the *Journal* daily, but we only were getting paid for about six hundred of them. Nobody had money in those days to buy anything, let alone newspapers."

Hugh Bancroft had been advised on more than one occasion to shut down the operation in the former Poodle Dog Café. He stubbornly refused. The Pacific Coast edition staggered on through the Depression years. The editors printed numerous "special issues" in which the contents were specifically selected to attract advertisers. Everyone on the staff was instructed to think up new angles to attract new readers and advertisers. Bottorff remembered writing every word of an "Alaska Special" in hopes of finding an audience interested in adventure and far-off places. He had never been to Alaska; he did all his research for the fifteen-column special in the *Encyclopaedia Bri-*

tannica, which he found in the San Francisco public library.

Kenneth Craven (better known as Casey) Hogate was assigned to study the Pacific Coast edition and decide whether or not to close it down. The strongest argument for keeping it open was that it was losing less money than it would cost to maintain a news bureau there. On that basis it was decided to continue the operation with the proviso that some way be found to make it a more profitable venture.

Hogate had two choices: He could cut corners, condense news coverage, and produce what would amount to a trade paper for the financial community. Or he could broaden the paper's appeal by expanding its coverage to report all the news that affected business; for example, President Franklin Delano Roosevelt's proposals for the New Deal.

Hugh Bancroft was growing less inclined to make decisions about the future of Dow, Jones; he was frequently away from the office and seemed discouraged and upset to find himself saddled with difficulties. Fortunately for Dow, Jones & Company, Kenneth Hogate was on hand to keep things going.

Hogate had been managing editor of *The Wall Street Journal* when Clarence Barron died in 1928. A beefy six-footer (he weighed almost 300 pounds), Hogate seemed like a happy-go-lucky type. He was, in fact, an awesome, somewhat aloof man, an indefatigable worker, and a genius at working out the important details in masses of disjointed information.

Hogate had come to Dow, Jones from the Midwest. Born in Danville, Indiana, in 1897, he had literally grown up in the newspaper business. His father ran the local paper. Hogate became editor of the college daily at DePauw University and spent his summer vacations working on various small papers in nearby towns.

Hogate had finished college and was working for the *Detroit Free Press* when someone mentioned his name to Clarence Barron as a possible staffer for *The Wall Street Journal*. The two men found they had a great deal in common, including their enormous weights. As Hogate said later, he accepted Barron's offer to get involved in a different kind of newspaper work because *"The Wall Street Journal* looked like a chance to handle history."

In 1921 a Dow, Jones news bureau was opened in Detroit with Hogate as bureau chief. He was transferred to New York within a year and became managing editor of the *Journal* in 1923. In the early 1930s he was elevated to the position of vice president and general manager of Dow, Jones & Company. By then Hogate was so highly regarded in the financial world that when the New York Stock Exchange voted to elect its first full-time salaried president, the board of governors pushed for Kenneth C. Hogate. Hogate, however, refused. He was more interested in following the bulls and bears than in leading them.

As the man in charge of Dow, Jones & Company, Casey Hogate faced a monumental task. The *Journal* had started to slip, and cutbacks had to be made. The Great Depression had left the American public with little love for the money moguls of New York. Wall Street was the cause of their troubles; the less they heard about the place the better.

An investigation into money market activities by the Senate Banking and Currency Committee struck a further blow to Dow, Jones's survival. The Washington probe was charged with deciding "whether the American buyer and seller has a fair market or whether it is rigged up and down and whether there is a movement on the part of bear raiders to destroy values."

The investigation was directed primarily at the New York Stock Exchange and its member firms, but Dow, Jones & Company came in for its share of scandal. Hauling a huge trunk full of canceled checks and newspaper articles into the committee room, New York Representative Fiorello H. LaGuardia appeared as a "surprise voluntary witness" and charged that certain financial writers and brokerage firms were pushing rigged stocks.

According to New York City's future mayor there had been collusion, primarily between A. Newton Plummer, a publicist for many large stock pools, and certain newsmen who helped place or rewrite Plummer's often erroneous information. As proof of this LaGuardia produced $284,000 in canceled checks, all made out to "cash."

LaGuardia testified that a Dow, Jones reporter named Gomber had received three checks for his services—$140.50 and $209 for promoting Savage Arms stock and $284 for publicizing the Pure Oil pool. All three bore Gomber's endorsement.

LaGuardia went on to detail the publicity given to the Indian Motorcycle Company at Plummer's behest. The story had originated in the Boston News Bureau and had appeared in *The Wall Street Journal* on January, 16, 1930.

"The American people have been defrauded out of $200,000,000 in South American securities, more than $200,000,000 in European investments and millions on such trash as has been presented here today," LaGuardia declared.

The *Journal* ran the story of LaGuardia's allegations on page eleven, but there were no further stories or editorials either defending or explaining his charges. Dow, Jones personnel records indicate, however, that Gomber resigned on April 26, 1932, the same day LaGuardia appeared before the Senate committee.

The Gomber affair was a blatant and disgraceful violation of the credo adopted by Charles Dow and Edward Jones, "The truth in its proper use." Although Casey Hogate stoutly agreed with New York Stock Exchange president Richard F. Whitney's contention that the Senate committee had failed "to prove against the Exchange its presumption of guilt," the Dow, Jones executive called for a renewed emphasis on ethical conduct in his own organization.

There were no rules against reporters playing the market for their own personal profit, but there was a regulation stating that staff members were to "bend over backwards to avoid any action, no matter how well intentioned, that could provide grounds even for suspicion." Dow, Jones staffers were instructed to guard against indebtedness to brokers, heavy market commitments that could lead to biased stories, writing to affect a stock's price, and the use of inside information before it became available to the general public.

The year 1932 was a period that Dow, Jones wanted to forget as quickly as possible. The scandal was only one of a number of headaches. A young Washington reporter, William Kerby, summed it up:

Wall Street was a dirty name to the American public, and few indeed wanted to venture into investing in securities or read news affecting them. Dow, Jones as a company eked out a precarious living from the eroded profits of its news service, by then its only solvent operation.

The election of President Franklin D. Roosevelt was more of a blow to Wall Street and the financial community than to any other sector of the economy. Rigid controls and new regulations were imposed on all stock market trading. But if Wall Street was the enemy of the New Deal, the reverse was also true.

During FDR's first months in office the *Journal* regularly railed against the expansion of bureaucracy. It criticized the formation of additional government agencies, departments, and bureaus. When the Interstate Commerce Commission announced its intention to regulate railroad holding companies in addition to railroads, a *Journal* editorial charged that the action reflected the "intense jealousy that 'bureaucracy' feels toward all power, political, economic or social . . . and furnishes their main impulse. . . . [Government] will never say of its power . . . it is enough!''

Nevertheless the *Journal* had some good things to say about a few of Roosevelt's actions. It endorsed his plan for resolving the crisis that had halted all banking operations—the quickly passed Emergency Banking Act, which aimed at reopening the closed institutions and making investment banks divest themselves of securities-marketing affiliates.

The *Journal* had been conservative throughout its history, but now, realizing that the nation's problems demanded innovative solutions, the paper shifted to a new stance. For the time being Hogate and his staff forswore allegiance to any political party. They agreed to give Roosevelt a chance to revive the nation's economy.

The grace period did not apply to Roosevelt's moves to regulate the stock market, however. The *Journal* pushed for honesty in the financial world, admitting the existence of charlatans, but continued to insist that Wall Street could, and should, police itself.

The paper gave its nod to such Roosevelt programs as the so-called Truth-in-Securities Act of 1933 and the replacement of the Federal Farm Board by the Farm Credit Administration. The Federal Farm Board—which had been subjected to the *Journal*'s editorial ire—had been formed to lend money to farmers; the new agency essentially bought excess cotton and wheat for the government.

The Truth-in-Securities Act reduced the ways insiders could use their privileged information to make personal profit and set strict regulations for information on initial offerings of securities. The *Journal* found the bill "so right in its basic provision that the country will insist on its passage." A year later, when the honeymoon with the new President was over, the *Journal* revised its judgment, calling for changes in certain aspects of the measure, which were later adopted by Congress.

On October 17, 1933, fifty-four-year-old Hugh Bancroft committed suicide. It was only natural that his widow would entrust the management of Dow, Jones to Kenneth C. Hogate. He was, in effect, already doing the job. It was not an easy one. Although the year ended with a small profit for the firm, morale was poor. A series of pay cuts did not improve it, but Hogate made no bones about the necessity for retrenchment. The firm's once substantial cash reserves, he reported to his employees, "have shrunk most drastically. They were chiefly in what appeared to be high-grade common stocks, and little more need be said."

Unpaid subscriptions piled up, advertising remained stagnant, revenue continued to decline. The Dow, Jones ticker service was the only thing that kept the company afloat. The situation finally bottomed out, and by the middle of the decade circulation took an upward swing. The newspaper's East and West Coast editions had a total of 28,000 subscribers. It was a far cry from the pre-Depression figure of 52,000, but it was substantially ahead of its 1932 low. The paper was not exactly booming, but at least it was still breathing.

Now that Dow, Jones had a new lease on life, Hogate felt it was time to revamp *The Wall Street Journal*. Turning an old paper into a new one is always difficult. For Hogate it was even more of a challenge. Since the *Journal* was unique, there was no pattern to follow. Hogate had to come up with new ideas, a new style of reporting for a drastically altered, far more diverse economy. Men had to be found, trained, and developed to dig out the news in factories, stores, transportation terminals, and research laboratories, on proving grounds, banking and warehouse floors, on the farms, in mines and forests, in the innermost sanctums of the states, the nation, and the world.

In the midst of overhauling the *Journal* Hogate decided in the summer of 1934 that it could not continue with both an evening and a morning edition. It was impossible even for Hogate's skilled staff to clothe the bare skeleton of the day's news with background and analysis before the evening edition went to press at 3:00 P.M. By cutting back to a single morning edition *The Wall Street Journal* would be able to run comprehensive articles on every significant business development.

In September Hogate simply dropped the evening edition. At the same time he promoted his crack Washington correspondent, William Henry Grimes, to managing editor. Twenty-five-year-old Bernard (Barney) Kilgore, a fellow alumnus from DePauw University, became Grimes's replacement in the capital, a post that had proved strategic as Franklin D. Roosevelt's New Deal politics became increasingly relevant to the business community.

Under managing editor Grimes's direction during the thirties the process of broadening the news content of *The Wall Street Journal* went on steadily and without much fanfare. The groundwork for the "fourth growth wave" was being laid.

The voice of *The Wall Street Journal* grew stronger and less enthusiastic about Roosevelt as the government moved into other areas. The paper reacted negatively to the President's call for a federal housing plan, for example, scoring it as a "further intrusion of Government-in-business for private enterprise." The government did not have the immense funds needed to do a total job—only private enterprise could carry it out—but this "emergency expedient . . . will check and discourage the movement of private capital into active employment."

The newspaper also damned the National Recovery Administration as "a nebulous mass of uncertainties . . . it would take all the Public Works Administration's money to build enough jails to hold all the NRA violators if they could, in fact, be caught, tried, convicted and sentenced."

Roosevelt's embracing of the Keynesian philosophy of deficit spending also drew *Journal* disapproval. In the face of continued applications of Keynesian doctrine and an ever-skyrocketing national debt, the paper warned against bookkeeping illogic. Unable to accept the theory that a budget could be brought into line "not by reduction in expenditures, but only by larger receipts," the *Journal* preferred (and still prefers) equal debits and credits within each fiscal year.

61

Casey Hogate kept up his journalistic assaults on President Roosevelt. Even FDR's famous "fireside chats" did not please the editorial staff; they were not specific enough. After one radio address the paper said that not only had the President spoken in vague terms, but some of his sentences were "totally innocent of meaning."

Although the *Journal*'s circulation was not as low as it had been in the depths of the Depression, it was not exactly soaring either. A new approach was called for; it came with the inauguration of special issues, an idea that had been tried on a small scale and with some success in the Pacific Coast edition. For the first time the *Journal* started carrying industrial and corporate advertising. It was sold on a one-shot basis for inclusion in the special issue, but since there were a number of these issues each year, some of the advertisers appeared with a certain amount of frequency.

Perhaps more than anything else these special issues convinced Casey Hogate that the old days of *The Wall Street Journal* were gone. It was time for still further changes, along with a gradual transition from a financial to a business daily.

When readers picked up their papers on the morning of September 4, 1934, they found a new feature on the front page. It was a column called "What's News," which offered capsule versions of national and international developments. The paper had also jumped from five to six columns. No reason was given for the change. However, the grouping of the top news stories in one column allowed readers to find out at a glance what was going on, and the standing headline "What's News" made for a neat front-page layout.

The idea for the new column was undoubtedly born out of the need to differ from other major newspapers and thus attract attention on the newsstands. Being different is always a gamble, and to some extent Casey Hogate's gamble paid off. "What's News" caught on immediately. It resulted in the addition of several hundred subscriptions and remains one of the paper's most salient features.

Unfortunately, the new column couldn't generate enough interest in the newspaper to make it a viable business enterprise. The Depression had not abated, and there wasn't enough business activity around the country to warrant the existence of an organization like Dow, Jones. Even the once profitable ticker was frequently silent. When this happened, staffers were apt to send out jokes and verse so sub-scribers would have something to read.

Hogate and the owners of Dow, Jones—Hugh Bancroft's widow and her family—debated the future of the company. There were rea-sons to believe that there was no further demand for the services they provided, but they agreed to try some last-ditch strategies.

Barney Kilgore, Hogate's college friend and Washington bureau chief, had a number of ideas to rehabilitate the ailing *Journal*. In early 1941 he left Washington and moved to New York as managing editor, the post vacated by Bill Grimes, who was made editor. Ho-gate gave the new team his enthusiastic support along with carte blanche to do whatever seemed necessary to give the paper a bright future.

Bill Kerby, who had been news editor in New York, was assigned to Washington as Kilgore's replacement. Kerby had worked out of the Washington bureau some ten years before. He was looking for-ward to returning to the capital and rekindling his old friendships. Shortly before his projected move, however, Kerby ran into Barney Kilgore in the New York office.

"What's this about Washington?" Kilgore demanded.

Kerby affirmed that he would soon be heading for the capital.

"But I want you here," Kilgore exclaimed.

Kerby's response came quickly: "I'll stay."

He was given the title of assistant managing editor, and the two men began a long and close relationship that was to mark a major change for *The Wall Street Journal*.

In Kilgore's estimation the principal problem with the *Journal* was that it failed to reach a specific constituency. Other newspapers ap-pealed to a region, city, or town. Kilgore believed that *The Wall Street Journal* had to address itself not to a location but to a popula-tion—businessmen and other interested parties all over the nation who wanted to keep abreast of the changing pace of commerce.

"For this community," said Kilgore, "there is no such thing as local news. If a story is of interest to a businessman in Portland, Oregon, it is of interest to a businessman in Portland, Maine."

Kilgore's concept had never before been tried in American jour-nalism. Would it pull *The Wall Street Journal* out of its ten-year decline? Or would it further strain its resources and sound the death knell for Dow, Jones & Company?

The answer gradually became clear. After almost a decade in the doldrums the *Journal*'s advertising and circulation revenues slowly but steadily began to climb. Upwards of 30,000 subscribers could read Thomas Woodlock's brilliant column reminding Americans, as fascism, communism, and totalitarianism became common terms, what democracy was all about:

Democracy, as a "way of life" for human society, by its nature is best conducive to the preservation of men's personal liberty and is therefore the most desirable form of government. For its success, however, it demands a high state of civil morality in the people, who must be educated to a relatively high standard of intelligence. In the absence of either it is almost certain to degenerate, and in that process liberty tends to disappear. Forms alone are not sufficient for its preservation; they must be animated by a deep popular faith in principles of liberty itself. These principles, arising as they do from the fact of man's personality, are ultimately religious, for man's personality necessarily implies God, the soul and the moral law.

World War II and Its Aftermath

War with Japan means industrial revolution in the United States.
The Wall Street Journal
December 8, 1941

ON MARCH 12, 1938, the day Hitler's army marched into Austria, *The Wall Street Journal*'s Paris bureau chief, Charles Hargrove, sent a wire from Berlin. In New York newsman Bill Kerby rewrote the brief cable. He fleshed it out with background and interpretation and prepared to have it appear prominently on page one.

Bill Grimes, managing editor at the time, insisted that this was "not the the *Journal*'s type of story." He wanted Kerby's effort cut and carried as a lead item in the "What's News" summary section.

By chance top man Casey Hogate read a copy of Kerby's article and declared enthusiastically, "This is just the sort of thing we need more of."

"You two are ganging up on me," Grimes groaned.

"Oh," said the unsuspecting Hogate, "what were you planning to do with it?"

"Page one, column one," lied the grinning, outgunned Grimes.

The story became the *Journal*'s first nonfinancial feature page-one column.

A short, gray-eyed man with a soft voice, Bill Grimes spent thirty-eight of the forty-eight years he was a newspaperman with the *Journal*. As editor he supervised the paper as it was reshaped from a narrowly based financial journal into a newspaper of national distinction.

Born in Bellevue, Ohio, in 1892, Grimes began his newspaper career in 1913. His first major story was an exposé of working conditions among itinerant farm laborers in Ohio. He got himself hired as a lettuce picker and, because he looked so boyish (he was not yet twenty years old), was able to gain the confidence of his employer. This led to a firsthand, highly dramatic account of how the workers were being exploited.

In 1918 Grimes was hired by United Press, serving first in their Washington bureau and later as head of UP's New York office. In a move to upgrade Dow Jones's Washington bureau Casey Hogate hired Grimes away from United Press. Hogate later transferred him to New York, where he became managing editor and, in 1941, editor.

Bill Grimes had been the man behind Hogate's 1934 decision to kill the afternoon edition of *The Wall Street Journal,* thus saving Dow Jones considerable money and offering readers more comprehensive information. Next Grimes turned to revising the newspaper's morning edition. For years the *Journal* had been printed around 6:00 P.M. each evening, thereby missing some important news breaks. Grimes ended this policy by instituting a three-edition paper, the last edition going to press around 11:30 P.M.

President Franklin D. Roosevelt is generally felt to have accelerated, even if he did not initiate, government intervention in the private sector. This plus his "welfare-state" program, as the *Journal* termed it, did not make him one of their favorites.

In 1940 Roosevelt's third presidential campaign was followed in a *Journal* column called "Presidential Politics." The column's focus alternated between Roosevelt and his Republican opponent, Wendell Willkie, depending on which of them was making news. As World War II thundered on in Europe, both Democrats and Republicans pledged aid to England short of war participation and expressed a desire to keep America out of the conflict. Bipartisan agreement ended, however, on domestic policy. To the *Journal* Willkie, a public utility president, would carry the banner for private initiative. Roosevelt, on the other hand, was moving the nation toward a managed economy. The paper's editors counseled that the voters could be deciding one of the most important questions in the country's history.

The third-term issue also bothered *Journal* editors. They did not question FDR's motives, but wondered "whether any man can safely be allowed to make this radical alteration in the presidency as an American political institution." They also cautioned that third-term-ism could lead the president to plan only for the next four years instead of for the long run.

The *Journal* followed the campaign's progress closely and said that Willkie's rising popularity could put him ahead by a wide margin. On the morning of election day the *Journal* carried Barney Kilgore's prediction of a Willkie victory. But page seven carried a two-column photo of Roosevelt with an editorial calling for unity and subordination of personal preferences for the general welfare. "Mr. Roosevelt remains the President of the United States of America," it said.

When Bill Grimes moved up to become editor of *The Wall Street Journal* in March, 1941, Bill Kerby was given the job of organizing all the Sunday news that would find its way into the newspaper's Monday edition. Until then the bulk of the Monday edition had been put together the previous Saturday, and only a handful of people could be found in the *Journal*'s offices on Sunday. A new schedule was decreed; Saturday became a day off, and most of the staff were required to report for work on Sunday.

The new schedule began on the first Sunday of December, 1941. Kilgore stopped by to see how things were going. Bill Kerby was sitting in the newsroom, working on copy for Monday's edition. Suddenly he leaped up and started charging around the office. All the bells on incoming wires rang at once. It was December 7; the Japanese had attacked Pearl Harbor.

With the instinct of seasoned reporters Kilgore and Kerby scrapped most of their Monday columns and ordered new ones based on the reports emanating from Washington. There were Secretary of State Cordell Hull's comments along with details of the Pearl Harbor attack, including a tally of the ships and planes destroyed.

In the midst of the furor Kilgore ordered Kerby to sit down and write a column on the attack and its implications for business. It took him only eighteen minutes to compose the paper's lead story, predicting with amazing accuracy what would happen over the coming four-year period:

War with Japan means industrial revolution in the United States. The American productive machine will be reshaped with but one purpose—to produce the maximum of things needed to defeat the enemy. It will be a brutal process.

It implies intense, almost fantastic stimulation for some industries; strict rationing for others; inevitable complete liquidation for a few. . . . War with Japan will be a war of great distances. Thus, certainly in its preliminary stages and probably for the duration, it will be a war of the sea and the air. This means unlimited quantities of ships and shells, bombers and bombs, oil, gasoline. . . .

Thus, American industry now divides itself automatically into war-useful and war-useless categories. And, again, particular emphasis must be placed on the modifying geographical character of an American-Japanese war. Because such a war puts great stress on planes and ships many industries will work to the limit of their capacity, expand and expand again. These include: steel, shipbuilding (warships and merchant vessels), aircraft (emphasis on long-range bombers), ordnance machine tools. Plus, of course, all the now familiar list of supplying and complementary industries.

Kilgore stood by, looking over Kerby's shoulder as he typed, and grabbing each completed sheet to rush to the wire for the presses. There was no time for editing or rewriting. Speed, energy, and talent were the important things. Bill Kerby demonstrated all three that Sunday afternoon.

Kerby was once asked what issue of the *Journal* was the most important in its history. He paused only a second before replying, "That edition of December 8, 1941." Other newspapers had captured the event for their Monday editions, but it was a special triumph for the financial newspaper. The *Journal* had proved without question that it was truly on top of the news.

If there was one single turning point that marked the public's acceptance of the *Journal*'s change from a stock-market-oriented publication to a national business newspaper, it would have to be the issue that reported the attack on Pearl Harbor. According to Bill Kerby:

We really had encyclopedic coverage on what that event would signal for business and the economy. We had enormous impact. My desk was just flooded with telegrams and I had dozens of phone calls from other newspapers requesting permission to reprint stories from that issue.

America's entry into the war brought significant changes to *The Wall Street Journal*. In addition to its old traits of reliability and thoroughness, it added briskness and brevity. It became human, at times, even humorous. Financial news was relegated to the back pages; business, Washington, and world news was pushed up front.

In 1942 a typical front page was devoted to such matters as the increasing role of women in America's railroads and the effect of the war on the Hollywood film industry. A third story reported on the federal government's wage-stabilization efforts.

To a greater extent than any other newspaper or magazine the *Journal* reported what Washington was doing and planning for the war effort. As an indication of the importance the *Journal* placed on Washington news its bureau there was by far the largest maintained by any business publication. Conversely, although President Franklin D. Roosevelt's reading of other major newspapers was done by his secretary, "Missy" Le Hand, she reported that the President "carefully scans" *The Wall Street Journal*. So did most of the top men in his administration.

Barney Kilgore took advantage of this fact to ask for a private meeting with FDR.

I called up Steve Early [Roosevelt's press secretary] and arranged for an appointment. The President was in a serious but friendly mood and he talked very frankly. He even said I could write about his ideas as long as I didn't tie anything so closely to the White House that it would make trouble among the regular Washington correspondents.

After I left . . . my head was buzzing with ideas and I sat down and wrote a piece about gold and silver money.

When the *Journal* broadened its news coverage during World War II, it made equally important changes in the way the news was presented to its readers. While major events of the day were packaged tightly for quick scanning by the reader in a hurry, important themes were covered in depth for those who wanted to know more about the subject than simply what happened.

During the war much of the *Journal*'s reporting dealt with defense contracts, war production, the effects of rationing, the trends of the European and Asian wars—all of which affected the economy. The most sensational news story of the war years, however, never got written.

In the spring of 1943 Bill Kerby met a young scientist at a New York cocktail party. The scientist was in the process of developing thick lead shields to protect people against massive explosions. Soon after that the *Journal* reported that the Canadian government had ordered trading suspended in two mining companies listed on the Montreal Stock Exchange. It turned out that these mining firms were the only North American producers of ores that would yield radium.

With his reporter's instinct Kerby connected radium and lead shields and soon concluded that a special project was under way. From several sources he heard whispered rumors that a superbomb was being built. Kerby kept his information and his conclusions to himself; he neither said nor wrote anything that might jeopardize the project.

On August 7, 1945, the "What's News" column carried word of the first atomic bombing in history. The regular-sized bold type said, "New Atomic Bomb Dropped on Jap City/ Is 'Most Terrible Destructive Force' "; 400 atoms would be the "Way to a New Source of Power for Industry." The *Journal,* as usual, had its eye on business.

Some years later Bill Kerby wrote:

The *Journal*'s war was fought on the home front. Ours was the story of shortages, manpower and materials allocations, rationing, price controls. And, for the first time in its long history, *The Wall Street Journal* recognized its readers as not only managers of business and finance but also consumers. So we tried to be as alert to news affecting them and their families as we were to events important to their business operations.

There were stories on the driving ban in the twelve northeastern states, which would allow only one vacation per family each summer, on the need for the average American to be satisfied with nine and a half pounds of ice cream each year, and on how to survive the cigarette shortage.

Once, when attempting to console Americans who found it difficult to purchase tires for their cars, the newspaper ran a picture of a large pile of used automobile tires along with some background information on the tire industry taken from the *Encyclopaedia Britannica*. The editors were rebuked by the Office of Censorship for extending "an invitation to sabotage." Even material culled from an established reference work was considered off limits, lest it fall into the hands of readers in Japan or Germany.

Fourth-termism became a major issue in the 1944 campaign, when Roosevelt and Governor Thomas E. Dewey of New York were vying for the presidency. The *Journal* was outspoken against Roosevelt's brand of government:

. . . there is in [Roosevelt's] mind no clear distinction between government by law which is the essence of democracy, and personal government, which is the essence of tyranny.

. . . Mr. Roosevelt has to his credit some accomplishments which his opponents accept—the securities acts, the labor relations act and social security. In each case they were won through established legislative processes.

The day before the election the editors ran a two-column page-one editorial, "The Overriding Issue." It began with a denial that the editorial could be "taken as an expression of opposition to any one man or any one administration." It said the first necessity was to win the war and then to decide whether the economy should be managed by government or private individuals. But it also declared that governmental control "is evil. It is an evil through and through, not just part evil."

The editors vowed to speak out against any attempt to substitute government judgment for individual judgment, noting that "silencing of speech is one of the final results of this evil."

Doubtless many readers saw these opinions as critical of President Roosevelt, but the *Journal* maintained that some of Governor Dewey's policies had the same basic fault. Even so—and despite the pa-

71

per's frequent disclaimer that it endorsed issues, not men—the *Journal* was obviously trying to put a Republican in the White House.

Roosevelt was acknowledged as the force behind the winning of the war. Wouldn't it seem appropriate to keep him in the White House? Apparently Dow Jones management did not think so. They were disappointed in the movement of the nation's economy and felt that a new administration would revitalize the stock market and bring significant profits to industry.

Roosevelt was reelected, but as it turned out, the entire country was on the verge of being revitalized. The war in Europe ended, and the atomic bomb was about to bring the Japanese to the surrender table. As victory neared, articles appeared on industry's conversion to peacetime production, on rebuilding Europe, on postwar job prospects for GI's, on housing for those same war veterans, on the specter of a managed economy, and on the war-related research discoveries that offered possibilities for new industries.

The United States was about to embark on a new phase of its economic growth, and *The Wall Street Journal* would follow suit.

Postwar Growth

Newswork is highly addictive. It is the cocaine of crafts.
WILLIAM F. KERBY, former chairman, Dow Jones & Company

THE WINDS OF CHANGE started blowing at *The Wall Street Journal* during World War II. Still further changes were made after Barney Kilgore became president of Dow Jones & Company in 1945. Kilgore is generally credited with putting more creative energy into the paper's development than anyone since Clarence Barron.

Kilgore was born on November 9, 1908, in Albany, Indiana. In 1925 he entered DePauw University, where he studied economics, became editor of the college paper, and earned a Phi Beta Kappa key. After graduating in 1929 he wrote to Kenneth C. Hogate, general manager of *The Wall Street Journal,* and asked him for a job. Hogate, a fellow alumnus, was influenced partly by the DePauw letterhead but mainly by Kilgore's credentials. He offered him a job at a starting salary of $45 a week.

Kilgore went to work in September, 1929, the day the stock market hit an all-time high. Two weeks later he was assigned as a rewrite man on the copy desk of the thriving *Journal*. Within another two weeks the stock market crash ushered in the Great Depression.

Kilgore was eventually sent to San Francisco to work for the *Journal*'s Pacific Coast edition. His talent for transforming difficult financial news into understandable terms was a decided asset for the new edition. It resulted in an immensely readable series called "Dear George," in which he decoded the complexities of the stock market for a befuddled, imaginary friend.

Kilgore became news editor of the Pacific Coast paper, but in 1932 he was called back to New York to be an editorial page columnist. A year later he wrote the first of the Hogate-inspired "What's News" columns, a sign that top management had singled him out for a promising career on the paper. In 1935 Kilgore was again transferred, this time to Washington, D.C., with the title of bureau chief. There Kilgore initiated the weekly feature, "Washington Wire." He originally envisioned it on the editorial pages, but his colleague William Kerby thought it would be better on page one—and so it was.

Barney Kilgore set the *Journal*'s Washington coverage on a course for expansion. Seeking to become known, he stretched his budget to rent a spacious apartment on Connecticut Avenue, where he could entertain and interview important political figures. It was he who pushed for extensive coverage by the paper of Roosevelt's New Deal policies.

FDR's secretary "Missy" Le Hand had admitted that her boss "carefully scanned" *The Wall Street Journal*. A story in a Washington newspaper indicated that he did more than that:

At a presidential news conference, when asked to explain a technical difference between two suggested ways of paying the soldiers' bonus, Roosevelt advised the reporters to "read Kilgore in The Wall Street Journal" because he had written "a good piece" on the subject.

And soon it happened again, when FDR was asked to explain a complicated Supreme Court decision on the National Industrial Recovery Act. The Journal tooted its own horn a bit with a story headlined: "President Tells Reporters to Read Kilgore Article."

When in late 1942 Casey Hogate became seriously ill and could no longer discharge his responsibilities as president, Grimes took the reins and appointed Barney Kilgore vice president and general manager and Bill Kerby managing editor, reporting directly to Kilgore. Grimes thus encouraged his juniors, both in age and position, to supersede him in the power structure of the *Journal*.

This proved to be a wise move. Grimes knew where his own interests and talents could best be used. His editorial skills were unmatched. In 1947 he received a Pulitzer Prize for his "distinguished editorial writing."

Some years later a more recent editor of the *Journal,* Vermont Royster, paid tribute to his predecessor's talents: He described Grimes as a man

. . . who sometimes had to keep enthusiasm from running riot and who in the meantime was slowly turning *The Wall Street Journal*'s editorial page into a voice of national influence. Not since the days of Dow had the paper had an editor who could use simple language to drive home a point with such force, but Grimes had a more wide-ranging mind than either Dow or Hamilton and a sharper pen than Woodlock.

In 1943 Kilgore became vice president of Dow Jones, and when Casey Hogate moved up to become chairman of the board on November 6, 1945, Kilgore was appointed president. He lost no time in establishing his goals. The image of a newspaper strictly dedicated to business and finance had to be discarded; World War II had convinced Kilgore of that. He wanted the *Journal* to offer broad national news coverage, report on topics not dependent on yesterday's news, and cover a wider format of subjects that might not strictly be considered as relating to the economy.

For Kilgore reader interest and profitability went hand in hand. He sought a broad spectrum of business news, one that included political and sociological trends. At the same time he believed in another axiom: "It doesn't have to have happened yesterday to be news." Kilgore maintained that if readers hadn't heard something, it was still news to them.

One of Kilgore's most urgent priorities was top-quality writing. Style and comprehensibility became his obsessions. He was determined to present complex matters in a way that everyone could understand, but he was frequently faced with terminology that was peculiar to a particular industry. Sugar commodity traders, for example, use the term "Bombay Straddle" to describe a particular type of price speculation. After the *Journal* printed one story that mentioned a "Bombay Straddle," Kilgore asked his staff what it meant;

no one knew. The normally calm Kilgore blew his stack. If his reporters didn't know what they were writing about, neither would anyone else who didn't happen to be a specialist in the commodities field.

Kilgore would not tolerate sloppiness, especially from reporters he knew could do better but weren't really trying. He was particularly fanatical about the use of clichés. He once sent a memo to one of his editors who worked on a lower floor of *The Wall Street Journal* building: "If I see 'upcoming' in the paper again, I'll be downcoming and someone will be outgoing."

No matter how talented the president of a newspaper is, he can only achieve great things if he has an equally gifted editor. Vermont Royster proved to be just such a man.

Despite his name—Vermont Connecticut Royster—the *Journal* editor was no Yankee. He was born in Raleigh, North Carolina, and educated at the University of North Carolina. To this day his conversation retains the accents of his native state.

He did not shed all his country ways in the big city. He kept his Southern drawl, the dry wit that takes people by surprise, and the name that's unusual even by New York standards. It started when his great-grandfather, for reasons best known to himself, decided to name all of his children after states. There was Iowa Michigan, Wisconsin Illinois, Arkansas Delaware, Virginia Carolina, Georgia Alabama, and Nathaniel Confederate States. There was also Vermont Connecticut, and the name was passed on. The present Vermont has been trying all his life to get people to call him by his proper name, but they seldom comply. His nicknames are Roy or Bunny.

Royster attributes his feeling for language to the fact that he was nurtured on Latin and Greek and the King James Version of the Bible:

I went to prep school—Webb School at Bellbuckle, Tennessee—where you had to have four years of Latin and two years of Greek in order to graduate from the damned place. . . . They had a fellow there and he'd make you write an essay of 265 or 389 words and you had to write it just that way. You had to go and count them because you couldn't have one word more or one word less. He taught me discipline.

Royster started writing about sports in high school. "I worked on the *Raleigh News and Observer,*" he recalled. "I'm a little fellow . . . and all those giants on the football team began to treat me like I was somebody. . . . The *News and Observer,* in a moment of aberration, even once gave me a byline on a little piece, and it was fatal."

At the University of North Carolina, Royster was on the staff of the *Daily Tar Heel.* One old friend remembered him as being "busy as the bumblebee he resembled."

Graduation did not bring a flood of job offers.

When I got out of school I found that a nodding acquaintance with Euripides was not a very marketable commodity. I came up to New York with my Phi Beta Kappa key and landed a job as a busboy. . . . I got a temporary job on this paper when it was a little one, with about 35,000 circulation, and I've sort of expanded with it, while it's grown to around 1,200,000 circulation.

Years later Royster asked his boss Barney Kilgore, "Don't you think we can make this job permanent?"

Replied Kilgore, "Let's not rush it."

Royster began as a copyboy in 1936 and went from there to being a reporter on the paper's Washington bureau. His beat included the Treasury, Capitol Hill, and the White House.

When the U.S. entered World War II in 1941, Royster became an officer in the navy. He served in both the Atlantic and the South Pacific; in each assignment baffled brass mistook his name for some kind of code. At the end of the war he returned to Washington as the *Journal's* bureau chief, then later moved to New York, where he wrote editorials, became associate editor, and in 1948, when William Grimes retired, took over the editorship.

In an editorial published on September 10, 1952, Vermont Royster described an editor's function.

He should express an opinion which the reader can judge. And that function is properly performed only if the opinion is an honest one. The minute an editor withholds an opinion for fear that someone may think it "irresponsible" or that he may be "out of step with the times," he ceases to perform his function.

77

One of Royster's earliest editorials was directed at President Harry S Truman. In September, 1952, Truman asserted in his message to the American Federation of Labor convention that, according to the *Journal,* Wall Street had plans to make the Taft-Hartley Act more "oppressive and unfair."

The *Journal* flatly denied the charge. Royster's no-nonsense editorial said the paper was unaware of any "Wall Street plot" to change the Act. He insisted, moreover, that the *Journal* was not antilabor, though its editor had expressed doubts "about many Government efforts to interfere with the processes of collective bargaining" in the past and expected to do so again.

Certainly the *Journal* had never been reluctant to speak out against the increasing involvement of government in the lives of its citizens. Vermont Royster believed in a business world as unrestricted as possible by government regulation. In one *Journal* editorial he suggested that industries anticipate federal moves by taking action on their own to alleviate problems: "Industry could do more to meet social responsibilities like pollution control before the Government takes over, although . . . industry cannot be expected to assume unlimited public responsibilities."

After noting that business and government are not equal instrumentalities, the paper continued:

Business, free enterprise, is the economic manifestation of the free society, the principal reason for America's preeminence. Overweening Government inherently tends to be repressive and coercive, as the nation is now witnessing. No natural harmony exists between the two.

The paper's editors recognized that the nation's ills must be cured, but they also asserted that "government spending and bureaucratic solutions favored by Democrats are simple and beguilingly easy to explain. The approach Republicans want to take make it ultimately sounder, but also more subtle and hard to dramatize even when it works."

The editorial went on to suggest a change in welfare laws to reward recipients willing to work, rather than penalize them. (In 1969 the Nixon administration proposed a welfare-reform program, formulated by Daniel Patrick Moynihan, that would do just that, but Congress failed to enact it into law.)

The *Journal* frequently railed against the excesses and wastefulness of welfare and ". . . the whole snowballing range of handouts for rich and poor, farmer and businessman, city and state and practically everybody except the ordinary, tax-ridden middle-class man." The paper insisted, however, that it was not against all federal aid; it simply urged "ways to make it effective and worthy of a free society."

The *Journal* reiterated its plea for the government to stay out of people's lives when a group of backwoods families in Appalachia resisted a plan that would have forced them to move to urban areas so they could qualify for federal aid. Protesting a study that had been authorized to find out why these residents of Appalachia did not want sewers, water systems, hospitals and vocational schools, Royster wrote:

A cardinal principle of democracy, the last we heard, was that the State serves the will of the people. These people want to be let alone. Since they are harming no one, it follows that the Government has every obligation to let them alone.

In July, 1952, the *Journal* asserted that it was Eisenhower Republican—hardly a surprise when approximately 80 percent of an editorial titled "The Candidates" was devoted to the former general. The paper referred to Eisenhower and his advisors as if the two were totally separate, the former pure, the latter tainted.

Mr. Eisenhower is a man about whom there can be built a positive campaign. He has shown administrative ability of a high order. He has a deep love for America and for things American and a desire to serve his country. These are the things that recommend him to a great many people. . . .

Here is a man of stature, a fine and able man willing and eager to conduct a campaign with a high level of discussion of public affairs. And he has been loaded down with a lot of third-rate amateurs whose idea of political tactics is a screaming denunciation of an opponent. A man who consented to be a candidate from a deep sense of service and duty has been made to appear as an ambitious self-seeker, struggling for delegates.

Despite the efforts of his friends, Mr. Eisenhower has a good chance of getting the nomination.

If he should get it, we suggest that his first action should be to shake his coattails vigorously.

In the first paragraph of its editorial the *Journal* maintained that it was continuing its traditional policy of "adhering to principles" and not making "commitments either to parties or to candidates." This disclaimer notwithstanding, the *Journal*'s treatment of Democrats tended to be harsh. Eisenhower's opponent, Illinois Governor Adlai Stevenson, got off lightly in one column:

Let us say immediately that we have no intention of attempting to brand Adlai Stevenson of Illinois as the proverbial, straddling, pompous old wind-bag who seeks merely to be a time server. Gov. Stevenson appears quite otherwise. But it is certainly true that he sees both sides of all issues on which he has commented. . . . You go and read the speeches and you get the picture of a man, a man of intellect rather than a man of action, who can analyze penetratingly but who seldom, if ever, caps that analysis with a commitment. . . . [The Republican party faces] an extremely articulate man of persuasion and charm.

The Democratic party and outgoing President Harry Truman came in for some rougher treatment:

To many people "Trumanism" and the Democratic party are one and the same, associated with graft, inefficiency, and sellouts to the labor leaders. . . . Even the Democrats know this.

Truman had claimed in a press conference that Stevenson, like all politicians, was running on his party's record. The *Journal* agreed the Illinois governor was indeed linked to the record of the previous twenty years: "No party can run away from its record any more than a man can run away from himself."

The *Journal* regularly praised Eisenhower for his understanding, moral courage, and patriotism. Stevenson was condemned for any number of failings, including a susceptibility to "alien ideas."

One of the new things with which Mr. Stevenson's party experimented was the idea that government is immune from laws of frugality . . . another of the new things roaring through the world . . . was the doctrine that the individual is incapable of ordering his affairs. . . .

Both of these doctrines—call them socialism or the welfare state or what you will—came swirling on the tide from overseas. The party of power for the last twenty years embraced these alien ideas and changed the character of the nation.

The character of the nation continued to change, of course, even with Eisenhower in the White House. The party in power is only one of many factors that influence a nation's attitudes and development.

When Eisenhower and Stevenson opposed each other again in 1956, Alan L. Otten wrote in the *Journal* that Stevenson might be as indecisive as he had been in 1952, because "he wants to be free to calculate the risks right up to the last moment." Otten described Stevenson as a "highly intellectual, moody person," "extremely self-conscious about having no permanent job," "quite likely to become depressed," "still given to soul-searching and to vacillation," and "still self-deprecating." No one will ever know whether this highly unflattering portrait contributed to Stevenson's defeat, but Dwight D. Eisenhower was elected to a second term.

The *Journal* was unusually kind to President Eisenhower, probably because everything seemed to return to normal during his presidency. The country was at peace. Wall Street was more confident and optimistic. The economy was strong and continued its upward movement.

As Barney Kilgore had undoubtedly foreseen, Eisenhower showed minimal interest in Wall Street and its institutions. His advisors looked on governmental regulatory agencies—particularly the Securities and Exchange Commission—as New Deal leftovers with little contemporary relevance. During the Eisenhower years *The Wall Street Journal* covered few corporate frauds or scandals, mainly because the SEC had so little clout. The agency had less than 750 employees at the time; most were clerks, typists, or rejects from other agencies. What few ambitious people there were had little chance to demonstrate their talents.

During Eisenhower's presidency the country was prospering, and Wall Street was riding one of its waves of popularity. The financial health of the nation was measured by increasing profits in the automobile industry, the bellwether of the American economy.

Henry Gemmill, whom Barney Kilgore called "the finest news-writing talent I have ever known," had become managing editor of the *Journal* in 1950. Visualizing the newspaper as the "conscience of business," Gemmill pioneered the concept of investigative reporting. One of his most resounding blockbusters was his historic confrontation with General Motors.

On May 28, 1954, staff reporter John D. Williams wrote a column with a Detroit dateline: "1955 Autos—The Most Makes Ever Will Get Restyling and Powerful New Engines . . . See Pictures on Page Ten." Williams wrote about the four giant automobile manufacturers—General Motors, Ford, Chrysler, and Packard—and presented a forecast of their 1955 models: "More makes will be thoroughly restyled than ever before in the half-century of automotive history. Under many of the hoods will be new, more muscular engines."

Traditionally the carmakers kept mum about their new models right up to the minute they stopped making the old ones. Under normal circumstances that announcement was months away. But the dies and tools required for creation of the '55 models were being made in May, when Williams decided to write about the new cars that would eventually be rolling off the assembly lines.

He managed to get his hands on some blueprints, and from those he projected what consumers would find in automobile showrooms some four months later. Pulling no punches, Williams described the leading models. The 1955 Chevrolet, he wrote,

. . . will look very much like the present Oldsmobile except that it, too, will have an "egg-crate" grille, hooded headlights and a different, larger tail light. The super deluxe Bel Air series will be even more super. A brand new V-8 engine will be offered, with more horses in it than the present 125 h.p. six cylinder motor. As has long been the case with Ford, however, the Chevvy customer will be able to take his choice between the V-8 and a six-cylinder engine; the latter won't be abandoned.

Having obtained the blueprints, Williams felt he had every right to go ahead and inform the *Journal*'s readers what the automobile industry had in store for them. Barney Kilgore and Henry Gemmill agreed. General Motors did not.

At 5:30 P.M. on the day Williams's story appeared the advertising

Broad Street, looking south from Wall Street, circa 1885. The first home of
Dow Jones & Company is toward the rear of the street.

Clarence Henry Dow (1851-1902),
co-founder of Dow Jones & Company.

Edward Davis Jones (1856-1920),
co-founder of Dow Jones & Company.

Charles Milford Bergstresser,
partner of Dow and Jones.

FURNISHED BY

DOW, JONES & CO.

Financial News Agents,

No. 15 WALL STREET.

FOR CUSTOMERS' AFTERNOON LETTERS

New York, Thursday, May 15, 188.

MORNING GOSSIP.

Windsor thronged last night. It was known that the investigating committee was at work for the Metropolitan Bank, and everybody agreed that the market to day would depend a good deal upon whether the bank would be able to resume or not.

If it was in a condition to be carried through by the Clearing House banks, other failures would be obviated and relief would be felt.

The announcement that the bank will resume is therefore assurance of a better feeling to day.

Everybody agreed that the action of the Clearing House saved the street and would prevent a money panic to-day.

The point was made that the loan certificates would act as an inflation measure. It would enable parties holding securities to borrow money on them, as the bank making the loan would be secured. Under these circumstances it was thought that the large operators could secure certificates to almost any extent.

Some of the large houses made arrangements last night for the certification of all their checks before 10 o'clock this morning.

9 A. M.—The Metropolitan Bank is open. None of the officers are down, but the clerks say they are told that the bank will open between 10 o'clock and noon.

President Rolston of the Farmers' Loan & Trust Company, laid particular stress on the action of the Clearing House. He said that each bank left to itself and forced to stand a run could be broken, but united by this action, none of them could be hurt. This action by the Clearing House had heretofore brought everything out all right.

Bank Presidents at the Windsor admitted calling loans and refusing to certify, private bankers did the same with the result of looking up money. This caused some of the failures. Customers would be helped to-day by certification and loans. Parties who could not respond to calls yesterday, would be allowed to renew loans to-day. Money would be eased by this action.

Large shorts covered yesterday, and in a good many instances went long in order to steady the market. Conspicuous among the buyers were H. N. Smith, Mr. Johnes, Mr. Van Emburgh, Mr. Chapin, Soutter & Company, and H. L. Horton & Company. Mr. Smith was a large buyer of Western Union.

Mr. Gould bought and sold, apparently keeping his account about even.

The withdrawal of support in Western Union Monday, was on the discovery by Mr. Gould of inside selling.

The *Tribune* interview with Dr. Green is worth reading.

One result of the disturbance is expected to be conservatism in railroad management. The disposition of the companies will be to make themselves as strong as possible financially and no risks will be run in paying unearned dividends or interest.

It was stated positively that the Metropolitan elevated difficulties were settled. Mr. Kneeland stated that a settlement had been nearly reached, the first time he has said anything of the kind. The terms of settlement were not obtainable. Rumour said that the Manhattan Company would issue some sort of bond for the purpose of retiring the Metropolitan stock. Another statement was that the arrangement would be similar to that made with New York Elevated.

9 A. M.—Cashier McGourkey, of the Metropolitan Bank, says: "We shall resume at 12 o'clock."

Atchison, Topeka and Santa Fe dividend 1½ per cent. payable to-day. Pullman dividend 2 per cent. payable to-day. Canadian Pacific books open to-day.

Mr. O. M. Bogart says he can give no statement as yet. If the Metropolitan Bank resumes it will help him.

One of the first Customers' Afternoon Letters printed by Dow Jones & Company.

THE WALL STREET JOURNAL.

VOL. 1—NO. 1.　　　　　NEW YORK, MONDAY, JULY 8, 1889.　　　　　PRICE TWO CENTS

Average Movement of Prices.

The bull market of 1885 began July 2, with the average price of 12 active stocks 61 49.

The one culminated May 18, 1887, with the same twelve stocks selling at 91 27.

Prices gradually declined for about a year, reaching the next extreme low point April 2, 1888, the 12 stocks selling at 75 29. The movement since then, counting from one turning point to another, follows:

Last low point	Apr. 2, 1888,	75 29
Rallied to	May 1, "	80 54
Declined to	June 13, "	77 12
Rallied to	Aug. 8, "	85 95
Declined to	Aug. 18, "	83 76
Rallied to	Oct. 1, "	88 16
Declined to	Dec. 5, "	81 88
Rallied to	Feb. 18, 1889,	87 77
Declined to	Mar. 18, "	84 12
Rallied to	June 22, "	91 78
Closed Sat. night	July 6, "	87 71

The Market To-Day.

There is some reason for believing that operators identified with the bear party sent early orders to London to depress Americans in that market as a preparation for the opening here. These orders were faithfully executed, and London at 9.30 was quoted as opening weak and as having become very weak. Prices, however, were only a little below New York closing figures.

Clearings Last Week.

Boston special—The Post's table of clearings shows gross exchanges of 41 cities for the week ending July 6, 1889, $1,127,114,829 against $968,993,314 last year, an rise of 27 5%.

Bankers Exerting Their Power.

The Position of Atlan.

Jersey Central Dividend.

Boston Money Market.

Philadelphia Market To-day.

Washington special

First copy of *The Wall Street Journal*, July 8, 1889.

Clarence W. Barron (1855-1928) purchased Dow Jones & Company in 1902 and founded Barron's in 1921.

William Peter Hamilton, editor (1908-1929) of *The Wall Street Journal* during Barron's presidency.

Hugh Bancroft, president of Dow Jones & Company from the death of his stepfather, Clarence Barron, until his own untimely death in 1933.

Kenneth Craven Hogate (1897-1947), vice-president and general manager of Dow Jones & Company following the death of Clarence Barron. He became president in 1933 after the death of Hugh Bancroft.

Centers of the News of Finance

Pacific Coast Edition of
The Wall Street Journal

New York Auxiliary
Plant - 1930

First Wall Street Journal
Building 1893-1931

First Home at 15 Wall St.
1882-1886

DOW, JONES NEW BUILDING
In New York—1932

26 Broad Street
1886-1889

41 Broad Street
(at extreme right)
1889-1893

Dow Jones buildings in New York City, 1882-1932.

Vermont Royster (second from left), editor of *The Wall Street Journal* from 1958 until 1971; Bernard Kilgore (second from right) (1908-1967), managing editor of *The Wall Street Journal* from 1941 and president of Dow Jones & Company from 1945; William Kerby (right) (1908-), president of Dow Jones & Company from 1966, chairman of the board in 1972.

William Grimes (1892-1972), editor of *The Wall Street Journal* from 1941 until 1958.

cancellations began to pour in. D. P. Brother & Company in Detroit dropped 840 lines promoting GM's New Departure division; the Kudner Agency in New York canceled two Buick advertising insertions totaling 800 lines; Campbell-Ewald in Detroit canceled four Chevrolet ads of 672 lines each, and Foote, Cone & Belding of Chicago dropped four ads for the Frigidaire division, totaling 1,437 lines. The loss in ad revenues came to some $11,221, a hefty sum in 1955.

If anyone needed proof that *The Wall Street Journal* was not controlled by its advertisers, this was it. General Motors, the country's largest automobile manufacturer and second largest corporation, had removed what could ultimately amount to a quarter of a million dollars' worth of annual advertising from its columns. The incident gave the *Journal*'s critics something to think about. It gave General Motors, the largest newspaper advertiser in the world, even more to ponder.

Initially the public knew nothing of the contretemps. Then, two weeks after Williams's article was published, there was an item in Walter Winchell's column in the *New York Daily Mirror:* "General Motors and Wall Street newspaper are feuding. Its reporters are now barred from GM press confabs."

With the news out Barney Kilgore realized that General Motors would be quick to defend its own position and attack the *Journal*'s. A June 16 editorial, headlined "A Newspaper and Its Readers," anticipated the car manufacturer's assault:

The burden of their complaint [letters from readers] is that any news of new models before the manufacturers are ready to announce them hurts the sales of current models; if customers know that 1955 models will be better they will postpone purchase. Similarly, news that one dealer is offering some special "bargain" will make other customers demand like bargains and this will damage the new car market. . . . The burden of their plea is that this newspaper should publish only such news as is approved by the manufacturers, the dealers or their trade associations. This would insure the proper kind of news being printed.

After refuting the theory that the *Journal* article would have a negative impact on 1954 auto sales, the editorial went on to deal with the more crucial issue: the idea that it was a disservice to business to

83

publish information that a particular branch of business didn't want published.

Would they wish us to print only the banking news approved by bankers, only the steel news approved by steel officials, only the real estate news approved by real estate agents? If we followed that practice would they not soon wonder how much information was not being printed and begin to doubt the usefulness of this newspaper's service?

Although the *Journal* was never formally notified that it was being cut off from General Motors news, press releases stopped coming in. When the paper's reporters directed queries to regional offices of the car maker, they were curtly informed that no information would be given to them.

General Motors' retaliatory stance soon came under fire from papers other than the *Journal*. The press around the country firmly backed Kilgore's stand.

The *New York Times* headlined its story "G.M. Blacklisting Wall Street Journal: Cuts Off News Releases and Advertising After Story on '55 Automobile Models." It reported that the automobile giant was even refusing to give the *Journal* the weekly production figures that it had heretofore furnished each Friday.

The *Journal* reprinted the complete *Times* article on June 21, with this explanation: "The following news story is reprinted with permission, from *The New York Times* of Saturday, June 19. *The Wall Street Journal* is one of the subjects of this story; we wanted our readers to have an independent news account."

It can be argued that General Motors had a right to be angry at the editors of *The Wall Street Journal* for publishing news about their new car models. But GM's sledgehammer retaliation through canceled ads and the cutoff of news releases seemed beneath the dignity of the mammoth corporation.

If, as it claimed, the auto maker had a "property right" to the blueprints of its new models, did such a "right" preclude publicity when the manufacturer itself was responsible for disseminating the plans "to industry sources and suppliers in the normal course of business only on a confidential basis" and, in the process, taking the risk of having them become available to others? In other words, how good was GM's security? The company charged that there had been "a breach of a confidential relationship.'' But the *Journal*'s reporter did not use information that was given to him by GM officials confidentially. The violated confidence was between GM and one of its suppliers.

There had been no complaint from GM that the facts of the story were inaccurate. The controversy arose only because the newspaper printed what the car maker considered ''trade secrets,'' news it was not ready to release.

This raised the question of whether a newspaper had to wait for official release of information before publishing it. General Motors believed that it did, a position predicated more on precedent, particularly in the automotive business, than on the traditional concepts of news reporting. Basically the argument was between adherents of the ''proprietary right'' theory and those of the ''news is where you find it'' school.

General Motors, like any other corporation, has the right to place its advertising where it will do the most good. It also has the right to cancel such advertising if it is not getting results. But to cancel all advertising in a publication because a news story does not meet with the advertiser's approval raises a serious question as to why the advertising was put there in the first place. Was GM advertising in the *Journal* because it was a good medium for its messages? Or was GM's advertising intended only to have an influence on news and editorial policies? If the former was the case, the automobile manufacturer could only lose by canceling its ads. If the latter was true, then GM would have to approve all news and editorial policies of every publication in which it advertised.

By the end of June public relations officials at General Motors were trying to explain and defend their actions and, at the same time, extricate themselves from the situation without appearing to yield on their basic point about property rights.

In an effort to reach a peace settlement, Kilgore and Harlow Curtice, president of General Motors, met on July 7, 1954. Kilgore described what happened:

I just told Curtice that much as we would like to be friends with General Motors and much as I hated losing all that advertising, I couldn't let anyone dictate what the *Journal* could or couldn't print. Besides that, I told him, if

85

I did what he wanted I'd lose two of the best editors in the United States. In time I could replace the advertising, but I'd be damned if I knew where to find new editors.

The matter was finally resolved by an exchange of letters between Dow Jones and General Motors. Both were dated July 9 and were printed simultaneously in the *Journal* on July 12. Curtice denied any intent on the part of the automobile giant to control or manipulate what any publication printed. He insisted however that GM owned a "common-law copyright" and therefore had property rights to the source material, the designs used to reproduce the 1955 Chevrolet. Kilgore reiterated his newspaper's policy of publishing anything its editors thought suitable and went on to declare that he saw no conflict between that policy and respect for the property rights of others.

The publication of these two letters served as an announcement that General Motors Corporation and *The Wall Street Journal* had "reached an understanding" on their differences. GM had resumed sending news releases to the *Journal* three weeks before, and *Journal* reporters were no longer being shunned by GM executives.

"Truce" was the title of *Time* Magazine's July 26 report of the incident. "Last week, with the misunderstanding straightened out, the W.S.J. was once again getting both the regular flow of G.M. news and the $250,000 a year in ads that G.M. had cancelled."

By the end of July things were back to normal, and General Motors was locked in a struggle with Ford to see which of the two companies would have the bestselling automobile in the United States. The 1955 models hit the market in late December, and the new year proved to be an excellent one for the entire automobile industry.

Things turned out well for *The Wall Street Journal* too. As Bill Kerby noted:

This dramatic incident, and the spate of national publicity it engendered, firmly established in the public mind, including millions who never had read *The Wall Street Journal,* and presumably never would, that here was a newspaper of unshakable independence and integrity. GM had done us a priceless favor.

6

The Sixties and Beyond

I do not mean to sound prideful or arrogant but it is the simple truth that the American economy literally could not function without an information such as the Journal*.*

WILLIAM KERBY,
Dow Jones president

IN THE 1960 PRESIDENTIAL CONTEST between John F. Kennedy and Richard M. Nixon the *Journal,* exhibiting its usual Republican tendencies, favored Nixon. Kennedy's New Frontier promises were too far out of line with the paper's philosophy:

Reliance on government is, indeed, the key to the New Frontier. More and more Government will solve all problems. The farm problem, for example, will be solved by taking over the farmers. . . . The nation is being offered the stagnant image of an outworn age—a New Frontier that looks increasingly like a dead end.

Nixon, on the other hand, was described as "not temperamentally a man who would charge into our established system to remake it to his own ends," implying, of course, that Kennedy was. The *Journal*'s editors conceded that neither administration would be frugal, but said that Kennedy "likes to spend," it was his "answer for almost everything." On economic problems—always of prime consideration—Kennedy was said to "play both sides of the street, but Nixon has shown that he does understand the relationship between one economic policy and another." On civil rights: "Mr. Nixon is no less passionate about correcting what social ills remain, but he is not bemused, as Mr. Kennedy is, by the idea that all can be put right overnight by putting a policeman's club in the hands of the Federal Government."

The *Journal*'s editors found still another reason to deny Kennedy the White House: he avoided the issue of "honest money . . . so the reality the country faces is that it either accepts the rigors of financial discipline or it turns to the fiscal irresponsibility of inflation."

The newspaper's business orientation has been invariably reflected in its interest in the candidates' fiscal attitudes. The editors have repeatedly emphasized sound money, a balanced budget, taxes, and the national debt. They are concerned about social-welfare programs and foreign aid because they worry about who'll pay the bills. Even in their arguments against excessive foreign involvement on the grounds that the United States cannot save the world, there usually has been at least one paragraph in the article touching on the financial side of the picture.

When, as it sometimes happens, the *Journal* finds fault with a Republican candidate, it is apt to criticize him for style rather than substance. During Nixon's first presidential campaign, for instance, the *Journal* declared:

The chief criticism to be made of Vice-President Nixon's campaign so far . . . is this: While he certainly talks sense on a number of issues, he does not seem to be getting across a clear and positive program. It sometimes sounds diffuse, imitative, and even defensive.

On November 8, 1960, voters put John F. Kennedy in the White House by the smallest margin of victory in the twentieth century. The business community, which had, for the most part, supported Nixon, began to worry. If the new President followed through on his campaign promises, they would be in for the greatest antibusiness crusade since Roosevelt's New Deal.

At first all went well. The Dow Jones industrials remained stable in 1961. Nevertheless, by year's end it was determined that only $2.7

billion in new funds went into the stock market, while $5 billion had been invested in corporate bonds, $5.1 billion in state and local bonds, and $5.2 billion in Treasury securities. In early 1962 the Bank of New York instituted a 10 percent cutback in its pension trust-fund stockholdings. Meanwhile Congress ordered an SEC inquiry into the runaway market, and its probe of the American Stock Exchange and the roles of specialists uncovered several instances of chicanery.

Most economists and Wall Street observers remained "cautiously optimistic" about financial developments, but a few began to talk of the "profit squeeze." Financial journals reported corporate profits increasing at only 3.3 percent, while federal spending had risen more than 20 percent, the GNP by 19 percent, payroll expenditures by well over 18 percent. For a brief period securities were being traded with little focus on the reality of the economy.

The *Journal* was never friendly toward the Kennedy administration and even less so after the President pressured U.S. Steel into holding the line on prices in 1961. The newspaper wrote: "We never saw anything like it. One of the country's companies announced it was going to try to get more money for its product and promptly all hell busted loose."

In early April, 1962, the Dow Jones industrials dropped to 685.67, creating what market theorists referred to as a "sell signal." At about this time the SEC began its investigation of the Billie Sol Estes scandal, and there were rumors that duPont would be distributing its holdings of General Motors. As the major glamour stocks began dropping in value, Kennedy was definitely seen as antibusiness.

By mid-May the bear market was in full swing. On Monday, May 21, the New York Stock Exchange posted 460 new lows for the year, against 5 new highs. By the end of the week the value of all listed stocks on the exchange had dropped $30 billion, the sharpest drop since the 1929 Crash.

Much of the investors' anger was directed toward Kennedy. One broker said bitterly, "This is what we get for putting a rich man's son in the White House."

Few corporate giants spoke out. Only J. Paul Getty, the oil tycoon, was heard from. He said that he had bought stocks during the troubling week. "When some folks see others selling they automatically follow suit. . . . I do the reverse—and buy. I don't think the slide will go on. In fact, I think there will be a rather substantial rise and very shortly.''

The following afternoon the market began its greatest rally since the end of the Second World War, registering a gain of nearly 5 percent. In the space of a few days the market had dropped nearly fifty points; now it rallied forty-one points. The near-crisis was over.

On June 20, 1962, the *Journal* estimated that during the previous six months Americans had lost nearly $100 billion; pension funds had dropped by $4.5 billion and life insurance firms had lost $1.3 billion.

Suspecting wrongdoing of some type, the SEC investigated the crash; its special committee reported signs of ''incompetence'' but none of ''malfeasance.''

Earlier stock market crashes had larger drops, but few had the potential for panic that existed on May 28, 1962. All the ingredients were in place: a runaway market, disenchanted investors, poor leadership. Fortunately there was no panic; instead there was a significant drop, a quick recovery, followed by another slide, and then a rapid bull market. Stability eventually returned, if only for a brief period.

On May 16, 1961, after the Bay of Pigs, John F. Kennedy's disastrous attempt to overthrow Castro, the *Journal* described a report on the administration's plan for ''undercover warfare.'' The story concluded with the pointed remark: ''Without going into secret details, indications can be reported that at least one such maneuver is being blue-printed at this moment for execution in a vital nation far-distant from Cuba.'' The reference was to South Vietnam. It made John F. Kennedy furious at *The Wall Street Journal*.

Perhaps the tensest moment of Kennedy's administration was the Cuban missile crisis in the autumn of 1962. Russia and the United States were having a showdown, and the *Journal* wondered in print what the outcome would be.

On September 5, 1962, Kennedy was quoted as calling Cuba's military ability ''defensive.'' If the U.S.S.R. had offensive missiles in Cuba, said the President, ''the greatest issues would arise.'' The *Journal* agreed with Kennedy advisors who felt that the incident in Cuba was being used to divert attention from Berlin. Writer William

Henry Chamberlain likened Nikita Khrushchev's choices to an option play in football. He could "run with the ball in Cuba or make a pass at Berlin."

As tension mounted, the *Journal* counseled that intervention in an explosive situation should be "swift, sure and with sufficient force to be effective." It also observed that "the Eisenhower record was not fully valued by everyone at the time . . . perhaps due to the fact its accomplishments were not dramatic. . . . If the Communist ambitions were contained for eight years, in twenty-one months they have come unleashed."

Four days later President Kennedy announced the United States blockade of offensive weapons being shipped to Cuba. The following day the *Journal* opined that the nation was firmly behind Kennedy, no matter what the consequences. Then, just as it had done at the start of World War II, the paper offered an assessment of the potential effects of a conflict on major industries: electronics, steel, transport, fuel and power, nonferrous metals, rubber, chemicals, machine tools, construction, food and fiber, consumer durables, and soft goods. A chronological account of events in the Cuban missile crisis was presented on October 24, including the fact that those who had warned about Cuba the summer before had been called "alarmists" by the President.

When Khrushchev capitulated and withdrew the missiles at the end of October, the *Journal* printed several articles analyzing the unprecedented Russian move. It hailed the incident as a "significant victory for the United States and President Kennedy in particular."

Yet the *Journal* continued to have strong objections to the way Kennedy exercised his executive power. A column described his conduct in harsh terms, as an effort to use "the pressure of fear—by naked power, by threat, by agents of the state security police."

Even before that, when the President-elect announced that he was planning to name his brother attorney general, *Journal* writer Robert Novak warned that Robert Kennedy could turn out to be an "unqualified disaster."

The White House–*Wall Street Journal* war had its lighter moments. The President once appeared before an audience of editors and publishers and in the question-and-answer session called on Vermont

Royster first. Royster promptly asked the kind of tough question for which he was well known.

Kennedy's press secretary, Pierre Salinger, was appalled. "Why did you call on him first?" he asked later.

"The little bastard was the only one whose name I knew," confessed Kennedy.

Like everyone else in the country the *Journal* mourned Kennedy's assassination, but they evinced little love for his successor. In describing Lyndon Johnson's presidency the paper said, "National politics today is pretty much a vacuum or at least a desert. It is arid of ideas . . ."

When Johnson ran for the presidency on his own in 1964, his Texas drawl and homey language were scored by many critics, but the *Journal* also had a few things to say about his opponent's oratorical style:

Barry Goldwater . . . more often has missed the mark because he has scattered his fire, aiming at so many targets in a single speech that concentrated and persuasive argument is brought to bear on no target. . . . Perhaps the times are out of joint for any but the easy catchphrases and the jury would not heed the best of advocates. But it is sad that for so many trials past none came forward to present the case, and now sadder still if a want of rhetoric should appear to the people a want of reason in the case at the bar.

Conflict between Lyndon Johnson and *The Wall Street Journal* was inevitable. The economic downturn during the Johnson administration prompted the President to conclude that if the method of calculating the Dow Jones industrial average were changed, the figures would give a brighter picture. White House pressure became strong and, according to Bill Kerby, "All attempts by editors to explain to White House surrogates why we couldn't and wouldn't comply with the president's wishes only served to intensify the campaign."

Finally Kerby flatly and decisively said, "No!" The President got his own way to some extent, however, when soon after that the New York Stock Exchange started its own more broadly based Index.

The press had started to chip away at Johnson in January, 1964. During his vice presidency he had accepted the gift of a $542 stereo set from his former aide, lobbyist Bobby Baker. How could a vice president accept such a gift from a dubious character like Baker?

In addition Louis Kohlmeier, Washington correspondent for *The Wall Street Journal*, wrote a series of articles on "The Johnson Wealth" in which he reviewed the rise of the Johnson fortune in general and the family radio and television empire in particular. On March 23, 1964, Kohlmeier wrote:

Unlike most businesses, a broadcasting enterprise can exist and expand only with governmental approval. From the very beginning and repeatedly thereafter, the fate of the Johnson family fortune has inevitably hung not only upon business acumen but also upon favorable rulings by the Federal Communications Commission. Yet FCC public records show not a single intervention by Representative, Senator, Vice-President, or President Johnson in quest of a favor for his wife's company.

The *Journal* had brought up an interesting question: How had a poor Texas boy living on government salary acquired all those millions?

Louis M. Kohlmeier won the 1965 Pulitzer Prize for "his enterprise in reporting the growth of the fortune of President Lyndon B. Johnson and his family." Kohlmeier's articles prompted public discussion of the Johnson broadcasting empire and led the President to provide a detailed audit of his finances.

The articles were based on facts painstakingly collected in Austin, Johnson City, and more than a dozen other Texas cities, as well as in Little Rock, Oklahoma City, Washington, and New York. Kohlmeier also dug into Federal Communications Commission files that were more than twenty years old and had long since been relegated to a government warehouse. He read yellowed copies of the *Congressional Record* from the days when Johnson was on the Senate Commerce Committee. He examined land deeds and bank stockholder lists at more than a half-dozen Texas county courthouses. He interviewed four of the FCC's seven commissioners, two former commissioners, and nearly a dozen FCC staffers. Kohlmeier also interviewed Johnson confidantes, broadcasters, brokers of television and radio stations, and present and past congressmen and senators.

According to Marquis Child, who met with Johnson around the time Kohlmeier's articles appeared, the President was furious: "Several times he spoke with contempt of the rich man's paper, *The Wall Street Journal.''*

During the Johnson administration the story was told of a white Lincoln Continental rocketing down a Texas highway. It was overtaken by a motorcycle cop, who waved the driver to the side of the road and, ticket book in hand, walked back to the car. The officer caught sight of the driver's unmistakable profile and gasped, ''Oh, my God!''

''Yes,'' growled a voice from inside the car, ''and don't you forget it again.''

Alan L. Otten of the *Journal*'s Washington bureau related this story in a long editorial and went on to recount some of the most often heard complaints about Johnson:

That the President drives people too hard, is too high-handed and arrogant, doesn't really want argument and independent points of view. That he is too preoccupied with his popular image, is too sensitive to criticism, spends too much of his time answering attacks he should ignore, that he tends to whine over his troubles and blame others for his mistakes. That when things go wrong he frequently turns nasty.

Veteran Washington reporters can't remember when it was so hard to obtain inside insight into an administration's short-term or long-term plans from the President himself, from the White House associates, or from Cabinet members and other high-level officials. The President and those few intimates who may know what's in his mind simply aren't saying anything much beyond self-serving platitudes, most other federal officials just don't know what the President has in mind.

Otten repeatedly attacked the President, whom he described as ''an abnormally egotistical man with a disturbing tendency to nurture and brood over criticism; his unhappiness roils with him until it bursts out . . .''

Henry Gemmill, chief of the Washington bureau, continued the onslaught. He described Johnson as an ''opportunist whose mastery of pure politics is devoted not to principle but to personal ambition or even profit.''

In August, 1964, two U.S. destroyers were ordered into the Gulf of Tonkin. What happened next triggered the escalation of the Vietnam War and the controversy that put a severe strain on national unity and policy.

It was three months before the next presidential election; press and public reaction seemed favorable on Johnson's decision to take the war to the North. The *Journal,* while regretting that the U.S. "is once again so enmeshed in so compromising a venture," concluded that "if the President's order means the government is at last on the road to firmness and decisiveness, it may be the best hope the circumstances offer."

Vietnam turned out to be far from the "significant victory for the United States" the *Journal,* among others, had hoped for. In the beginning American involvement was barely noticed by the press or the public, but attention grew when more troops were dispatched and the U.S. moved from its advisory role to a more active one. The *Journal* watched Vietnam developments but offered no solutions and subscribed to no definite policy, either hawk or dove. Eschewing all the various strident positions, the *Journal* discussed the war in essentially quiet, reasoned tones.

Although questioning the advisability of military programs in Southeast Asia, the *Journal* was not antiwar because ". . . to teach that war is always bad . . . is to teach that nothing is worth fighting for, which in turn is to say that freedom is not worth fighting for. Most Americans think it is, and they would not want their children indoctrinated in the contrary view."

In 1965, Vermont Royster wrote about some of the complexities the U.S. faced in Asia, noting:

. . . it's hard to keep sanguine about the chances of keeping a physical military fulcrum on that continent if the millions of Asians are determined to throw us out. If that be the case, the cost of staying would be staggering.

Royster added that the United States might not be able to control Asia but could nevertheless influence it.

In a March, 1965, article, "Diplomacy and Vietnam," *Journal* staff writer Philip Geyelin foresaw no possibility of negotiations because the United States was not a strong enough threat, and ideally countries negotiate from strength.

As the controversy over the war grew more heated, an editorial called "Hysteria Over Vietnam" observed that there was a great deal of ignorance about the war and its conduct, and that certain valid questions had arisen. Characterizing their position as little more than a "feeling," the editors warned against the possibility of the U.S. overcommitting itself in Vietnam by "trying to hold the place, by whatever tactics, without regard to costs and risks." They went on to say:

Should the Vietnamese war finally be deemed unwinnable, that would be a warrant for withdrawal. But the U.S. government must not be persuaded that deliberately handing over a people to communism is somehow a fulfillment of moral imperatives.

In early June, 1965, President Lyndon Johnson announced that American troops would engage in combat, a role that unquestionably went beyond "advising." The administration denied, however, that there had been a change in policy, saying that advisors had always been allowed to fight guerrillas defensively but not offensively. America's commitment in Asia was growing stronger by the day.

On January 29, 1968, the Vietnamese celebrated Tet, the lunar new year. A truce was declared in honor of the holiday. But the Vietcong violated the ceasefire and launched a series of all-out offensives. On January 31 the U.S. Embassy in Saigon was attacked and held by Vietcong for six hours, an embarrassing occurrence, both diplomatically and militarily.

A *Journal* editorial on these developments appeared on February 6. Calling Vietnam an "American dilemma," it placed the responsibility for defending itself on South Vietnam's shoulders, saying that "in the long run the U.S. cannot effectively give military aid to another country unless that country is determined to help itself stay out of the communist grip." The editorial declared that the onslaught "raises in the starkest form not only the question of weakness in Saigon but of whether the U.S. effort is reaching a point of diminishing returns."

At the end of March President Johnson startled the world by announcing that he would not run for the presidency again in 1968. On April 2 three page-one *Journal* columns dealt with the Johnson decision. One analyzed the reasons for his action, another assessed the gains he would reap from being the lame duck, while the third was a lighthearted examination of the problems created for cartoonists, campaign-button manufacturers, and weekly magazines with stories already set in type that made no mention of Johnson's move.

Editorially the *Journal* called the resignation a confession of failure:

There is not only Vietnam, which has grown worse not better during his term, but the social breakdown, the rioting in the streets, the erosion of our foreign alliances and the near breakdown of our monetary system. If they are not all due to Johnson policies, none have been ameliorated by his actions.

The editors said that Johnson had not inspired confidence, but that history would remember him as the first President "willing both to acknowledge his hopes confounded and plainly say the country would do better to choose another man." An analysis on the same page concluded that the new Democratic candidate Vice President Hubert Humphrey would have to call attention to his own policies to avoid being identified with Johnson's.

The *Journal* felt that Johnson's foreign policy lacked "clearly defined direction" and called for a priority list of projects facing the nation. It blamed the protests of various activist groups on LBJ's domestic philosophy: "that the Government can, if it only spends enough money, do just about anything for anybody." As for the Vietnam War the *Journal* stated that neither Eisenhower nor Kennedy had expected the U.S. to become involved to the extent it did after the Tonkin Gulf resolutions.

In late October, 1968, the U.S. halted its bombing of North Vietnam. The *Journal* took a wait-and-see attitude toward the presidential order. The paper considered the war a "Democratic war, in the sense that Democratic Presidents vastly deepened and enlarged the American involvement," but it did not leap at the chance to brand Johnson's announcement as a last-minute policy ploy designed to aid Hubert Humphrey in his quest for the presidency.

If the move did help Humphrey, it was not apparent in the election results. Seven months later President Richard Nixon was coping with the war. One of his first moves was to announce the withdrawal of 25,000 troops (less than 5 percent of the United States forces in Vietnam). The *Journal* was pleased to see the men coming home but questioned the "sizeable practical difficulties":

Saigon's military record gives no reason for confidence. . . . At best, also, Saigon would require American logistical support, and perhaps airpower as well, on an essentially permanent basis.

When the administration announced that it would withdraw an additional 35,000 men, the paper called the decision the "sensible thing to do under the depressing circumstances." But it also suggested that the Nixon administration publicly reveal "the broad policy the withdrawals are intended to serve." It conceded that the President must have options and not be held to a strict timetable, though noting that "the costs of an ambiguous policy include creating an impression there is no policy at all."

As the United States began to wind down its role in Vietnam, Vermont Royster wrote of the psychological effects of the defeat:

What we have to face now as a country is what men sometimes have to face in their private lives, an agony for which there is no balm. We are going to withdraw from the war in Vietnam not because it is a good solution but because we cannot do otherwise.

The *Journal* cited mistakes in Vietnam as one reason for what it saw as the collapse of liberalism "under its own deficiencies." The editors also blamed rising crime rates, urban unrest, and disorderly demonstrations on liberalism, which, they said, had "come to mean dependence on the powers of central government to solve nearly all problems." The liberal left, they said, was motivated by a "naive view of man, the search for frantic short-cuts, the devotion to commitments ahead of effectiveness, and excessive materialism." The declaration appeared a month before the 1968 election and prompted so much mail, pro and con, that the "Letters to the Editor" column had to be expanded.

Although the voters did choose a moderate conservative in 1968, Richard Nixon's mandate was so slight it could hardly have been interpreted as a death blow to the left. Even the *Journal* termed his win "a mushy mandate."

The editors may have been disappointed at the slimness of Nixon's victory, but they could be consoled by the fact that the electorate shared their sentiments. This was not often the case in the past. In the face of *Journal* disapproval Franklin D. Roosevelt had been elected to four terms, and in the previous fifty years Democrats had spent more time than Republicans in the White House.

Over the years *The Wall Street Journal* has been on the losing side in all sorts of political controversies. It has seen virtually uninterrupted deficit financing, continued expansion of the federal bureaucracy, and the proliferation of government "give-away" programs. Through it all the paper has maintained its conservative stand and fulfilled an editorial function that is vital to a free society: to challenge, not to echo.

The *Journal*'s editors applauded Richard Nixon's policies, particularly his handling of the war in Vietnam. In October, 1970, an editorial praising the President's new major peace initiative declared, "However Hanoi finally responds, in fact, the President has put forth an American position so appealing and so sane that only the most unreasonable critics could object to it."

When Nixon finally did end the war in Indochina, the *Journal* joined the rest of the country in breathing a long sigh of relief.

In 1966 the paper marked its seventy-fifth anniversary. It had become the third largest daily newspaper in the country with a circulation of 844,824 (exceeded only by the weekday editions of the *New York Daily News* and the *Chicago Tribune*).

The Dow Jones team at the time consisted of Bernard Kilgore, president; William F. Kerby, vice president; Buren H. McCormack, vice president and general manager; and Robert Bottorff, executive editor of all Dow Jones publications. Each had come out of the news department, and each had served as managing editor of the *Journal*.

It was a time of unprecedented prosperity for Dow Jones. The company now employed more than 2,150 people full time and operated a private communications system with 101,926 miles of leased lines for the transmission of news and information. *The Wall Street Journal* had a staff of 196 reporters and editors in 15 U.S. news offices and 6 foreign bureaus.

99

In 1965 Barney Kilgore learned that he had terminal cancer. "I have cancer, but I am going to live my life as though I didn't," he told Bill Kerby.

Kilgore immediately began to develop a plan for reorganizing the management of Dow Jones & Company. Kerby would move up to the presidency, while Kilgore would become chairman and chief executive officer. The line of succession would continue in the years to come. Eventually Kerby would become chairman of the board and Buren McCormack would move up to the presidency.

Eager to show his regard for his longtime associates, Kilgore told Kerby, "It would be nice for all the top people before they retire to be able to say, 'I was president of DJ.' "

Then he added, "And find something important for Roy [Vermont Royster] to do. He's lazy, but he's smart as hell."

After Kilgore died on November 14, 1968, Vermont Royster, then editor of the *Journal,* memorialized his old friend with eloquent simplicity, "If you ask what manner of man he was, his friends can only tell you he had a touch of genius and was to the full measure a gentleman."

William Kerby became chief executive officer of Dow Jones in the spring of 1966, just a few months shy of his fifty-eighth birthday. As Kerby tells it: "I was born on T Street in the Northeast section of Washington, D.C., in a house shared by my parents, grandmother Kerby, and my father's sister, Mary, and younger brother Robert."

At the age of eighteen, through the good offices of his father, a reporter with the Scripps newspapers, Bill got a summer job as a junior reporter on the *Washington Daily News.*

Early in the morning of July 5, 1926, I set out to report for my first day's work. Walking up Pennsylvania Avenue, I saw smoke pouring out of a Chinese restaurant. In a moment, scantily clad Chinese began jumping out of windows; obviously the help slept on the premises. I ran to a phone booth and called the *News* city desk.

Kerby wrote his first feature story and was praised by his editor for "alertness" and also for keeping his story short.

At the University of Michigan, Kerby joined the staff of the *Mich-*

igan Daily, at that time the premier college newspaper in the country. The summer after his sophomore year his father's friend and golfing partner, William Grimes, who was at that time the *Journal*'s bureau manager in Washington, offered young Kerby a job as a summer trainee. In late August, as Kerby was getting ready to return to Ann Arbor, Grimes gave him a pocket dictionary as a parting gift. "You have a job here next summer," he said, "but it would be nice if you would just learn to spell."

Kerby graduated from the University of Michigan, Phi Beta Kappa, in 1930 and declined several other job offers to work for the *Journal*. He returned to Washington only to learn that Dow Jones was beginning to feel the effects of the Depression and was desperately cutting expenses. Bill Grimes's promise of a job had to be broken. Instead Kerby went with the *Federated Press* and later became a dictation typist with United Press for $35 a week.

In his book *A Proud Profession* Bill Kerby recounted how he finally returned to the *Journal* in the spring of 1933. Bill Grimes arranged for him to meet Casey Hogate at a Washington club:

We lunched at the "members restaurant." Casey's appetite matched his size. The restaurant was famous for its seafood pie, an enormous dish composed of creamed lobster, crab, oysters, shrimp, and filet of sole, topped with a baked mashed potato cover and embellished with a full two ounces of beluga caviar. I recommended the dish. Casey ordered it; finished it; and ordered a second. "Don't ever mention this to my wife; I'm a refugee from a diet."

Then Hogate asked Kerby his birthplace.

"The District of Columbia," was the reply.

"That's terrible," said Hogate. "Where were you brought up?"

"Mostly in and around Washington," Kerby admitted.

"That's even worse! Where were you educated?"

"The University of Michigan."

"Well," said Hogate with a broad grin, "there may be some hope for you yet. The salary is fifty-five dollars a week to start, and when can you start?"

Kerby stayed at the *Journal* until not long after his marriage in 1935. By then he had managed to win a $5-a-week raise, but it didn't seem adequate to support a wife. "For the first time in my young professional career," he recalled later, "my salary became more important than my job." When he asked for a raise at the *Journal,* Grimes replied briskly, "No one is getting a raise."

Kerby left the newspaper to join the public relations department of the American Liberty League, which he described as a "well-heeled organization formed to do battle with the Roosevelt New Deal." His salary jumped from $60 a week to $105.

Happily, Fanny Kerby was astute enough to see that her husband had made a mistake. "I don't care about the money," she said, "you'll never be happy doing anything else." Bill soon returned to the *Journal* for the same $60 a week, but transferred to its New York offices, where he manned the copy desk on the 2:00 P.M.-to-midnight shift. Kerby never regretted his decision to return to Dow Jones. The *Journal*'s sales were shaky, but it had achieved considerable respect in Washington.

In 1938 Bill Grimes, who had also moved to New York and became managing editor, made Kerby assistant managing editor of both the newspaper and the Dow Jones News Service, the "ticker." Kerby was presiding over the copy desk on October 1 when Hitler's army entered the Sudetenland, the German-speaking area ceded to Germany by a Czechoslovakia left impotent by the Munich agreement.

Grimes, a late riser, usually arrived at the office around noon, but a Dow Jones News Service printer had been installed in his Brooklyn Heights apartment to keep him in touch with the news. On the morning of the Sudetenland takeover, and in the midst of the uproar created by reports, later proved false, of fighting between Czech and German troops, the copy desk phone rang.

An apoplectic Grimes was on the other end of the line. "Why in the goddam hell didn't you call me?" he roared.

"Too busy and still am," Bill Kerby replied, slamming down the phone.

An hour later Grimes was on the scene. He marched over to the news desk, a roll of ticker copy in his hands, but instead of berating Kerby for his rudeness he said simply, "Nice job."

Bill Kerby was instrumental in building *The Wall Street Journal* to its present eminence and in transforming Dow Jones from a small financial publishing firm to a large and widely diversified company with interests in business publications, daily community newspapers, books, worldwide news wire services, newsprint manufacturing and other fields. Kerby himself held every major position on the news staff of the *Journal* before becoming an executive of Dow Jones. He was made news editor in 1938, assistant managing editor in 1941, and managing editor in 1943. In 1945 he became executive editor of Dow Jones publications and news services. Four years later, on January 1, 1949, he took on the additional responsibilities of treasurer of Dow Jones. On June 6, 1951, Kerby became vice president. From 1958 until May 1966 he also served as editorial director of the Dow Jones publications. He was elected executive vice president in 1961, president in 1966, and chairman of the board in 1972.

Kerby felt that his "success story" was based on "throwing away the rules." It was his judgment that good newspapers and good newspapermen needed a certain amount of daring; any paper or reporter who fell into a routine operation was doomed to flounder or fail.

When queried about one of the most significant events of the 1970s, publication by the *New York Times* of the Pentagon Papers, Kerby was quick to reply:

I have often been asked what I would have done if fortune and good reporting had brought the Pentagon Papers my way instead of to the *Times*. My answer is very simple. I would have published the news. I would have published on the same grounds that my colleagues at the *Times* published, through a firm belief in the right of the American people to know what their government is doing. . . . This is the only basis on which a democracy can function and a free people maintain their freedom.

A strong voice at Dow Jones & Company for forty-five years, Kerby was a member of a select group whom Vermont Royster dubbed "The last of the Mohicans." Explained Royster, "Bill Kerby is the last of that little band who made the modern *Wall Street Journal*."

Royster was one of the *Journal*'s outstanding reporters during Kerby's reign. Another is Edward R. Cony, who today is vice president/news at Dow Jones. He was awarded the 1961 Pulitzer Prize for reporting of national affairs for his analysis of a timber company's wheeling and dealing, which drew public attention to problems of business ethics.

The award-winning article, which appeared on August 15, 1960, described how officers and directors of Georgia-Pacific Corporation, a large timber and plywood concern, had used their relationship with the company for personal gain. Cony disclosed that Carrol Shanks, a director of Georgia-Pacific and president of Prudential Insurance Co. of America, had realized a substantial saving on his income taxes as a result of a personal transaction with Georgia-Pacific. It seems that Shanks had purchased 13,000 acres of Oregon timberland and then immediately sold it to Georgia-Pacific for the same price he paid for it, plus the costs of financing the transaction. Shanks financed the purchase with a $3.9 million bank loan. Since interest on this loan would be tax deductible, it was estimated that Shanks might save as much as $400,000 on his tax bill over the five-year life of the loan.

While maintaining there was nothing unethical about the transaction, Shanks subsequently disposed of his interest in the financing and resigned from Prudential, citing as a reason "my highly publicized personal transaction" with Georgia-Pacific.

Another Pulitzer Prize winner (in 1964) "for a distinguished example of local general or spot news reporting" was Norman C. (Mike) Miller. In an exclusive story on December 2, 1963, and in a series of follow-up articles, Miller exposed the multimillion-dollar swindle that became known as the "salad oil scandal." He told how more than $100 million worth of vegetable oil, pledged by Allied Crude Vegetable Oil Refining Corporation as collateral against loans, had never existed.

The first hint of the scandal occurred in late November, 1963, when Allied, the nation's largest supplier of edible oils for export, filed a bankruptcy petition. As investigators delved into the company's affairs, they discovered that some of the oil Allied was supposed to have stored at a Bayonne, New Jersey, tank farm was missing.

Mike Miller was the first to report that the oil was more than just missing, it was wholly imaginary. He was also the first to disclose the huge amounts of money involved and to unravel the tangled strands of the swindle and explain how it had worked. His Pulitzer was awarded for his comprehensive coverage of the scandal as it unfolded as well as for his initial stories.

The upshot of this incident was that Anthony De Angelis, president of Allied, was indicted on charges of transporting forged warehouse receipts for the "phantom oil."

The swindle also resulted in substantial losses to brokers, banks, and others holding the phony warehouse receipts, and to an American Express Company subsidiary that was supposed to be storing the oil on behalf of Allied. One brokerage house, Ira Haupt & Co., was forced out of business. A second, J. R. Williston & Beane, had to merge with another concern. The American Express subsidiary filed for protection under the bankruptcy laws.

In May, 1967, Monroe W. Karmin and Stanley W. Penn of *The Wall Street Journal* won the Pulitzer Prize for reporting on national affairs for their story "of the connection between American crime and gambling in the Bahamas."

In an article headlined "Las Vegas East" Karmin and Penn explored in detail how a big gambling casino was allowed to open in the Bahamas, thanks to an exemption from local laws granted by a group of top Bahamian political leaders known as the "Bay Street Boys."

The superstar of the *Journal* was Vermont Royster. When he was awarded the Pulitzer Prize in 1953 for editorial writing, the committee made the following comment:

An ability to decide the underlying moral issue, illuminated by a deep faith and confidence in the people of our country, is the outstanding characteristic of the editorials of Vermont C. Royster which won for him the 1953 award for editorial writing.

Under the general heading, "Review and Outlook," Royster's comments on the daily events of the world today are a regular feature of one of the country's outstanding financial publications. In his editorials, he has ranged from the Robinson-Maxim prizefight through such political events as the election campaign and the seizure of the steel industry by President Truman up to the significance of the New Testament's teaching in our daily life.

His warmth, simplicity, and understanding of the basic outlooks of the American people is illustrated by the closing paragraphs of his editorial of November 12, 1952, "The Quality of Morality": "We do not think Americans are immune to human frailties. Other things being equal they can be grateful for bread and circuses and express their gratitude at the polls. But present them a moral issue and nothing else is equal. . . . Once convince the people of a moral issue, be it at city hall or Capitol Hill, and they will set aside even cupidity. Long is the list—and now longer—of the would-be buyers of the electorate who have had their power snatched from them by the people's moral indignation."

"Roy" won tremendous respect among his coworkers. He was known for his solid approach to the world of finance and for his talent for taking any subject and finding an appropriate way to connect it to the economy of the day.

Royster was senior vice president of Dow Jones when he decided to retire at the age of fifty-six. He later confessed that he was never sure exactly why he did it. He was in line for the presidency when Bill Kerby retired, but that was years away. By then Royster would be sixty-two, leaving him only three years in the job before his own retirement.

New York City was becoming a less attractive place to live for him, and a winning bout against kidney cancer had temporarily sapped his strength. But in the long run it was probably his attachment to his native North Carolina that persuaded Royster to retire. He stepped down in mid-January, 1971, and became William Rand Kenan Professor of Journalism and Public Affairs at the University of North Carolina in Chapel Hill.

A reporter and writer for *The Wall Street Journal* for thirty-five years and the paper's editor for twelve of them, Vermont Royster's public voice was far from silenced by his retirement. He continues to write a column, "Thinking Things Over," that touches on a wide range of subjects. The veteran journalist once summed up his basic philosophy with the pungent remark, "I'm always pessimistic about the immediate present, but I'm always optimistic in the long run, however long that is. After all, the Dark Ages only lasted 500 years."

The post-World War II era had seen a distinguished team at the helm of *The Wall Street Journal*—Kilgore, Royster, and Kerby. Kilgore revived the *Journal* and brought it national acclaim, Royster gave it journalistic prestige, and Kerby prepared the way for still further progress and diversification, thus pointing Dow Jones toward an even more promising—and profitable—future.

The National Observer—
"America's Liveliest Newspaper"

It is a young publication and its evolution is by no means finished.
HENRY GEMMILL,
editor, *The National Observer*

IN 1961 BARNEY KILGORE and his executive team at Dow Jones & Company decided to launch a weekly national newspaper for a general readership. After a survey campaign and a drive for new advertisers, *The National Observer* made its debut on February 4, 1962. Within a year it had a circulation of approximately 220,000, an impressive figure for a fledgling newspaper.

The National Observer's first editor was William E. Giles, who grew up in Plainfield, New Jersey. He worked for a local newspaper during summer vacations from college and after graduating from Columbia went on to earn a graduate degree at that university's School of Journalism. He was hired fresh out of school by Dow Jones & Company as copy editor on *The Wall Street Journal*'s New York desk. From there he went on to become a reporter and rewrite man and eventually wound up in Dallas, Texas, where he was bureau chief and production supervisor for the plant that printed the southwest edition of the *Journal*. After three years in Texas, Giles was again promoted, this time to news editor at the Washington bureau.

In July, 1961, Barney Kilgore chose the thirty-three-year-old Giles to head the *Observer* and gave him free rein to get the weekly off the ground. Seven months later the first issue appeared.

It was an unusual kind of paper, one that did not report the news as it occurred, but instead summarized and analyzed it later and also carried feature articles on topical subjects. There was a story that went around in the early days of the paper that Kilgore had balked at giving *National Observer* reporters telephones. Gathering the news firsthand was not their business, he supposedly said.

The *Observer* was one of the first publications to write about national trends. As early as 1962 it began publishing articles analyzing the Vietnam situation. It also emphasized civil rights and education— in fact, almost everything but business—which was left to *The Wall Street Journal*.

Basically, we were writing for fairly young, intelligent, well-educated people living in the suburbs and smaller cities and aware of what the world was about. But one of the reasons the paper had problems was that there was never a time we could define our reader sharply enough for our national advertisers.

The newspaper was full-sized, usually running about twenty pages, with a front page that had large pictures or drawings and three feature articles. In a typical June issue, for instance, the lead articles were "The Music They Call Punk Rock," "Nutrition Fights Cancer," and "Farm Life Lures the Young," the last with a subtitle, "Hayseed image fades as students, many city-bred, jam ag schools." Inside there was a summary entitled "Top News of the Week," an analysis of the Helsinki agreement, questions and answers on natural gas reserves, and articles on sports, religion, and health.

Nine and a half years after he had launched *The National Observer*, Bill Giles was promoted to assistant general manager of Dow Jones & Company, and fifty-three-year-old Henry Gemmill took his place as editor of the weekly.

Although Gemmill looked more like a university professor than a journalist, there had never been much doubt about what he wanted to be. A poor boy who managed to get through Yale, Gemmill got his first real taste of journalism through his summer jobs as a reporter on the *Washington Evening Star*. He joined the *Star* after his graduation in 1939, but soon grew tired of "chasing ambulances and fire engines." Eager to report on national affairs, he jumped at an opportunity in 1942 to move to the *Journal*. During World War II Gemmill covered war agencies for the Washington Bureau of the *Journal*. In a 1971 Dow Jones newsletter he said, "Since I was green enough I got the knack of these new things more rapidly than most veteran reporters at the time. I was hauled indoors in Washington, and later to New York, to edit other people's 'leaders.' " Thus, after writing an occasional story for the front page, he found himself in a managerial role, becoming managing editor of the paper in 1950. By the mid-fifties, when the *Journal* had emerged as a national journalistic phenomenon, Gemmill was becoming uneasy. "I felt that I had been robbed of my youth as a reporter," he said. "They had needed editors so I had agreed to become one. But I got restless, and they finally agreed to let me go back to reporting."

After four years as managing editor, Gemmill went to Paris as European news editor. He traveled extensively, reporting on the vast area from the Scandinavian countries to the Middle East. Then he returned to the United States to an assignment on the West Coast. In 1957, when the *Journal* began a major effort "to get on big breaking national news stories," Henry came back to New York. Before long he was again sent to Europe as chief of foreign correspondents for what was supposed to be "a prolonged stay." But a year later, in 1960, he was called to head the *Journal*'s Washington bureau, where he spent the next ten years as an associate editor.

After a brief sabbatical to begin writing a "whodunit" novel, Gemmill was ready for his newest challenge: editor of *The National Observer*. He was quick to compare the young publication with the *Journal* of the 1940s: "It's still in the formative and interesting stage, but with one enormous difference. On the *Journal* originally we were starved for talent, so it was a back-breaking task to get anything done. Here with the *Observer* we are rich in talent, and the back-breaking time is mostly past. We have a great staff and we can quickly begin to accomplish most things we set out to do."

Gemmill set out to do several things, all of them aimed at attracting more readers and advertisers.

The most dramatic change was in the layout of the front page. Gemmill put fewer stories on it. Previously there had been at least six—now there were rarely more than three. The editor explained:

A time-motion study would show it is a tremendously inefficient thing for readers to follow the paper back and forth pursuing jumps. There is really no good reason for it in a publication like ours. Starting a lot of stories on the front page is okay for most dailies because they are trying to give readers a chance to scan headlines and quickly see what happened the day before. In our case, we are not going to report events of the previous day. So we are treating our front page as a cover to some extent. We are giving readers a showcase sampling of the kind of "goodies" that they can find all the way through the *Observer*. The billboard on the bottom of page one is the "ballyhoo" strip. It is aimed at the man who picks up his first copy on the newsstand and at the trial subscriber—to draw them into reading the whole issue and get hooked.

Under Gemmill the paper's editorial page also underwent alteration. Each of the "Observations" was now signed by its writer. Asked if this might signal a more controversial stance, Gemmill responded, "We are going to be prepared to dash off in all directions. I think people like to read opinions as well as facts. We are going to give them a broader and perhaps more vivid spectrum of opinion." In one article that typified Gemmill's approach staff writer Patrick Young began an inquiry into the Warner-Lambert Pharmaceutical Corporation. It was prompted by the news that the company's shareholders had voted down a recommendation that drugs sold overseas be labeled with the same safety precautions required by the United States Food and Drug Administration.

Chloromycetin, an antibiotic, was the primary drug in question. Young noted that it could cause intense pain and, in some cases, trigger a fatal blood disease known as aplastic anemia. Using FDA statistics, he calculated that 1 percent of the 25,000 to 40,000 users of Chloromycetin annually would develop the disease. Although the drug was often used in underdeveloped countries to treat typhoid fever, its manufacturers saw no need to warn foreign physicians of its potential side effects. "Warner-Lambert officials contend it is up to each foreign government to set drug-labeling requirements," Young reported. "So if a government doesn't require that its physicians be told Chloromycetin, or any other drug, may kill a few patients, Warner-Lambert isn't going to tell."

Gemmill never hesitated to take on controversial subjects; no theme was off bounds as long as it pertained to the "business of living" and stirred the minds and imaginations of *Observer* readers.

The results of this attitude were clearly demonstrated in the quantity and content of the paper's letters to the editor. The tones ranged from praise to contempt. The *Observer* made it a point to print as many as possible of both kinds. "Letters to the editor are potentially the best reading on the editorial page," Gemmill insisted.

The news staff of the *Observer* worked out of White Oak, Maryland, not far from Washington; the paper also had some eighty correspondents in other cities around the country. Their mission, as they saw it, was to help readers cope with the business of living on a very direct and personal level.

In keeping with this mission, the *Observer* embarked on a dialogue with its readers unique in contemporary journalism. Contributions from readers were solicited, encouraged, and published in a variety of ways.

A regular column, "Off Hours," for example, was devoted to essays from readers on the unusual ways in which they spent their leisure hours. From time to time readers' opinions were solicited on specific topics such as coping with higher prices, and the entire front page was turned over to their responses.

In addition there were page-one "plebiscites"—nonscientific polls of readers' opinions on subjects in the news. While not conducted by bonafide pollsters' methods, the plebiscites nevertheless reflected the intensity of interest in a given subject as well as the broad spectrum of opinions about it.

The smallest response—2,300 ballots—was to a question about the media's coverage of sex-oriented scandals in the government. The largest—72,632 ballots—was generated early in the Watergate affair by a question asking if President Nixon should resign from office. The outpouring of sentiment on this subject represented about 15 percent of the *Observer*'s subscribers at the time. It was estimated that they spent more than $5,000 in postage to participate in the plebiscite.

The question of Nixon's resignation drew mixed reactions from across the country and, in one case, the living room.

A letter published on June 30, 1973 stated:

Please cancel my subscription to the National Observer effective immediately. From my viewpoint The National Observer is but one jump ahead of the St. Louis Post-Dispatch—full of foolishness. For your own good why not sponsor constructive action in Europe, they think Watergate a foolish joke.

Harlan A. Gould
Kirkwood, Missouri

The following week another letter appeared:

I see in your letters accompanying the Plebiscite results that my husband has asked you to cancel our subscription to The National Observer. But it is not *his* subscription. It is *my* subscription and I do not want my subscription cancelled. Thank you.

(Mrs. Harlan A.) Jane Gould
Kirkwood, Missouri

Mrs. Gould continued to receive her *National Observer*.

The *Observer*'s commitment to reader involvement occasionally reached unusual extremes. Jim Driscoll, who traveled the country collecting material for his column, "Survival Tactics," once wrote a piece in which he dismissed watermelon as "watery mush."

Soon after the article appeared, he received a letter from Robina Bagwell of Spartanburg, South Carolina, who claimed that he had ". . . maligned that peerless product of the South." Intending to fill a gap in Driscoll's Yankee background, Robina challenged him to a duel with carving knife and teaspoon.

"We should meet under a large wateroak, by a rough wood table spread with *National Observers,* with a committee of knowledgeable growers who selected the melon," she wrote.

Remarking that he couldn't think of a better way to spend an afternoon, Driscoll accepted the challenge.

The Yankee, the challenger, the carving knife, assorted onlookers, and one large watermelon met near Spartanburg on July 19, 1971. A pecan tree replaced the wateroak, a local minister said grace, the watermelon was dissected, and the duel began. After several bites

Driscoll conceded defeat. "I pronounced the melon superb," he admitted publicly and, further, "that it cooled better than any drink I've tried."

Claiming to be the only publication in the nation that had devised a technique for making all of its readers mad at least some of the time, the *Observer* consistently refused to formally support any candidate for President of the United States. "We wouldn't if we could . . . but anyhow we can't" was its statement on the matter. During the Nixon-McGovern campaign Gemmill wrote:

Having abolished editorials, our publication . . . as an institution . . . no longer takes a position on any issue. Our *Observations* column continues with the same label but an entirely different function: expressing the personal opinions of individual members of the staff. Since the staff is varied, the opinions are diverse, inconsistent, contradictory; each item printed represents the view of the man or woman who signs it.

I have little doubt political opinions reflecting upon Nixon and McGovern candidacies will be printed during the campaign. I expect some will lean in one direction and the others the opposite way. I hope some rough balance will be struck in the *Observations* column. To help in sustaining a balance of opinion, we'll be printing plenty of reader letters on the same page.

Underlying all this is a basic calculation: We don't feel our readers want to be told what to think. The most we can do is stimulate their thinking. We think offering a diversity of highly personal opinion, whatever its imperfections, is more stimulating than presenting the predictable monotony of an institutional editorial line.

At the high point in *The National Observer*'s history it employed nearly fifty newspeople, including editors, writers, assistants, and desk copyists: "What we have done, among other things," said Henry Gemmill, "is to hold mass meetings of the entire staff, mostly on Tuesday mornings, and we often go over everything; we will continue to do so. An awful lot of the very best ideas have come not from me, but from the staff." Edwin A. Roberts, Jr., was a favorite columnist with subscribers. "Politics by Perry" signed by James M. Perry drew passionate followers, as did Douglas S. Looney's articles to "The Sports Observer." The *Observer* also presented stories on music, poetry, movies. Art columns were usually written by Bill

Marvel, while Michael Putney and Clifford Ridley covered books.

Most people felt that the staff was what made the *Observer* special. They were all young, most of them in their early twenties, and they approached their assignments with an enthusiasm that came through in practically everything they wrote.

One of the *Observer*'s most outstanding reporters was Nina Totenberg, who covered the U.S. Supreme Court. In 1970 she got the names of six men selected by President Nixon as possible court nominees, and broke the story on the Dow Jones ticker. Even *Time* was obliged to publicly credit Totenberg and the *Observer* with the scoop. When pressed to describe her quest, she said: "A little sexism in the pursuit of a story is a virtue."

On a rainy day several weeks ago, I sat closeted in a phone booth at the U.S. Supreme Court dialing my index finger off and running up a fantastic long-distance phone bill. I had learned that the American Bar Association had just received President Nixon's list of six potential nominees to the High Court, and I was wild to find out who they were.

After about 50 phone calls and one lucky break I had the names and I sat in the press room moaning because I couldn't figure out what to do with them. I knew by the time I got them in the next *Observer,* the story would already be out. Then Barry Schweld from the API wandered in and asked me what I was in such agony about. "The list, the list," I groaned, "I've got it, but it will never hold for our paper." Barry, being the decent human being he was, shrieked at me: "Put it on your own wire, dummy!"

Totenberg had the usual skills required for making an outstanding reporter, but she also knew how to use her femininity. "I do confess that being a girl is a definite asset," she once said. "I daresay I am the only Supreme Court reporter who ever asked the Chief Justice to dance. He was quite the gentleman as he waltzed me around the ballroom floor—lecturing me on the evils of Women's Lib."

Nina Totenberg also put her feminine charms to work at a White House correspondents' dinner:

I played dirty pool with a very low-cut evening gown. At a party afterward I was drinking straight ginger ale while the Deputy Attorney General and three Assistant Attorneys General clustered around me. They were not drinking ginger ale. Ron Ostrow of the *Los Angeles Times* and Fred Graham of the *New York Times* called across the room: "Hey Nina, let us see your notes tomorrow." Little did my two competitors know that at that very moment I had just nailed down the first press interview with Robert Mardian, Assistant Attorney General for internal security.

In 1972 Totenberg won her second American Bar Association Award for outstanding coverage of the U.S. Supreme Court. This marked the first time since 1963 that the award had been given to the same writer two years in a row. The Silver Gavel was presented to Totenberg "in recognition of her exceptional series of features and spot news articles on the United States Supreme Court in transition." Her 1971 award was for interpretive reporting on the Supreme Court.

One of *The National Observer*'s unique attractions was its concern for the consumer. This policy began with its first edition. An article on the Paris fashion showings made the point that the expensive designs would soon be copied and would show up in the readers' favorite department stores.

A major article a few weeks later reported on President Kennedy's consumer-legislation proposals. It took some time for the proposals to become law, but the article was the first in the paper's continuing coverage of developments in the area of consumer-protection laws.

Formalized consumer-news reporting began in 1964 with "News to Note," a column containing practical tips and information about new products and helpful publications. Gus Gribbin, who later became a writer of major consumer articles, initiated the column. In June, 1968, Bill Giles appointed a formal consumer-news staff. The emphasis at that time was on how-to articles, ranging from picking a physician to choosing Bourbon whiskey.

When asked why he had allocated so much talent and space to consumer news (it was the largest group assigned to any area), editor Gemmill said:

Consumer and coping stories, particularly those found on pages eight and nine, are at the very heart of what we consider to be the *Observer*'s specialty, know-the-business-of-living coverage. The kind of material found on those inside pages is roughly comparable with the main corporate news stories found inside *The Wall Street Journal*—that is, the *Journal,* despite its far-ranging scope, does still have as its specialty the coverage of business news for managers and investors. The *Observer* strives for comparable utility in its specialization, which is providing information useful to the atomic individual, either as a free atom or in a molecule of family or community.

Certainly no other daily or weekly newspaper provided such a thorough investigation of consumer products and services. Readers were told how to recognize and avoid the bait-and-switch automobile trap; how tenants' unions had been organized and how they sometimes improved the renters' lot; the hazards of buying property in desert land developments; how Madison Avenue used something called "psychographics" to target advertising messages at specific groups; the safety hazards at children's summer camps; how to buy pantyhose that would last; and, on page one, how to thwart burglars by engraving identifying marks on valuables.

Always an innovator, Henry Gemmill was constantly searching for new ideas. The *Observer* called itself America's liveliest newspaper. Much of its vitality came directly from its editor. "Not much sleep last night. Up early to type this column. And late to bed because of a lively party . . ." ran the lead on one of his "Post Script" columns.

The column was a must for Gemmill. No matter how much time he spent supervising his staff, going over budgets, meeting with advertisers, and conferring with Dow Jones executives, he was determined to keep his imprint on the *Observer*. "Post Script" gave him the chance. It ran at the bottom of the back page and enabled its author to chat directly and informally with the readers of his paper. He talked to them about the story behind the story, the personality behind the byline, the thought behind the action. Gemmill was proud of his staff, and he believed readers would like to know more about them as individuals, about what went into their work for the paper.

Occasionally he wrote about his own experiences, displaying the same vivid style he encouraged in his staffers:

Here on business. At this early-morning moment I'm sitting alone in my room, in a hotel I would perhaps never have known were I not a loyal reader of our *Observer* ads. It turns out to be modest, clean, and friendly—the sort of place I like—but what I especially prize is my balcony. When I step out there I'm tempted to shout an inspiration oration to the crowds below.

They'd never hear me, though—15 stories down. Instead, it is I who listen. No doubt this roar is partly human and partly mechanical, but as it reaches my ear it carries the energy of a huge animal. I cannot tell whether the beast is bellowing in triumph or distress.

In agony, I think, after scanning the local newspapers. I read of water mains bursting, cops on the take, dogs making sidewalks unfit for human tread, taxes destroying mom-and-pop stores, homeowners defaulting on mortgages, street gangs invading hospital operating rooms, art dealers swindling art lovers, the Metropolitan Opera falling millions in the red, Con Edison failing even to measure its pollution of the air, an NAACP chief found slain in the Bronx, and the whole city's master plan denounced as "no plan at all."

Who am I to doubt the printed word? New York must be in its death throes. Still, the air on my balcony seems brisk and fresh—at least this morning. As is my habit when away from home, I have walked the streets both by day and night; I have never been mugged nor slain. I notice the women, of course. These New York women, half my bulk, stride past me at double my speed; some look driven, but most appear eager to get somewhere. The small shops seem well stocked, well patronized. Cigarets are taxed beyond belief, but I have my pipe. I have purchased no paintings, but I did buy eggs and coffee at a counter around the corner; in my preoccupation with the morning paper I offered a second payment on my check—and the proprietor declined it. My shoes thus far remain unsullied, though I really do not watch where I step. Like a country boy, I'm staring at skyscrapers—not at the familiar older ones (after all, I did once live here), but all those young ones, with their inviting plazas and splashing fountains. And at numerous others even now under construction, gaunt cranes perched in their soaring upper branches.

I stare with fascinated lack of understanding. If New York is falling, why is it rising? Joining sophisticated New Yorkers for lunch, I pose that question. They shrug.

Our own *Observer* staff members often fly into New York. They come to talk with young John and Yoko Lennon, and old Arthur Godfrey. They report horrifying things going on in Bellevue Hospital, and amazing happenings on Broadway. They interview political fat cats, population experts, basketball players, and poets. When I get back home, I must remember to ask them: If New York is dying, why is it so alive?

Advertising is the lifeblood of any newspaper, so Henry Gemmill went after the buyers of space with a vengeance. At first it seemed to be paying off. A 1971 intensive target market promotion campaign in Detroit had some highly positive effects. In late September the eight-week target-city campaign moved to Chicago with an enlarged program. "Before" and "after" campaign research indicated that the probability for future use of the *Observer* increased by 17 percent among all advertising prospects. Ad agency decision-makers with a positive feeling for using the newspaper climbed by 25 percent, and among agency clients the increase was 55 percent. An overall increase of 39 percent was registered among account executives who indicated they "might use" the paper in their future advertising schedules.

A multimedia campaign in New York City followed in the spring of '72. Through direct mail, magazines, radio, television, transit ads, and trade papers the *Observer* was introduced to potential readers. Gemmill believed New York City would become *Observer* country by mid-June. The campaign was on its way to the other big cities of America—Los Angeles, Cleveland, Washington, Pittsburgh, Philadelphia, Louisville, and finally Boston.

The initial cost of the campaign was $400,000, but despite some signs of success it just never worked. The accent on "uniqueness" failed to capture advertisers. Circulation was also beginning to slide, but Henry Gemmill remained optimistic:

It is a young publication and its evolution is by no means finished. I do think the main line of our strategy is quite clear—this emphasis on news that is close to the reader. But there is a great deal of creativity still open to us. We are not finished changing things by any means.

Despite Gemmill's optimism the picture did not improve. In reality it had been growing darker for some time. The paper's deficit had been reduced from nearly $2 million in 1965 to $300,000 in 1974. But then the losses began to inch up again. The costs of acquiring new subscribers had risen sharply and could not balance out the loss of readers—even though renewals were 70 percent, a high rate for the publishing industry. To make matters worse, second-class postage delivery rates had climbed over 200 percent since 1971; this proved to be the highest percentage increase of any cost category.

By the summer of 1977 circulation had fallen to 401,933 from

429,652 a year earlier; the figure was 483,727 at the end of 1975, down from a peak of 560,000 in 1973.

Dow Jones & Company announced that it was stopping publication of *The National Observer* with its July 4, 1977, issue.

"The long effort to make *The Observer* self-sufficient hasn't succeeded, and its future prospects don't give sufficient encouragement to continue the battle," Dow Jones president Warren H. Phillips said in his statement to the *Observer*'s staff.

Henry Gemmill was more precise in his reasons for the paper's failure:

We were a smashing success with people who read us. Some of them got emotionally hooked. Our trouble was converting nonreaders into readers. There are myriad explanations for that. One may be the name of the paper. It didn't denote anything special, or convey the nature of the publication.

Whatever the explanation, *The National Observer* was gone, but it was by no means unmourned. Heartbroken readers wrote letters and sent Mailgrams to protest its passing.

I can't begin to tell you what this loss means to me. This was the only intelligent and fully informative-entertaining weekly newspaper, and my life will be duller because it is gone.—*Shaker Heights, Ohio*

After we have learned to love *The Observer,* are we now supposed to read a weekly news magazine, for heaven's sake? That would be like a lifetime sentence of eating junk food.—*St. Petersburg, Florida*

With *The Observer*'s passing I lose lots of friends—all your staff writers and contributors. I lose my finest source of thought-provoking news. I lose the best in book and movie reviews—and the best damn crossword puzzle going! *The National Observer* turned "Monday blues" into "Can't Wait for the news!"—*Silver Spring, Maryland*

In its fifteen years of existence $34 million in pretax income was poured into the *Observer*'s struggle to survive. The irony is that one nationwide poll found *The Wall Street Journal* to be America's most trusted newspaper, with *The National Observer* tying the *New York Times* for second place. The weekly's major problem, experts agreed, was that it failed to attract advertising. Looking back, some of those same experts also agree that the *Observer* was a first-rate idea whose time had simply not yet come.

Barron's National Business and Financial Weekly

The Frenchman leads the world in knowing when he has enough. He will retire at 30 if he has a competence. The Englishman will retire at 40 and serve his country. The American will never retire. He finds his rest, his recreation and his sport in business.

CLARENCE W. BARRON.

Barron's, The National Financial Weekly (*Business* was added in 1942) was first published on May 9, 1921, nineteen years after its namesake took over Dow Jones & Company. The new publication and its name were Hugh Bancroft's ideas. Bancroft's daughter, Jessie, recalled her father walking into her step-grandfather's office and saying: "C.W., I am going to start a weekly, and Harry Nelson [a highly respected financial writer who had been with Dow Jones for ten years] is going to write a column called 'The Trader' in *Barron's*."

"I think the name is preposterous," Barron replied, "but a wonderful idea to have Harry write 'The Trader.'"

Soon after that *Barron's* was born. It was not the most auspicious time to start a financial weekly. The U.S. Labor Department had recently put the number of unemployed at nearly six million, the worst figure of the post–World War I depression. Wages were being cut in many large industries. The National Conference on Unemployment was advising manufacturers and retailers to cut prices as well and had also proposed a program of public works to provide jobs. Nevertheless, *Barron's* was launched.

The first issue sold for twenty cents at the newsstands, $10 for a one-year subscription. "What we want is confidence," the weekly's first editorial boldly declared. "A fresh financial publication based on sound sources of information and policy should be a helpful factor in assuring return of confidence in the world of business."

Barron's had no trouble attracting advertisers. All of the Dow Jones papers—*The Wall Street Journal,* the Boston News Bureau and now *Barron's, The National Financial Weekly*—were read for dollars-and-cents reasons. "Not every reader is a millionaire," Clarence Barron liked to say, "but there are few millionaires who do not read religiously one of these papers."

The publisher offered "blanket rates" to advertisers interested in appearing in all three publications. "This means that if you are an advertiser, are desirous of reaching people of more than average means, you can do it through these media, with no waste circulation," Barron announced. Lest anyone miss his point, the slogan for his ad campaign was "To reach all the 'Millionaires' in the country. . . ."

Barron's subscribers included a fair share of the nation's company presidents, board chairmen, directors, owners, and partners—all the leaders in finance and industry. The weekly was among the first publications in the country to create subscribing profiles, which are now considered an indispensable advertising tool.

Barron's slogan was "For Those Who Read for Profit." Its aim was to inculcate sound investment principles in the public mind. To this end it offered special articles, analyses, reviews—a profusion of interesting and informative financial features. When readers began asking for the same material in more permanent form, *Barron's* extracted some of its best articles and compiled them into separate volumes bearing such titles as *Buying a Bond, The Stock Market Barometer, Investing in Purchasing Power, National Government Loans, Practical Hints for Investors, The Art of Speculation,* and *Forecasting Stock Market Trends.*

Barron's first editor was Clarence Barron, then in his middle sixties but still as energetic and enthusiastic about his work as he had always been. Barron took some of his news and statistics from his daily Boston News Bureau report. He also drew on the material that was available through his other enterprises—*The Wall Street Journal,* the Philadelphia News Bureau, the Financial News Bulletin Services in New York, Boston, and Philadelphia, and the news ticker in New York.

International news was stressed. The first issue introduced a series called "European Unsettlements," which dealt with the reparations problems and was written by Barron from Paris, London, and Berlin. Another piece, "British Soviet Smashed," was written by Herbert N. Casson from London. On the home front were features on "Frisco Bonds," "The Steel Stocks," "Union Pacific's Recovery," "An Inside View of Wall Street," and "Investment Suggestions."

Barron's owner used every possible technique to bring it to the public's attention—direct mail, house ads, magazine space, and outdoor advertising. The first direct-mail piece used many sales techniques that are still considered effective. The first promotion was in the form of a letter from publisher Hugh Bancroft stressing the exclusiveness of *Barron's* investment coverage. The publisher offered free trial subscriptions and gave a special reduced rate to charter subscribers.

The Wall Street Journal was one obvious advertising medium for the new Dow Jones publication. It was used along with outside publications, such as the *Literary Digest*, to promote subscription sales. Outdoor advertising, on billboards, also trumpeted the new weekly "For Those Who Read for Profit." As a result of these efforts *Barron's* attained a circulation of 27,000 by 1925 and well over 30,000 by 1927.

The most famous of *Barron's* direct-mail promotions was the "widow" contest it sponsored in 1925. Participants were asked to work out an investment plan using a hypothetical $100,000 belonging to a fictitious widow with two small children.

The contest was promoted in major magazines and newspapers throughout the country with point-of-purchase entry blanks available at key metropolitan newsstands. Announcements of the contest were also sent out to brokerage houses and their customers. Over 1,000 entries were received, out of which three prizewinners and eleven runners-up were named. Perhaps most important, everyone started talking about *Barron's*.

Clarence W. Barron died at the age of seventy-three, seven years after his national financial weekly came into being. The paper's new editor was none other than Harris J. (Harry) Nelson, the man Hugh Bancroft had selected to write "The Trader," the column that had been the cornerstone of the new publication.

When Nelson graduated from Harvard in 1910, he had no idea what to do with himself. Then a friend told him, "There's more ignorance on Wall Street than in any other part of the world." It struck Nelson that a man who had majored in English and economics might be just the person to dispel some of that ignorance. C. W. Barron agreed. He hired the young man and put him to work keeping a scrapbook of Barron's press clippings. Nelson was so bored that ". . . one night I stayed late and wrote an article about the relative activity of U.S. Steel common and preferred stock." The bureau chief, impressed by what he read, ran it on the front page.

With Nelson at the helm, *Barron's* editorial offices shifted from New York to Boston. Four days each week the editor caught the 7:57 train from his home in Manchester, Massachusetts, so he could be at his desk when the stock market ticker clicked into action.

Totally absorbed in his work, Nelson seldom had time for small talk. Barney Kilgore once visited Dow Jones's Boston offices and found Nelson with his eyes glued to the ticker. He was chewing on some paper—a favorite habit of his—and talking to his boss, but his eyes never once left the ticker. The president of the company departed, unimpressed. He visited Nelson on a number of other occasions, and each time the same scenario took place. Kilgore remained baffled until one of Nelson's coworkers told him, "You have to understand. His whole world is the stock market and the ticker."

If further proof was needed, Nelson continued to write his "Trader" column until he was well into his eighties. He retired in 1974 after sixty-four years with Dow Jones.

Lawrence A. Armour, then associate editor of *Barron's* and now director of corporate relations for Dow Jones, used to fill in for Nelson at vacation time and took over the writing of "The Trader" after Nelson's retirement. The column is still going; it appears in the mid-section of *Barron's* under "The Market Week" and its author is Steve Anreder.

In the early 1930s the problems of editing a financial weekly like *Barron's* fell into two main categories: (1) the securities and commodity markets themselves, and (2) the drastic changes in basic economic rules that occurred in the early days of the New Deal.

Statistically the low points of the Great Depression and of the stock market occurred in the summer of 1932; the restoration of financial confidence came very slowly. Since the Depression had left few people with any funds to invest, interest in stocks, bonds, and mortgages was minimal. Only those who lived through this trying period are not staggered by the fact that the Dow Jones average dropped from a high of 381.17 to a low of 41.22 and that the banking structure was so precarious that banks had to be shut down for the "bank holiday" of early 1933.

All during the early 1930s the financial weekly ran articles on the many changes that were taking place in finance and economics. Most of the reforms initiated by the Roosevelt administration were highly controversial, and many of them were anathema to Wall Street. Outlining and discussing their impact rarely made for light reading. Nevertheless, the bank holiday, new banking legislation, the devaluation of the dollar, suspension of the gold clause in bonds, the NRA, and the Reconstruction Finance Corporation—to name just a few— deeply influenced the economic and psychological climates against which the markets operated. *Barron's* felt obliged to report at length on all of them.

During this era the weekly maintained a very small staff, relying mainly on special articles by reporters on other Dow Jones publications. Particularly helpful were the foreign correspondents for *The Wall Street Journal*. They contributed articles on such timely topics as the growing power of Hitler and the complexities of currency relations between Europe and the U.S., which had been severely disrupted by the Depression.

In 1939 *Barron's* announced its second "Investing for a Widow" contest. The theoretical performance of one plan submitted for the initial contest in 1925 became the basis of a direct-mail package that proved to be one of the most successful circulation boosters in history.

In 1949, twenty-four years after the first "widow" contest, *Barron's* ran a third one. It was a direct-mail effort; a letter was sent to potential contestants describing the investment plan submitted by a runner-up in the 1939 contest, Mr. A. Vere Shaw. The letter showed how the value of the securities Shaw had selected had grown over the years and offered a free booklet, "Ten Rules for Investors," along with a subscription to *Barron's* to contest winners.

The "widow" contest has remained *Barron's* most effective direct-mail marketing technique and has been the "control" or standard letter of the paper's direct-mail program for years. New letters and packages have been periodically tested against the "widow," but none has been as consistently successful.

A number of individuals have contributed to the success of *Barron's* and Dow Jones & Company. One was George F. Shea, Jr. Born in Paris in 1902, Shea might have grown up there, but his parents fled to the United States at the outbreak of World War I.

The elder Shea, the son of a founder of Joseph Horne Co., the Pittsburgh department store, had been the first American male to sing in French opera. His wife was a singer, too, but their son's interest lay in other directions.

After graduating from Princeton in 1922, young George got a job as both a copyreader for *The Wall Street Journal* and a copy editor for the Dow Jones News Service. He became a reporter for the paper, then one of its assistant managing editors. From there he went to *Barron's,* where he was editor for eleven years. During this time Shea expanded the weekly's domestic economic news to include international events and their effect on the national economy. Under his guidance *Barron's* retained its reputation for solid, reliable reporting. Trading on Wall Street was somewhat different in the late 1940s from what it is today. The stock exchanges were open on Saturday mornings, and the average volume was one million shares a day, compared to the several million shares that now change hands in one hour.

"The leisurely pace tended to be reflected in the contents of *Barron's*," says Bob Bleiberg, now editorial director. "Whether a story ran on any given week, or five or six weeks later, really didn't matter, because not much was happening in the market. From 1946 through 1949, the Dow Jones Industrial Average didn't move more than fifty points up or down. Circulation was running about 40,000."

In 1949 Barney Kilgore decided to give *Barron's* readers a wider view of the financial world by modeling the weekly along the lines of the London *Economist*, England's influential financial periodical. Kilgore hired John Davenport, who was on *Fortune* magazine's board of editors, to do the job. Lean, intense, and articulate, the forty-five-year-old Yale man was an alumnus of the *New York World*. When Davenport became *Barron's* new editor, George Shea, a crack corporation analyst, became financial editor of *The Wall Street Journal*.

Davenport widened the scope of the weekly to include more political commentary, both national and international. Circulation began to climb—by the end of 1954 it was over 50,000. With that accomplishment under his belt Davenport returned to *Fortune,* and thirty-year-old Robert Bleiberg took his place as editor of *Barron's*.

In all, *Barron's* has had ten editors: Clarence Barron, Harris J. Nelson, Hugh Bancroft, Sherwin C. Badger, Cyril A. Player, Thomas W. Phelps, George F. Shea, Jr., John Davenport, Robert L. Bleiberg, and Alan Abelson, who currently holds the job.

Bleiberg was the youngest and also held the position longer than anyone else. Nicknamed "the contemporary Mr. Barron," the bald, chubby Bleiberg bears a certain physical resemblance to his illustrious predecessor, but the similarity is most apparent in his penchant for hard work.

Born in Brooklyn, New York, on June 21, 1924, Bleiberg graduated with honors in economics from Columbia College and earned an M.B.A. from New York University in 1950. In between he saw service in the Army during World War II. Bleiberg's first job after he and Uncle Sam parted company in December, 1945, was as associate editor of *Prudden's Digest of Investment and Banking Opinions*. Within a few months he was looking for a better position.

Drawing up a list of several top publishing organizations, Bleiberg sent his résumé off to each of them. His shotgun approach included three newspapers, the *Sun,* the *Herald-Tribune,* and the *Telegram* two magazines, *Life* and *Look* and *Barron's.* (Except for *Barron's* and the recently revived *Life,* all of these publications are now defunct.) Bleiberg received a call from George Shea within a few days, and within a few more days he was an associate editor at *Barron's.* By the time he became editor in 1954, Bleiberg had his own ideas about where the paper should be heading.

My first editorial decision was to part company with our Washington and foreign correspondents, and to begin to shift the focus from politics to the kind of down-to-earth, hard-nosed financial coverage we feature today. I had decided long before that the major opportunity for *Barron's* and its readers lay in the world of finance. On this score, of course, a weekly magazine, which has the time to cover stories in depth, has a great advantage.

Under Bleiberg's direction *Barron's* won a number of awards for reporting, its circulation grew from 50,000 to more than 250,000, and his own weekly editorials became famous in business and government circles.

In January, 1980, Bleiberg was named vice president of the magazine group (a new position created when Dow Jones was reorganized into several principal operating groups) and now reports to Dow Jones vice chairman Donald Macdonald.

"Reports" is probably not the right word to describe Bleiberg's role, for he is freer to make decisions than most corporate presidents. His independence is based on his track record and bolstered by his strong, verbal personality. "Our profitability can be judged solely on circulation figures," boasts Bleiberg.

The contemporary Mr. Barron, like the original one, is firmly committed to getting the government off the back of business. As he sees it, deregulation and more deregulation are essential. For instance, numerous government officials have been urging some form of supervision over the spread of investment letters. Bleiberg insists that's not the way to do it. These advisory firms "should have First Amendment protection," argues Bleiberg. History and time will be the levelers. The good ones will survive, the others will fold. "The free market is the yardstick of perfection," Bleiberg insists, "and will be the judge of survival."

Each issue of *Barron's* contains three or four major stories, but Bleiberg's voice is most often heard in the editorials he continues to write. Commenting on Reagan's presidency and his high hopes for supply-side economics, Bleiberg feels it's "the best way to go now. We've got to cut capital gains, evolve more tax reform, and enhance productivity." He is quick to point out that this effort is really bipartisan. According to Bleiberg the Democrats began the process in 1978 under President Carter, and the new administration is simply continuing it.

Some professionals claim that *Barron's* moves Wall Street every Monday morning. Bleiberg, however, "is more interested in what happens six to eight months later, to see if we were right in our analysis."

Robert Bleiberg regularly castigates the SEC for its incompetence and failure to go after the big frauds. While the SEC was dealing with what he scornfully refers to as "small stuff," *Barron's* "broke" the Equity Funding case, "without question, the greatest swindle since World War II," says Bleiberg. "And where was the SEC all the time?" (See the story on Equity Funding in Chapter 16 for the answer.)

Each week *Barron's* presents an assortment of useful statistics, including the major stock market averages and indices—Standard & Poor's, New York Stock Exchange, and the Wilshire Index, which combines the sum of the market value for all shares listed on the Big Board, Amex, and those actively traded over-the-counter.

Barron's was the first financial paper to regularly show the Quotron change, the percentage shift of the entire list, on both the Amex and Big Board. Also reported in the weekly's "Market Laboratory" are the Dow Jones hourly averages, Dow Jones weekly averages, Dow Jones price-earnings ratio, *Barron's* 50-stock average, shares traded on the New York Exchange, weekly trading by markets in

NYSE listed stocks, NYSE odd-lot trading, stock exchange volume trends, and the week's market statistics.

"Barron's," Bob Bleiberg once wrote, "has always carried an incredible amount of grist for the technicians' mill." It has also pioneered in the writing of technical analysis. Garfield A. Drew first described the odd-lot approach to the stock market in *Barron's,* and Richard Russell wrote a lengthy series on the Dow Theory in the late fifties.

Many other specialists have written articles attempting to explain and predict the future movement of the market. Bleiberg has supported their work and is pleased to note that more often than not they have been on target. Says Bleiberg, "Such a track record compares very favorably with that of the nation's economists, who, with one or two notable exceptions, for years have been consistently wrong."

Prior to 1955, ads promoting *Barron's* as a market were a "catch-as-catch-can proposition." Bleiberg met this problem head on by announcing a four-part mission to "inform, interpret, sum up, and sell." Sales literature began stressing that *Barron's* was "read for profit and it is the profit motive that creates advertising acceptance." A brochure was created showing eleven major business situations of 1955, demonstrating that *Barron's* had "scooped" other publications in all of them. Later that year the weekly's ad linage topped the 500,000-line mark for the first time in its history.

The idea that *Barron's* subscribers "read for profit" was subsequently interwoven into advertising promotion, with such tag lines as "where advertising, too, is read for profit" and "advertising in *Barron's,* too, is profitable."

"Finance Spoken Here" first appeared in 1959, and the provocative question, "Have You Discovered the Wonderful World of Money?" set the tempo in 1961.

The ferment that had begun in Wall Street in the early fifties offered the perfect setting for a weekly like *Barron's*. For the first time in a generation new companies were going public, presenting new opportunities for investors and new fields for *Barron's* to cover. The weekly began to find an increasingly receptive audience as the stock market went into a long period of more or less uninterrupted advance. "We started to expand the statistical section of *Barron's,*" said Bleiberg. "This, I felt at the time, was far and away our most valuable single asset. Actually, it grew almost automatically with each new listing on the exchanges and over-the-counter."

Bleiberg used the "News and Views of Investment" section to provide background on various companies. He also initiated an informal prospectus on company operations, which looks ahead for six to nine months. Over the years the "News and Views" section has covered an impressive number of growth companies, many of which started out as small over-the-counter ventures and went on to achieve blue chip status on the Big Board.

"Such coverage is basically aimed at stimulating or prodding the reader into making an investment decision on his own. It is as close as *Barron's* comes to a recommendation. We do not give advice, but we do give information sometimes so pointed that it's hard to avoid drawing the correct inference on whether to buy or sell," wrote Bleiberg.

When asked for a definition of his publication, Bleiberg called it "a magazine of finance." Although *Barron's* is technically a newspaper, he prefers to consider it a magazine because it does not offer "spot news"; its information is contained in in-depth articles.

Bleiberg contends that his readers are involved in managing money, their own or other people's, and that his weekly reports deal with the "business of business." His focus is much narrower than that of *The Wall Street Journal*, but the image it gives in its own field of public investments is "sharper."

The editorial page of *Barron's* was greatly influenced by John Davenport, who, like myself, is a firm believer in freedom of choice and the free market. Since *Barron's* beat, so to speak, is the marketplace (whether for stocks, bonds, real estate, commodities or what have you), I have always regarded our editorial policy as uniquely appropriate. In a totalitarian society, to put things crassly, we would sell precious few copies.

Within the last three decades *Barron's* has cultivated a technique of developing stories by watching the stock market action. "We get a lot of stories that way. A case in point is our scoop on the imminent collapse of the Bernard Cornfeld empire, Investors Overseas Services, Ltd., which we began to suspect from the strange action of I.O.S. stock on the London market."

Another story highlighted some discrepancies in the annual report of the New Haven Railroad. Dated January 24, 1955, it told how the management of the railroad had just changed hands. "The new team reported a net income, before sinking funds, of around $9 million, compared to $6 million the year before, suggesting a major turn for the better in the New Haven's fortunes," said Bleiberg.

The *Barron's* piece went on to probe the financial background and emerged with a very different conclusion. "If certain extraordinary adjustments, credits and special dividends are deducted from last year's income, it appears the New Haven earned not $9 million but something less than $2.5 million," it said. "Even this sum, it's clear on further analysis of the road's financial statement, is entirely the result of heavy cutbacks in maintenance."

It was obvious to *Barron's* that without such cutbacks the New Haven would have been awash in red ink. Instead of an improved earnings picture, the weekly suggested that the New Haven was actually losing money—a theory that was borne out not long afterward when the railroad filed for bankruptcy.

Bleiberg reflected on another major *Barron's* story, "Discount store retailing woes," *dated February 5, 1962:*

Oddly, this story is remembered not for its impact after it appeared, but for the stir it caused prior to publication. This article was one of the first real indications that *Barron's* was destined to have a major impact on the movement of stock prices. At the time, discount stores were the glamour industry of the Street. The story, which was merely a gentle warning that capacity was threatening to exceed demand, was originally scheduled to appear on Monday, January 28th. On Thursday, January 24th, the *Barron's* switchboard was swamped with callers trying to confirm rumors that *Barron's* was going to publish an adverse article about discount stores. Throughout the day and the one following, January 24th and 25th, discount store stock prices dipped 15 to 20 percent just on the rumor that the *Barron's* piece might appear. The story was eventually held an additional week "until the heat was off." Ironically, in the 1962 bear market, which set in shortly thereafter, the slide was led by discount houses who were plagued, at least temporarily, by the sort of trouble *Barron's* had forecast. But the real story here was the overwhelming reaction to what the weekly might say.

Barron's was never reluctant to point out potential trouble spots. In the early 1960s its readers learned that the market's enthusiasm for bowling balls and transistors was getting a little out of hand, and similar warnings—which proved to be justified—were issued against "irrational enthusiasm for the boat makers, nursing homes, color TV producers, land developers, computer leasing and computer peripheral firms, to name just a few."

In early 1966 Robert Bleiberg realized that a great deal of material that was funneling into *Barron's* offices wasn't finding its way into print fast enough. Accordingly he put staffer Alan Abelson to work on "Up and Down Wall Street," a lively, informative, no-holds-barred column that added still another dimension to *Barron's* coverage of the financial world.

The column began at an ideal time, just as hedge funds and the resulting pressure on performance became major preoccupations on Wall Street. Abelson collected his facts and carefully checked them for accuracy. As a result he was able to zero in on scores of frauds—"perhaps more than the Securities and Exchange Commission has uncovered in its entire history," says Bleiberg.

One story, dated January 14, 1967, discussed Canadian Javelin, Ltd., a mining promotion that was being highly touted among investors. Its price had gone from around six to around twenty-six and seemed likely to go much higher. Abelson cautioned *Barron's* readers to beware of the company's promotional claims. It proved to be excellent advice; the president of the company was subsequently convicted of securities fraud.

Alan Abelson, a native New Yorker, graduated from the City College of New York in 1946. The following year he earned an M.A. at the University of Iowa's Writers' Workshop. After a year as a freelance writer he became a copyboy on the *New York Journal-American*. He later worked as a reporter, then moved to the financial desk, and in 1951 became the paper's stock market columnist.

Abelson joined *Barron's* in 1956, editing the Investment News and Views section and writing corporate and industry features. In 1965 he became managing editor and the following year started the weekly column, "Up and Down Wall Street." He was named editor on December 1, 1981.

Barron's stories are often interesting, but the main criterion is that they be informative. Like his predecessors, Abelson operates on the assumption that his readers want to know where to turn and—equally important—where not to turn.

The record here is quite impressive. In April, 1967, for instance, one of Barron's "Talking Money" interviews featured a portfolio manager from Enterprise Fund, which at that time had assets of about $50 million. The fund went on to dominate and outperform all other mutual funds for two consecutive years as it developed into a $1.5 billion organization.

Several years ago *Barron's* noted that because the deterioration of newsprint is so rapid, the average life expectancy of a typical weekly issue was 21.6 weeks. In 1973 an Illinois man, Phillip Niederman, informed the publication's Chicago office that he had been a subscriber since 1937 and had every last copy of *Barron's*—1,900 in all—neatly stored in his basement in perfect condition. Even more remarkable, Mr. Niederman, an engineer, had retired in 1946 and had lived off his investment income ever since, using *Barron's* as a guide to manage his portfolio.

A sore point with any reputable publishing company, particularly a financial one, is its integrity. In 1975 Dow Jones & Company sued McGraw-Hill, Inc., for $20 million in a libel action charging that a story in the April 28 issue of *Business Week* (a McGraw-Hill publication) impugned the integrity of Dow Jones and Alan Abelson, then managing editor of *Barron's*.

The story concerned the activities of James Corr, a speculator accused by the Securities and Exchange Commission of a number of securities laws' violations, including manipulating the market in shares of American Agronomics Corporation.

Corr told *Business Week* that he had "a golden news leak" that enabled him to know in advance what Abelson was going to publish in his column and that he used this advantage to make money in the market. In addition, the article quoted Corr as saying that a small group close to Abelson was also feeding *Barron's* positive stories on certain companies and that "I was told in advance that the stories were coming."

In instituting his company's suit for libel Warren Phillips, Dow Jones president, declared:

The charges published by *Business Week* cannot be supported because they are totally false. . . . *Business Week* refused to publish a retraction acknowledging the charges were false, or to express any regret for the reflection on the reputations of Mr. Abelson, *Barron's* and Dow Jones. We prize our reputation above all else. It has been sullied unjustly. We welcome an opportunity to demonstrate that.

A McGraw-Hill representative countered with:

We do not believe there is any merit to the claims made by Dow Jones in its legal action which was served on McGraw-Hill today [April 24, 1975]. . . . In the May 5 issue of *Business Week* being mailed [April 24], Lewis Young, editor of the magazine (and a co-defendant in the suit), points out that *"Business Week* did not say, or mean to imply, that advance information came from Abelson, *Barron's* or Dow Jones and has no reason to believe the columnist, the magazine or the company has ever acted unethically or illegally with financial or other information in its possession." The magazine stands on its original story. It should be pointed out that *Business Week* exercised due care and diligence in researching, preparing and publishing the material to which Dow Jones takes exception. McGraw-Hill intends to defend this action vigorously.

Two months later the two giant publishing houses announced jointly that the libel suit was discontinued. Attorneys for both parties agreed there was no evidence that advance information on the contents of *Barron's* was intentionally leaked to investors by Abelson, *Barron's,* or Dow Jones. Harold W. McGraw, Jr., chairman and president of McGraw-Hill, said that *Business Week* didn't state in its article or mean to imply the existence of such a leak. On June 28 the lawsuit was formally terminated.

In another lawsuit a few years earlier *Barron's* was the defendant. In 1970 Telex Corporation filed an action in a state district court against Dow Jones & Company and Abraham Briloff, Emanuel Saxe Distinguished Professor of Accountancy at City University of New

York. The action asked for $5 million actual damages and $5 million punitive damages to the company and $100 million for actual and punitive damages to the stockholders as a result of "libel published and caused to be published . . ." Briloff's statements were shown to be accurate, and the suit was dropped.

A more recent case against Dow Jones & Company and *Barron's* occurred in the late 1970s. Robert B. Nemeroff, a dentist in New York City, was a shareholder of Technicare Corporation, a manufacturer of medical equipment. He commenced a two-count class action on March 25, 1977, in the Southern District of New York against twelve defendants, including Alan Abelson, Robert M. Bleiberg, Dow Jones & Company, and nine investors.

In Nemeroff vs. Abelson it was charged that the publishing defendants gave advance warning to the investor defendants that Abelson would make negative comments about Technicare, and that these comments caused, or tended to cause, a decline in the price of Technicare stock. Nemeroff also charged that the publishing defendants did this in order to enable the investor defendants to trade at a profit, and that the investors profited from the information by selling Technicare short prior to publication and making covering purchases at a depressed price after publication of the *Barron's* issues.

Barron's carried a series of articles beginning in May, 1976, which mentioned Technicare and the CAT (computerized axial tomographer) scanner market. All but one were written by Abelson. To the extent that these columns were negative—and not all of them were— they stated that the market for CAT scanners was going to level out because of various factors, including their high cost and the increasing concern over the rising cost of medical care, increased competition, and state regulation of hospital expenditures. The columns indicated that Technicare would be particularly vulnerable, due in part to its proportionately large reliance on CAT scanner sales.

On April 18, 1979, the Federal District Court for Southern New York held that the action had been commenced in bad faith by Nemeroff against Abelson, Bleiberg, and Dow Jones & Company and awarded them $50,000 in attorneys' fees and expenses to be paid by Nemeroff.

On appeal, decided March 17, 1980, before the U.S. Court of Appeals, Second Circuit, it was held that the district court's finding that the action was commenced in bad faith was erroneous. This court held that a reasonable attorney could have concluded that there was indeed a relationship, in some cases a close relationship, between Abelson and the investor defendants; that Abelson had made comments critical of Technicare; that the price of Technicare had declined during the period in which Abelson's columns were being published; that the investor defendants had sold Technicare short; and that the New York Stock Exchange had found a correlation between the Abelson columns and the pattern of short trading. The court of appeals also reversed the district court's award to the publishing defendants of $50,000.

In April 1982, federal District Judge Robert Carter reaffirmed that Nemeroff and his attorneys must pay $50,000 in legal costs to Dow Jones because they unjustifiably pursued the suit. Abelson said, "Judge Carter once again has struck a blow for the first amendment and against abuse of the court process."

There will be further appeals and counterappeals, and the case probably will not be settled for some years, but Dow Jones and *Barron's* are determined to see that their reputation is untarnished.

It sometimes seems as if suing *Barron's* is an annual event. In the summer of 1981 SafeCard, a company that provides a loss-notification service for credit-card holders, accused a competitor and nine other defendants, including Dow Jones & Company, of trying to run it out of business. They were accused of conspiring to "destroy the business" of SafeCard by "disseminating publicly and privately misleading information." The suit sought damages of more than $30 million, in part directed against the then managing editor, Alan Abelson.

Specifically, the Fort Lauderdale, Florida, firm complained of statements that its success "can be found less in the service it offers than in the manner in which that service is marketed."

SafeCard claimed that *Barron's* articles precipitated a drop in the over-the-counter market price of the company's shares from $31.35 to $16 in one week.

"Baseless," said Editor Bleiberg. He insisted that on three occasions articles on SafeCard had run in *Barron's* and that a fourth article by Professor Abraham Briloff would soon appear.

In our view it's no coincidence that the suit was filed last Friday, just four days after Briloff, as part of his preparation for the article, met with top executives of SafeCard and their lawyer and auditor.

It's equally significant that the company recently filed an offering of one million shares of common stock, almost half of the proceeds of which will go to the two principal officers Peter and Steven Halmos. This is the latest in a series of efforts by the company to discourage *Barron's* from commenting on SafeCard. . . . From the outset, our sole purpose was to enlighten our readers and give them a better insight into the company's workings. The allegations against us have been made up out of whole cloth. They are baseless and clearly aimed at suppressing fair comment. As in the past, we will vigorously defend our right to print the truth.

Briloff noted that SafeCard never wrote a check to the Internal Revenue Service for corporate income taxes, "nor is it soon likely to." He maintained that the company was engaged in an assortment of "accounting no-no's" and had departed from a fair application of generally accepted accounting principles, with a consequent distortion of the company's financial statements. *Barron's* was vindicated in May 1982 when a federal court dismissed the suit, stating that Dow Jones and editors of *Barron's* had not violated any antitrust law or antifraud provisions of securities law.

Barron's was readied for printing every Friday (an off night for *The Wall Street Journal*) at about 6:00 P.M. Copy went to Chicopee, Massachusetts, to be printed. The next morning copies were sent off to newsstands and subscribers around the nation by plane, truck, and mail. Newsstand copies were often available on Saturday morning; subscribers usually got their copies in the Monday mail.

In 1977 the weekly began printing by satellite at Riverside, California; in 1979 satellite transmission was extended to the Orlando, Florida, plant; in 1981 the Naperville, Illinois, facility was added.

Barron's current advertising slogan is "Today is history; tomorrow is *Barron's*." There is no question that the weekly has been a barometer of market trends. During the 1970s, columns were added on commodities, options, international stock exchanges, and the domestic real estate market. As interest in the equities markets waned and investors sought alternative investment avenues, the weekly increased its coverage of such nontraditional investments as coins, diamonds, antiques, and art. The focus will undoubtedly change in the years ahead. When it does, *Barron's* expects to be the first to report it.

The Ottaway Newspaper Empire

I've always figured that if we put out a good quality editorial product, the business end will take care of itself.

JAMES H. OTTAWAY, SR.

JAMES H. OTTAWAY, SR., the founder of Ottaway Newspapers, Inc., is a tall, slender, extremely personable man. He was born in St. Clair, Michigan, on July 8, 1911, and spent his childhood years in Port Huron. The son of Elmer Ottaway, a cofounder of the *Port Huron Times-Herald,* Ottaway attended the University of Michigan and Rollins College in Winter Park, Florida, where he majored in journalism and edited the school newspaper, the *Sandspur.*

There he met Ruth Hart, who was one of two women on the *Sandspur*'s staff. Ruth and her fellow coed had written an article on the female students' perception of the college. Ottaway accepted it for publication and then discovered that the reporters had not interviewed any women, as the article stated, but had, in fact, made up the whole story.

"Well," said Ottaway, "the paper has gone to press. We'll have to pull it out and print a new issue. I hope you two girls have enough money to pay for it." Fortunately, they did.

In spite of this unpromising beginning Ruth Hart and Jim Ottaway continued to work together on the *Sandspur.* Their relationship grew closer, and by the time they graduated from Rollins in 1933, they had decided to be married.

The wedding took place in 1934 in Ruth's home neighborhood, Brooklyn Heights, New York, just across the river from lower Manhattan. For the next two years they lived mostly in Michigan, where the Ottaway family still owned the Port Huron paper. In the fall of 1936, Jim recalls, "Ruth came up with the idea of going east."

Through a newspaper broker came word that a semiweekly in Endicott, New York, might be for sale. "I'll never forget it," says Ottaway, "The paper was owned by a man named Harry Freeland. Harry sat there, his feet on his desk, a big pipe in his mouth, and he said, 'Young man, are you prepared to pay cash?' "

The answer was no. Instead, Jim Ottaway had a plan that was something of a novelty at the time. "I tried to sell him on the idea of terms," says Ottaway. Harry Freeland wasn't buying it.

Fortunately, Ottaway was relatively experienced at financial matters. During his childhood his father had mapped out a program to teach him and his two brothers how to manage money. The elder Ottaway set up an investment fund and printed certificates representing units in the fund, and these were sold to the Ottaway boys in $100 lots. "We all saved our money and put it in the fund," explains Ottaway, "and then my dad would invest it in securities."

When Harry Freeland refused to accept terms, Jim Ottaway had to come up with cash. Using money of his own plus some borrowed from his mother (who "insisted on absolute security; I even had to sign over my life insurance as collateral"), Ottaway scraped up the $50,000 necessary to buy the paper.

Ottaway's idea was to convert the paper into a daily and build its circulation base, which was then about 4,000, up to about 7,000. The *Endicott Bulletin* became a daily in 1937 and promptly dropped in circulation. Endicott's dominant shoe industry was going through some rough times, and this depression caused enough of a decline in the paper's revenues to make it vulnerable to competition from the daily paper in Binghamton, twelve miles away.

The experience taught Jim Ottaway two lessons he has never forgotten. One was to make relative isolation an important factor in acquiring newspapers. The other was not to buy papers in locations where the economic base is tied to a single industry.

Shortly after Pearl Harbor Jim Ottaway volunteered for service in the U.S. Navy. He was still in the service when he began negotiating for another newspaper. In 1944, with a nominal down payment and twenty-year terms, Ottaway purchased the *Star* in Oneonta, New York.

Thus began one of the more remarkable newspaper-empire-building sagas. Ottaway purchased the *Pocono Record* in Stroudsburg, Pennsylvania, in 1946, and by the end of the seventies he had acquired a total of twenty daily newspapers.

No matter what the paper or where its location, all the Ottaway publications strongly reflect their owner's style of doing business. That style includes, among other things, the delegation of editorial policy and complete fiscal responsibility to the local publishers, editors, and general managers. As one good example of this, in the 1976 presidential election seven Ottaway papers endorsed President Gerald Ford, while five supported Jimmy Carter. One, the *Union Gazette* in Port Jervis, New York, didn't endorse either candidate. In 1980 the twenty daily newspapers split their endorsements, twelve for Ronald Reagan, four for John Anderson, three for President Carter, and one uncommitted.

"The one thing we do insist on is an active—not strident, but active—editorial policy," says Ottaway, adding, "I've always figured that if we put out a good quality editorial product, the business end will take care of itself."

The emphasis on quality is strong, despite the fact that it usually means higher production costs. Ottaway never complains about that. His son, Jim, Jr., expresses the company's philosophy: "Local autonomy isn't a license to publish a lousy newspaper, but the freedom and responsibility to publish a great one."

As part of the Ottaway operating procedures, both the elder Ottaway and his son, plus the handful of other top managers, always make themselves available to the local publishers and managers, lending a hand where needed to maintain editorial quality, improve financial controls, or upgrade production techniques. "We've tried to develop the attitude that we're working for the local publishers

141

and general managers, not the other way around," says the elder Ottaway.

Ottaway Newspapers, Inc., has its headquarters in Campbell Hall, New York, a rural hamlet about sixty-five miles northwest of New York City. Jim and Ruth Hart Ottaway live on a ninety-five-acre farm a few hundred yards from the Ottaway offices, which are in an old farmhouse that has been enlarged and remodeled. Until the winter of 1980 Ruth Ottaway was a director of Ottaway Newspapers. Jim credits her with making major contributions to the company's corporate growth and development. Others say she has also had considerable influence on her husband's gentle management style.

Jim Ottaway's personal characteristics have occasionally been the subject of some good-natured comments. Jim, Jr., for instance, says his father sometimes tends to be slightly vague. "He thinks fast and talks even faster," he says. "Sometimes he talks in giant ellipses— and leaves it to you to fill in the blanks. . . . Sometimes you just have to say, whoa. Wait a minute. You've lost me."

On the other hand, Malcolm Mallette, former director of the American Press Institute, has said of Ottaway: "One of his great talents is getting straight to the heart of things. He can rip away the underbrush as fast as anyone I've ever known."

Perhaps nothing tells quite as much about Jim Ottaway, the man and the manager, as his behavior during an acquisition. In 1976 Ottaway Newspapers, Inc. acquired a daily paper in Joplin, Missouri, the *Globe*. Fred Hughes, the newspaper's president, said that as soon as Ottaway arrived (along with his son and J. Allan Meath, a company vice president), any anxiety that *Globe* personnel were experiencing began to evaporate. "After we had gone through the plant meeting the people," Hughes recalled, "Jim invited all the department heads, right down to the head of the maintenance department, to join us for dinner."

The group, totaling about twenty people, met at the Rafters, a well-known restaurant in Joplin. "There was no pontificating on the part of the Ottaways. They just explained how they liked to work and that the local people would still be in control," said Hughes. "They were

142

very down to earth about everything, and they answered everyone's questions.''

As one of the owners of the Joplin paper, Hughes said he could list four major considerations involved in his decision to join the Ottaway group. The first was their attitude toward people, particularly the personnel on the papers they acquired.

The second was their practice of being among the first to adopt technologically advanced equipment and processes. Next came the Ottaway insistence on community leadership and involvement on the part of both the newspaper and its key personnel.

Last and perhaps the most persuasive, Hughes noted:

The first thing Jim Ottaway wants is a quality product, and that's the first thing we want. After all, I've lived in this community all my life, and I intend to go on living and working here. I didn't want somebody who would come in and rip up the paper and the staff. I wanted to be able to walk down the streets of Joplin and not have people come up to me and say, "What the hell have you done with our newspaper?" With Jim Ottaway, you know that the only changes we would ever consider would be for the better.

By chance, Jim Ottaway and Bill Kerby, then president of Dow Jones & Company, had vacation homes and frequently golfed together at Buck Hill Falls, Pennsylvania. Kerby was determined to expand his firm. His principle was, "A company that doesn't grow withers away."

In the spring of 1968 the Dow Jones executive phoned his summer neighbor. "Jim," he said, "you've had a lot of experience buying newspaper properties, but you tell me you have all you can digest right now. If you hear of anything good that you aren't interested in, let me know."

"How about a group?" Ottaway responded quickly. "How about the Ottaway papers?"

Years earlier Kerby had attempted, without success, to merge Dow Jones with the Gannett newspaper chain. Since then he had been looking for a similar company. He was not interested in big-city papers; suburban and rural ones seemed like a better bet. Ottaway Newspapers made good sense to Kerby.

Now Jim and Ruth Ottaway had to contemplate both the assets and the liabilities of selling their "empire." The advantages far outweighed the disadvantages: an alliance with one of the world's leading publications, easier access to financial backing, technological capability by the parent organization, and a massive world-wide research unit.

Long and arduous negotiations followed, and in August, 1970, Dow Jones & Company announced that it had acquired the Ottaway group of nine daily and three Sunday newspapers by exchanging approximately 914,000 shares of Dow Jones common stock for all outstanding capital stock of the Ottaway company. James H. Ottaway, Sr., was elected to Dow Jones's board and would serve as chairman of the new subsidiary. His son, James H. Ottaway, Jr., became president of Ottaway Newspapers, Inc., heading a group of papers with a combined circulation of 242,695. The plan brought Dow Jones & Company—which had been predominantly in the business and financial fields—into the general newspaper publishing arena. Within ten years Ottaway Newspapers would gain control of twenty.

Jim Ottaway and Paul Miller, chairman of Gannett Co., were the first men named as members of the New York State Publishers Association Hall of Fame. "They are unusual and rare men, devoted to the profession of journalism and its highest ideals, men who cast large and inspirational shadows . . ." said the citation.

The newspapers Ottaway presided over also won their share of awards. In 1971 the staff of the *Oneonta Star* received two first-place awards from the New York Associated Press Association. One of the prizes, for newspapers under 40,000 circulation, was for a spot news story by a three-man team on the drug death of a student at the state college in Oneonta. The other prizewinner, a feature by editor Frank Perretta, was about a wild and successful ambulance ride from Oneonta to a New York City hospital to save the life of a day-old child.

The *Oneonta Star*'s famous police-probe story, for which the Ottaway daily won a Distinguished Community Service Award from the New York State Publishers Association, began one hot, rainy night in June, 1972.

An unhappy police sergeant asked for a secret meeting with city editor Bill Gates on Webb Island, an isolated spot in one of the city parks. The sergeant, Leland Higgins, told Gates that he was disillusioned with the leadership of Oneonta's police department. He accused the police chief and his assistant of "incompetent and gross negligence and dereliction of duty."

Higgins revealed that he had already met in secret session with the public safety board, but the three members of the board remained mum even after the *Star* published its first story. Other stories followed throughout the year. The safety board retaliated by forbidding the town's policemen to talk to the press, but before the order could be posted, Sergeant Higgins turned over some tape recordings he had made of his secret session with the board.

The *Star* published extensive excerpts from the tapes and followed them up with an editorial crusade. Eleven editorials, written by editor Frank Perretta, appeared over a five-month period. The editorials criticized the public safety board's handling of the case and called on it to drop its shroud of secrecy.

Some Oneonta residents praised the *Star,* while others damned it, but the constant pressure of the news stories and editorials made city officials realize they could not ignore the case. The *Star* got the mayor to admit that he was "relieved" the story was out in the open, but the safety board still refused comment.

The mayor wanted to appoint a citizens' committee to investigate the police department. This met with vociferous objections from many quarters. Finally, after a great deal of argument, the Oneonta Common Council retained a private investigator who interrogated policemen and witnesses. His 200-page report was made public—at the *Star*'s insistence—and was highlighted in a series of news stories over the next several days.

By this time the public safety board found its tongue and resigned en masse, after issuing a laconic statement. A new board was appointed, and open hearings were held. The *Star* reported fully on the proceedings but saw no need for further editorial comment. Ironically, on the very day the paper won its award the new board voted to suspend the police chief's pay for one month and to formally reprimand his assistant.

The Middletown, New York, *Times Herald-Record* is the largest daily (65,747) and Sunday (69,675) circulating newspaper in the Ottaway group. It was acquired by Ottaway in two transactions—the morning *Times Herald* was purchased in November, 1959, and the afternoon *Record* in April, 1960. The papers were consolidated into a morning daily in October 1960.

At the time of the acquisition the dailies had a combined circulation of about 33,000 and no Sunday edition. By 1976 the *Times Herald-Record* boasted a circulation of 57,118, and the Sunday paper, started in 1969, had a circulation of 63,199.

"You know," remarked Warren Phillips, Dow Jones president at the time, "the *Times Herald-Record*'s daily circulation is more than *The Wall Street Journal* has in forty-two states. It's about the same as the *Journal* has in Pennsylvania and New Jersey. And in only two cities—New York and Chicago—does the *Journal* have more daily circulation." The *Times Herald-Record* has also had a 28-percent jump in circulation since 1970, a period when the circulation of U.S. dailies generally was declining.

The paper's main turf is Orange and Sullivan counties, a fast-growing farming and livestock area with diversified manufacturing operations—apparel, leather goods, electrical equipment, machinery, metal fabricating, and textiles. Middletown itself, originally a railroad hub, is sixty miles northwest of New York City and eighteen miles west of the Hudson River.

The *Times Herald-Record* is a chunky, tightly edited, sprightly tabloid with a pedigree of distinction. One of its forebears, the *Daily Record,* was among the first newspapers in the country to be put together by photocomposition (cold type) and printed by the offset process. Cold type is a speedier, lower cost way of producing a newspaper, and offset printing provides superior printing and reproduction. The *Record* pioneered in these new technologies in 1956; today, of course, most newspapers use both photocomposition and offset.

The technological innovation that marked the early years continued at the *Times Herald-Record*. Today it has an advanced system of electronic news processing, and the entire production and business operation is computerized.

The *Times Herald-Record* office in downtown Middletown is a study in modern electronic journalism. In the news, advertising, and production areas are video display terminals (VDTs), Selectric typewriters, scanners, photocomposition units, and two computers.

When a reporter completes a story, the copy is put into a scanner that "reads" the words into a computer. An editor then retrieves the story on an editing terminal at his desk, makes changes as required through a typewriterlike keyboard, adds a headline, then pushes a key putting the story back into the computer. The computer supplies the data to a cold-type-setting machine, which produces the headlines and columns on paper for pasting up on a page.

Once the page is completely made up, a huge camera takes a picture of the page, and the negative is used to make a plate for the press. Press start is midnight for the first of three editions, but stories can be added to the final edition as late as 4:00 A.M. The press run consumes more than fourteen tons of newsprint each day.

Some 258 people work on the *Times Herald-Record* (including about 55 in the news operation), 753 youthful carriers help deliver the paper (30,000 copies "every day before breakfast"), and it's sold by 679 newsdealers.

The paper carries a couple of banner headlines on national events and a large photo, usually local and sometimes in color. The wire news, which makes up 25 to 30 percent of the news content, is organized into various packaged columns—around New York, around the region, around the nation, with major pieces (about three or four to a page) and photos spread liberally throughout.

Recognition of the paper's quality is widespread. It's a four-time winner of the N. W. Ayer Award for makeup and reproduction; its reporters and editors have won numerous prizes. In 1976, for the second successive year, editor Al Romm won the New York State Publishers annual award for editorial writing.

The electronic newsroom and the new equipment and processes are to some extent responsible for the success of the newspaper. But they are a minor factor compared to the imagination and dedication of the people who work there. "The gadgets are great," Warren Phillips observed, "but without the people and the high quality of their effort they wouldn't mean a thing."

Another interesting daily in Ottaway's stable of publications is the *Cape Cod Times,* which is very much a small-town paper even though it serves the entire Cape. Its publisher, Scott Himstead, rates the oil spill from the *Argo Merchant* in the 1970s as the biggest story of his career. Runner-up was the "Rose Parade" held in honor of Rose Kennedy's ninetieth birthday.

Himstead, who lives in Barnstable Village, graduated from Oberlin College. He joined the Ottaway group's Danbury, Connecticut, paper in 1967 and later moved on to Campbell Hall, where he became assistant to James Ottaway, Sr. He was made publisher of the *Cape Cod Times* (originally the *Cape Cod Standard-Times*) in 1972, when it had a daily circulation of barely 20,000. That figure has increased substantially in the past ten years. The paper currently has a daily circulation of about 33,000, which jumps to 41,000 during the summer months. The Sunday edition sells about 37,000 copies off season and another 10,000 in the summer. No other daily sells more widely on the Cape except the Boston papers, the *New York Times,* and *The Wall Street Journal.* This is in spite of the fact that the paper competes with five radio stations, five paid-circulation weeklies or semi-weeklies, and innumerable throwaways.

The paper is one of Cape Cod's largest employers. It carries news of the entire Barnstable County region plus the town of Wareham across the canal. The *Times* wades into local issues in the fifteen towns it covers only when they are pertinent to the entire area. If a Dennis town meeting votes for a modified "manager system," for instance, the paper congratulates it. If the state threatens to put an unwanted boating ramp into Pleasant Bay north of Chatham, the *Cape Cod Times* raises an indignant voice.

Himstead regionalizes his Cape Cod news, offering three wide-open pages for Upper Cape, Mid-Cape, and Lower Cape items. The paper's main office is in Hyannis with bureaus in Buzzards Bay, Falmouth, Orleans, Provincetown, Nantucket, and Edgartown. The staff numbers 146 full-time employees and 66 part-timers. Fifty-one full-timers make up the news department.

As in many local papers the newswriting leaves something to be desired. The articles are apt to be wordy and cluttered with trivial details:

The annual meeting of the Federated Church of Hyannis was held recently in the church sanctuary with Walter H. Fish, president, presiding. Charles C. Dolloff, retiring from the position of Church Collector, after 25 years in that position, was presented with a Paul Revere bowl inscribed with fitting tribute to his faithful and loyal services in that office. . . .

This story was followed by fifteen inches of type listing the names of everyone elected to every committee in the church. This was reminiscent of the era when small-town editors used to print a page of names out of the phone book every day just to flatter the local citizens.

In a critique of the daily press in New England a committee of journalists and press analysts wrote about the *Cape Cod Times* with a searching and questioning eye:

The account of a school committee hearing on the truancy of a boy in the town of Bourne ran 25 column-inches, reporting the minutest details of the conversation. It is not just that there is no time for rewriting such a mountain of news copy every day; this is what the Standard-Times deems its job to be at present. But the result is that every reader has to wade through 20 columns of such material to find one or two stories that may interest him.

The committee also felt that the paper does a first-rate job of giving the community what it wants.

But despite its sometimes helterskelter appearance, the paper has a tone of vigor and sound principles. The publisher and editor seek genuinely to make the public's voice heard at every opportunity through full reporting, published letters, and an excellent "Write-to-Know" column which fills two columns twice a week. They play the news straight and reassess their own performance constantly. . . . That is at least a good start toward building a character and a tradition.

Ottaway reporters periodically uncover instances of corruption that have national overtones. In 1973 the Ottaway News Service put the pieces together and linked Bill Brock, the Republican senator from Tennessee, to a high-pressure vacation home development called

Sherwood Forest in the Pocono Mountains of eastern Pennsylvania.

The story started with a tip from Bert Walter of Ottaway's *Pocono Record* to Knight Kiplinger of Ottaway News Service's Washington staff that a local man was suing Brock for allegedly reneging on a land deal. The case was eventually settled out of court, but Kiplinger, sensing there was more to the story, kept digging. First he found that the land in question was part of the former estate of "five and dime" millionaire Samuel Kress and had been bequeathed to Bucknell University. Then he found that Brock had purchased 800 acres of land from Bucknell and that the senator, through a dummy corporation, also owned at least half of the company that was developing Sherwood Forest.

While there is nothing illegal about a U.S. senator developing land on the side, some further legwork by Kiplinger turned up the information that Sherwood Forest had been cited several times by the Land Sales Office of the U.S. Department of Housing and Urban Development for questionable sales tactics and advertising. Specifically, HUD pointed out that Sherwood Forest had been advertising ski lifts, swimming pools, and a golf course as if they existed—which they didn't. HUD also ordered the developers to cease and desist from high-pressure sales pitches (in which potential purchasers allegedly were not permitted to read land-description forms).

To top it off Kiplinger discovered that two of Brock's senate staff aides were listed as officers of the dummy corporation. Moreover, Brock sat on the Senate Banking, Housing and Urban Affairs Committee, which is supposed to keep an eye on interstate land offerings like those made by Sherwood Forest and also has jurisdiction over the regulatory activities of HUD's Land Sales Office.

Another member of the Ottaway group, the *Sunbury* (Pa.) *Daily Item,* faced its most severe crisis during the disastrous floods of June 21–24, 1972. Though shorthanded and exhausted, the paper's staff got editions out on all but one day of the crisis. From Saturday, June 24, to the following Monday special flood editions—eight pages, no ads—were distributed free throughout central Pennsylvania.

The Ottaway executives at Campbell Hall backed up the beleaguered paper by authorizing the hiring of a private helicopter to ferry newspapers, flood victims, and food back and forth across the rampaging Susquehanna River. In addition two Ottaway News Service reporters were dispatched to supplement the regular staff.

Daily Item sports editor Bill Toland typified the spunk displayed by the daily's employees. Though his home was devastated by flood waters and he was living in an evacuation center, Toland showed up each day to put out his sports page. Other staffers, physically unable to make it to the office, filed daily roundup stories from their areas by phone.

In 1975 the *Standard-Times* of New Bedford, Massachusetts, served as an ombudsman in a consumer complaint case.

A local couple purchased a Volkswagen "Thing" for $3,263.50 on the basis of an ad that described the vehicle as "a car that goes anywhere. Use it on the beach, dune buggy style . . ."

When the owners drove to Cape Cod, however, they learned that beach authorities would not allow them off the pavement because the "Thing" "was not equipped for over-the-road sand operation."

The couple complained for eight months to their dealer, Volkswagen of America, Inc., the Massachusetts Attorney General's office, and the Federal Trade Commission—but no one would listen. The one person who did was Karen J. Karolczuk, assistant family living editor of the *Standard-Times*. She wrote a story on the couple's plight with the following results: First, the day after the story appeared Volkswagen of America approved refunding the couple the full purchase price. Second, Volkswagen was ordered by the State Consumer Protection Office to stop all advertising and recall all promotion material describing the "Thing" as a beach vehicle. The company was also ordered to provide restitution to persons who purchased the vehicle under that impression.

Traverse City, Michigan, "The Cherry Capital of the World," was a sawmill town once upon a time. Huge pine logs used to roll out of the surrounding Grand Traverse Bay forests to be sliced into planks, loaded aboard schooners, and shipped to other Lake Michigan ports. By the turn of the century the pines were gone, and local folks, looking for a replacement, took to growing cherries. Today the Traverse

City area produces more than half the annual U.S. tonnage of cherries.

About the time the cherry industry began to take hold—1897, to be exact—Traverse City got a new newspaper. It blossomed into the *Traverse City Record-Eagle,* which in 1972 became the eleventh daily newspaper in the Ottaway group, and its first publishing venture outside the Northeast.

Distributed each weekday to approximately 22,179 subscribers in five northern counties of the Lower Michigan Peninsula, the *Record Eagle* was sold to Ottaway for $3.9 million in cash. Transfer of ownership became effective September 29, 1972. The September 1 edition, which carried the acquisition story spread across three of the front page's eight columns, was a typically hefty issue. Its thirty-two pages of news, ads, and features and a special sixteen-page "Back to School" ad supplement were put together by the fourteen-member news staff.

The issue also contained a message from Jim Ottaway, Sr.: "I am particularly happy about returning to newspaper publishing in Michigan where I began to learn this exciting business as a boy working in my father's newspaper, the *Port Huron Times-Herald.*"

In 1979 Martin D. Sommerness of the Michigan State University School of Journalism wrote a master's thesis in which he examined the *Traverse City Record-Eagle* before and after its purchase by Ottaway Newspapers. Editor John Kinney was quoted as saying that the *Record-Eagle* "has become more of a local newspaper under absentee ownership." Sommerness's study supports this statement. Under Ottaway ownership and management the newspaper's total content increased to include more local information, a greater variety of opinion and entertainment matter, and more aggressive editorials.

Other improvements include an increase in news staff members, a switch from letterpress to offset printing, and a more active, locally oriented news and opinion policy that has enhanced the paper's ability to serve the five-county Grand Traverse region.

Sommerness concluded that "a chain-owned newspaper not only has the potential to serve the readers better than its independent predecessor, but in at least one case, did, and continues to provide its readers vastly improved daily accounts of the world in which they live.''

Among the many prizewinners in the Ottaway newspaper family is the *Medford (Ore.) Mail Tribune,* which in 1976 won the First Amendment Award of the Society of Professional Journalists, Sigma Delta Chi. It was the first newspaper to be honored; the two previous awards had gone to the Reporter Committee for Freedom of the Press and to former Supreme Court Justice William O. Douglas.

''Since it came to us 'out of the blue,' without application, we were doubly pleased,'' publisher Steve Ryder wrote Dow Jones president Warren Phillips. ''The special joy is in knowing that we are the first newspaper to be so recognized.''

The newspaper, whose circulation is 26,985 daily and 29,667 Sunday, was cited for its action in obtaining an injunction to forbid the sequestering of criminal records in its home county. This was necessary because in 1975 the Oregon legislature had passed a law designed to limit unwarranted access to criminal records. Inadvertently, certain exceptions were dropped from the bill. The law as passed banned the release of any criminal information about arrests, trials, detentions, previous records, releases, and paroles.

Just hours before the new law went into effect, the *Mail Tribune* obtained a temporary injunction against its enforcement by officials in Jackson County. The law was repealed four days after it became effective, but Jackson County was the only area in Oregon where criminal information was available for those four days.

The Sigma Delta Chi award cited the paper's ''strong and continuing effort to preserve and strengthen freedom of the press and The First Amendment to the Constitution.''

In March, 1978, Ottaway News Service (ONS), the wire network serving the Ottaway newspapers, launched a series of journalistic and technological innovations. The month began with the establishment of a full-time Washington bureau. This was followed by the replacement of ONS's teleprinters with video display terminals, allowing speedier, more accurate transmission of news to the various Ottaway newspapers stretching from Cape Cod to Oregon.

Creation of the Washington bureau was a landmark in the development of the news service. For twelve years Ottaway newspapers had received specialized Washington coverage from the Griffin-Larrabee News Bureau, an independent operation that serviced other clients. But the Ottaway group had grown so big and busy that it now required its own exclusive coverage in the nation's capital.

The new ONS transmission network linked Ottaway newspapers to transmission points at Washington, Boston, Albany, Harrisburg, Ottaway headquarters at Campbell Hall, and New York City. The relatively slow and cumbersome teleprinters at sending locations gave way to Goss Image III "tubes," which are easier to operate, transmit ten times faster with a higher degree of accuracy, and operate more quietly. Other features allowed selective distribution of stories, storage and recall of stories from a central computer, movement of stories among bureaus, more extensive editing, and repeat transmission with greater ease. The new system delivered upper-and-lower-case copy (instead of all caps) to all locations in a form that could be taken directly into a computer or used to produce paper tape to drive automated typesetting equipment.

One of the most common complaints about newspaper chains is that news and editorial policy can be dictated from afar with little or no concern for the individual newspaper or the community it serves. Ottaway is an exception. Each of its newspapers functions independently. Operating results and editorial quality are the specific responsibility of the local publisher and general manager. They are assisted by a small, headquarters management division staff at Campbell Hall, which provides management consulting and general financial services as needed; supplemental news coverage including Dow Jones news stories; national and regional advertising sales representation; production and mechanical counsel; and personnel development and training services.

To maintain a one-family concept the parent company publishes *Ottaway News Extra,* an internal bimonthly report on editorial performance by all the newspapers, and the *Ottaway Market Letter,* a bimonthly newsletter on business and financial activities in the areas served by the newspapers.

On August 1, 1976, James Ottaway turned the job of chief executive officer over to his son, James, Jr., and announced a reduction in his activities as chairman of the board. He retired from that post on July 31, 1979, but continues as a member of the board of directors of Ottaway Newspapers, Inc.

The younger Ottaway was born in Endicott, New York, in March, 1938. He started his newspaper career at Yale where he was chairman of the *Yale Daily News*. In the family tradition Jim has worked in all departments of a newspaper (a younger brother David, formerly a foreign correspondent for the *New York Times* and *Time-Life,* is assistant foreign news editor of the *Washington Post*). For eighteen months Jim Ottaway was in an on-the-job management-training program at the *News-Times* in Danbury, Connecticut. He served successively as a reporter, bureau chief, and special editorial assistant at the *Middletown Times Herald-Record,* where he covered the state legislature in Albany.

In 1963 Ottaway was named editor of the *Pocono Record,* and two years later he returned to Danbury to become associate publisher of the *News-Times*. In early 1966 he became vice president and a director of Ottaway Newspapers-Radio, Inc., and publisher of the newly acquired *Standard-Times* in New Bedford, Massachusetts.

James Ottaway, Jr., became president of Ottaway Newspapers on August 1, 1970, and on August 1, 1976, added chief executive officer to his title. When his father stepped down, Jim, Jr., became chairman of the board, and on January 16, 1980, he was named a vice president of Dow Jones & Company.

With the purchase of Ottaway Newspapers, Inc., in 1970 Dow Jones became the ninth largest newspaper group in the country in terms of daily circulation. By the mid-1970s it had risen to seventh largest.

The combined circulation of the twenty community newspapers published by Ottaway Newspapers passed the 500,000 mark for the first time in 1980. Its earnings that year were $8,659,000, up 4.7 percent from 1979. Ad revenues rose to $103,548,000, an increase of 10.4 percent over 1979.

In April 1982 the twenty-first daily newspaper, the Santa Cruz *Sen-*

tinel, was added to the Ottaway group, with a weekday circulation of 26,600 and a Sunday circulation exceeding 30,200. The newspaper serves the area around Santa Cruz, California, 75 miles south of San Francisco.

Recently five of the Ottaway papers installed either Associated Press or United Press International receiver dishes on their roofs to receive high-speed wire service news by satellite. Other papers will soon follow suit. The Ottaway tradition has always involved keeping up with the times as well as with the news.

10

The *Journal's* First Section

All copy for *The Wall Street Journal* ends up in one of three places: on the
inside of the paper, on the outside, or in the wastebasket.

"What's News"
Dow Jones & Company house organ

BARNEY KILGORE'S CONVICTION that economic news is more than
high finance was the basis for the important changes made in *The
Wall Street Journal* during his tenure. "Financial people are nice and
all that," Kilgore said, "but there aren't enough of them to make
this paper go." He saw the business community all over the country
as a single community. Thus it followed that all businesspeople could
be interested in one source of information, if it were competently
presented. To attract this segment of the population Kilgore set about
developing a newspaper that would be different in appearance and
content from other dailies.

The *Journal*'s front page is unique in three ways: First, wide columns are used instead of the usual narrow ones. Second, there are
almost no photographs. At one point illustrations were attempted for
the "What's News" columns, but were abandoned when it was decided they were a waste of space. Third, there is no traditional mul-
ticolumn headline in the upper-right-hand corner. All front-page stories
are run in one column and, if necessary, continued inside.

Kilgore also saw no need for his paper to run big headlines: "Why should we? We are not shouting about the news with headlines. It is a noisemaking device. If your paper is competitive, it might help, but probably not that much."

From the time Kilgore became president in 1945 he made few changes in layout, finding it best to work within the six-column style adopted "permanently" by his predecessor, Casey Hogate. "What's News," for example, has appeared in columns two and three for more than forty years.

When color printing for newspapers became technically feasible in the late 1940s, Kilgore was asked when the *Journal* would go color. "Just as soon as we learn to print in black and white," he responded, "and I don't expect to live that long."

Members of the *Journal*'s news department do triple duty in the course of their news-gathering efforts. Their first responsibility is to get a breaking news story onto the ticker (the Dow Jones News Service) as quickly as possible. Then, if the editor deems the news sufficiently important, the reporter races to the typewriter to write a story in greater detail for the inside pages of the paper—the hard business backbone of the *Journal*. Simultaneously the news staff is almost always working on major stories for page one, fitting the preparation of these in-depth features into their regular workload.

The news in the *Journal* is compiled, written, and edited by a staff of more than 400 reporters, editors, and copyreaders located in 25 news bureaus throughout the world. They fill 34 columns of white space each day—there are between 75 and 125 separate news items in every issue, all of which cross the national news desk.

Like the *New York Times* and other major newspapers the *Journal* maintains bureaus in numerous cities. The New York and Washington bureaus operate on a "beat" system—that is, reporters are assigned to cover specific areas of interest. Thirty-eight of the forty-five New York City reporters have beats that include the retailing, airline, food, securities, and publishing industries. Others cover resources, oil, mining, and so forth.

One advantage of having beats in New York is that a news editor can receive a story filed from Los Angeles on, say, an airline company and buck it over to the airline beat reporters for a fast review. The news story is thus filtered through an expert in the field in addition to the scrutiny given it by the news desk. The beat reporter can frequently offer ideas, suggestions, and contacts for follow-up by the reporter who filed the story and can also check the original to see if anything should be added and/or make sure nothing important is missing.

"What's News"

Without question the most widely read portion of the *Journal* is the double-column space on its front page titled "What's News." The feature has probably led to more paper sales than any other.

"What's News" has been on the front page ever since Kenneth Hogate instituted it as an experiment to pull the newspaper out of its decline during the early years of the Depression. The initial column was written by Barney Kilgore, who was then a young reporter. "What's News" takes up two of the six columns on the front page. Under the subheading "Business and Finance" are ten to twenty brief summaries of major economic news items, each generally directing the reader to a detailed story on an inside page. At the end of the column a succinct market report offers data on the previous day's stock market trading.

In the column to the right of "Business and Finance," under the subheading "World Wide," are brief summaries of major national and worldwide events. Here, however, there are no page numbers for more details. The *Journal* chooses not to develop these stories, leaving the reader to seek other sources for further information. To expand on stories of this type in the *Journal* not only would take up too much space, it would also require reporters to shift their focus from business news.

"World Wide" and "Business and Finance" have proved to be a boon to busy executives. A quick perusal is sufficient to keep them abreast of world events. As might be expected, however, the conciseness of "What's News" makes it unusually difficult to write. It also takes a team of reporters and editors to determine which topics will have priority.

"A-Heds" and "Leaders"

Glynn Mapes, since 1980 the page-one editor of *The Wall Street Journal,* is responsible for three of the newspaper's six front-page columns—column one on the far left, the story that runs under the daily chart in column four, and column six. Mapes also handles the feature story that appears on the back page of the second section.

Officially the page-one staff consists of Mapes and some seven rewrite people, but virtually every one of the paper's reporters contributes in some degree to one of the four articles that appear each business day.

These four daily features, particularly the three on page one, embody the newspaper's special brand of journalism and have contributed to the *Journal*'s reputation for quality reporting and writing.

Columns one and six and the back-page feature are called "leaders," or "leders," a British newspaper term for the story that "leads" or "led" the paper and/or was considered the most important. A *Journal* "leader" has a three-part formula. The story must be significant or have some strong appeal for a broad segment of the paper's readers; it must originate with the *Journal;* and it must be comprehensive and analytical. "Leaders" are the paper's showpieces; the best reporters and the most widely read articles appear on page one.

Every "leader" that comes to New York from any bureau around the world is subject to the law of supply and demand. The demand is steady at two leaders a day, five days a week (less holidays), 506 leaders a year. The supply fluctuates drastically. At vacation periods, in late August and early September, for example, the editors often sweat to get the leader columns filled. Two weeks later they may be faced with a horrible glut.

Vermont Royster, who retired from the *Journal* in 1971 after thirty-five years with Dow Jones, made some interesting comments appropos of the "leader" concept:

I think the newspaper business is already moving in the direction of interpretive reporting. When we first started our leader-type stories, we were innovators. This is no longer so. There are other large metropolitan newspapers that have adopted this technique and adapted it to their own needs. The *New*

York Times and the *Los Angeles Times* are good examples. You can even see signs of it in the small town newspapers.

. . . I think one of the tasks of journalism in the future is to devise ways and means of backing off a bit from these immediate day-to-day crises and trying to give them some perspective. Actually, on the *Journal* we have done more in that direction than most other newspapers. Our front page leader stories are very frequently connected with spot news developments. But, by and large, they are not spot news stories. They are an endeavor, maybe not always successful, to take a current situation, back off a bit, and try to tell the story in some depth. Maybe the leader doesn't run the first day the crisis breaks. It may come along two or three days later.

In actual fact, many leaders take weeks, sometimes months, to research and prepare. The basic concept is that a newspaper can carry both hard and soft news; the hard news has to be reported as quickly as possible, while the soft news can be held back until a propitious moment, perhaps even after the story has been more fully developed.

Column six is the weightiest column in *The Wall Street Journal* in terms of content. It is devoted to a business, financial, or economics story, although sometimes it is given over to an "investigative" report, a genre known to the staffers as the "cops-and-robbers" story. Column-six stories are generally regarded as the most important features produced by the page-one staff.

A story that appears in column four is called an "A-head," or "A-hed," for the headline style that runs above it. These articles tend to be lightweight, sometimes given to sheer frivolity. Aside from their entertainment value, however, they can usually be counted on to introduce readers to subjects they might not otherwise have given a second thought.

The A-heds are as much the responsibility of the page-one desk as the leaders, but the A-heds are secondary; the leader columns have to be filled first. The requirements for the two are the same. In fact column four sometimes carries stories that, in a tighter supply situation, would appear as leaders.

On any given day the story that appears as the A-hed is one that struck the editors as being of less general interest and significance than the two leaders. Still, the one-angle A-heds, telling of a blunder by a big corporation or describing some new and unusual development in merchandising, are among the liveliest reading in the paper.

About two-thirds of the ideas for front-page feature stories originate with the reporters whose bylines eventually appear on them. The others are proposed by the editors in New York, by other news bureaus, and occasionally by readers.

As on most newspapers, reporters get an idea, discuss it first with the bureau chief, then, if given the green light, submit it to an editor in the form of a brief memo. This memo, a typewritten page or two at the most, outlines the story, lists the sources for it, tells what the main points would be, and why it would interest readers.

On the newsweeklies reporters submit their stories in memo form to be fashioned into articles by the rewrite staff. At the *Journal* the reporter stays with the story. The rewriters remain anonymous, and the reporter gets the byline.

The time allotted to *The Wall Street Journal*'s reporters and editors and the frequent, thorough scrutiny given their articles distinguish the *Journal*'s reporting style from that of other publications. Time is the most precious gift a newspaper or magazine can bestow on its staff. At the *Journal* accuracy, quality of writing, and comprehensive coverage of a story are prime considerations. The many readings each story receives—from the bureau chief, page-one editor, rewriter, assistant page-one editor, and senior managing editor—are designed to ensure these qualities.

Inside and Outside

"What's News," Dow Jones's house organ, states, "All copy for *The Wall Street Journal* ends up in one of three places: on the inside of the paper, on the outside, or in the wastebasket." In the 1970s Mike Gartner (now editor of the *Des Moines Register & Tribune*) handled the outside—page one and features—and Bill Kreger handled the inside—everything except editorials.

Like many of the news-department people Bill Kreger came to the *Journal* from the Columbia University School of Journalism, which he attended after spending three years as a city-side reporter on the *Dubuque* (Iowa) *Telegraph-Herald*.

Kreger joined the *Journal* in May, 1952, when he was twenty-seven years old. He started on the copy desk and was running it by

1954. He was named a news editor in 1960 and took over the whole inside operation in late 1961, becoming assistant managing editor in 1965.

A large, moody man, Kreger had no patience with anyone who interfered with his concentration or his obsession with doing a first-class job. At 5:30 one afternoon, Ed Cony, a vice president of the company, was standing around chatting with a reporter in front of the desk where Kreger was hard at work. Suddenly Kreger looked up at Cony, his boss, and snapped, "Cony, if you'd get your ass out of here, I could get a paper out tonight."

Cony left.

Kreger's workday began some time between 10:00 and 11:00 A.M., when he clumped in after the trip from his home in Summit, New Jersey, sat down, often at someone else's desk, and read the paper to see if the printers had laid it out his way or theirs.

Kreger spent the rest of his day smoking cigarettes, chewing antacid tablets, drinking iced tea, and making decisions. He saw nearly every piece of copy that ran on the inside of the paper, decided what size headline it should have, how long it should run, and whether additional information was needed. He had an amazing memory and could recall that such-and-such a story was a follow-up on something that ran on page eleven in an issue years earlier.

In addition to overseeing copy—an eight- or nine-hour-a-day job— Kreger was head of a fairly large department. Although the dozen or so people who reported to him were often at odds with Kreger, they all liked and respected him. He was the kind of boss who stood up for his people when they were right and let them know when they were wrong.

In all his years at the *Journal* Bill Kreger never had a byline, although he had written an estimated five million words that had gone into print. Whenever a big story broke late in the evening and reports started coming in from the staff and the wire services, Kreger would grab a typewriter and announce that it was time for "Bill Kreger, boy writer" to go to work. Then he would quickly pound out a well-organized 800-word story that would tell more and be clearer and more concise than the versions that appeared in the *Times* or the *New York Post*.

In June, 1980, Kreger was appointed senior assistant managing editor, helping managing editor Larry O'Donnell put out the newspaper each day. Kreger was the final reader of page one, the front pages of the second section, and the other major features in the paper. He also helped coordinate feature coverage aimed at page one and served as the *Journal*'s chief language stylist.

When Bill Kreger died of a heart attack on August 1, 1981, his friend and fellow editor, Mike Gartner, memorialized him in the *Journal*:

For those of us who grew up in the *Journal* newsroom, Bill Kreger remains the best editor we've ever known. To copy editors—his favorite people—he was a selfless, patient teacher. To reporters, he was a probing, impatient quizmaster. To all of us, he was the resident expert. On everything.

Here are some of the things Bill Kreger knew: He knew that indictments are handed up (the judge sits on an elevated bench, higher than the grand jury) but decisions are handed down. He knew the difference between flaunt and flout, between uninterested and disinterested, between which and that.

He knew how to make a long story short, a fuzzy story crisp. He knew how to explain complicated points so deftly that the reader never knew he was in a minefield. He knew how to make a young man try harder. "Let's try it this way," he'd say and he'd cross out a phrase here and a sentence there, add just the right word at just the right place (in a beautiful penmanship) and then quietly move to the top of the story the needed paragraph that somehow had been hidden below. "How about that?" he'd say, and he'd make you think you did all those things yourself. Then he'd take a drink of iced tea, light up another cigaret, eat a sweet roll and move on to the next problem.

He was a great speller. He could spell accommodate and idiosyncrasy without looking them up, and he knew there was only one "e" in sizable and one in judgment.

Bill Kreger could spell judgment, and he had it as well. He could sense when something was wrong with a story. He knew when a reporter had been sold a bill of goods. He frowned—and then excised—when a copy editor wrote a bad headline or, worse, one in bad taste. He was firm but fair. He was honest. I remember one evening when a reader called and asked him if such and such a story was going to be in the *Journal* the next day. "Sir," he said, "I wouldn't tell my own grandmother what's going to be in this paper tomorrow." He slammed down the phone, sputtered, gulped some iced tea and lit a cigaret.

Also, he seemed to have total recall. When did that little item on Texaco and what's his name run in the paper, Bill? He knew what year, what day, what page, what column.

"One reason our library is so old fashioned," says Fred Taylor, executive editor of the *Journal,* "is because of Kreger. We've never needed a modern library. He remembered everything we ever printed."

Another thing. It was wonderful to watch Kreger get mad. "He goes from pale to pink to crimson, all the way down the chromatic spectrum," a colleague said a few years ago. "Then it's like Old Faithful."

One final thing: Bill Kreger was a terrific fellow. I'm sorry you never knew him . . .

Column Five

The fifth column of the *Journal's* front page carries the "special reports," covering different topics each day. On Mondays four editorial staffers from the news department—specializing in economics and finance—take turns writing "The Outlook," which examines the business environment from every conceivable angle. Inflation, recession, capital spending, interest rates, exchange rates, government policy, employment, upturns, downturns—all of the relevant forces at work in a modern economy are surveyed and subjected to a variety of statistical indicators and approaches.

Tuesday's column, the "Labor Letter," carries ten to twelve items on current developments in the employment area, policy from Washington, labor union news, and labor-management relations.

On Wednesdays the "Tax Report" is run. Written for managers who have to keep on top of taxes and accounting, it contains tax court decisions, IRS releases, technical articles, and comments by tax attorneys and tax accountants.

Thursdays are devoted to "Business Bulletin." Its objectives are twofold: to present facets of the business world and to spot emerging trends in any area—industry, marketing, advertising, production—before others do.

On Fridays "Washington Wire" offers the reader a reliable behind-the-scenes look at the workings of government.

The National News Desk

Since all the bureaus of the *Journal* submit their copy to New York for editing, a continuity of style is maintained. Once a story has been processed through the national news desk in New York, it is turned over to the copy desk. The desk itself is a horseshoe-shaped structure. The outside, around which the copyreaders and editors sit, is called the rim. There are places for seventeen people on the rim. Only two—the chief copy editor and an assistant—sit in the slot, the center of the horseshoe.

Completed articles are received by the slot, where they are rated on importance, given the size and type of headline they should carry, and estimated as to length. The editor in the slot then passes the copy out to the rim, whenever possible giving it to the editor who is most knowledgeable about that particular subject.

The denizens of the rim are professional copyreaders and editors—people who prefer to work inside rather than outside chasing stories. They can improve the language of a news item without ruining the style, have a sense for good spelling and grammar, and can write headlines to fit stringent space requirements.

Some writing is done on the rim—a rewrite of a lead, perhaps, or of a paragraph to clear up a particular point. The bulk of the work, however, involves improving language and correcting misspellings. The object is to see that the story reads clearly and is grammatically correct. If extensive rewriting is necessary, the story is turned over to specialists on that particular subject. Because of the workload and the pressures no one stays in the slot all day; the more experienced rim people take turns at the job.

When the rim finishes with a piece of copy, it's handed back to the slot for checking. The slot people make sure the headline fits and is a good index to the content of the story. They then move the finished copy along to have it set in type. The next time the editors see it is in the *Journal*.

The national news desk also monitors the ticker continually so as not to miss any news items. Not all of the thousands of stories carried on the ticker merit development and inclusion in the paper; a great many more are filed than the *Journal* has room for. The news desk's editors are the ultimate arbiters of what readers will see, but they do follow certain guidelines.

News of mergers, company expansion plans, or financing, for example, all have to be in the neighborhood of $3 million to merit coverage. National news editor Norman Pearlstine explains:

. . . our main guideline on giving the green light to a story is if it's news that will "move the market"—for example, a change in earnings or dividends that will affect the company is perceived by the business and financial communities and, consequently, affects the price of its stock.

Once a story has been filed and the decision has been made to include it in the paper, the next step is to determine its importance and assign it one of three grades: "Must, "Try," or "If." "Must" stories, as the name implies, are those that must run in all editions of the *Journal*. Stories graded "Try" are less compelling than "Musts"; the national news desk would like them included in the paper only if space permits. "Ifs" (short for "if room") are items that are sent out almost as insurance. On slow days, when nothing much is happening, the news desk editor falls back on the "Ifs." They are all good news items, but if they didn't appear, they wouldn't be missed.

At noon and again at 4:30 P.M. each day a dozen *Journal* officials, mostly editors, gather to review projected stories for the following day's edition.

"Corrections and Amplifications"

Some years ago a *Time*-Louis Harris poll found *The Wall Street Journal* to be the most trusted publication in the country. The "Corrections and Amplifications" column helps explain why.

Only a handful of items appear under this heading, but they are often the most important ones in the paper. Because so many major decisions are based on news reported in the *Journal,* decisions that affect both corporate treasuries and individual pocketbooks, accuracy is vital. A misplaced decimal point can totally distort the financial picture of a corporation; the transposition of two figures can impute greater earnings than a company reported.

"Corrections and Amplifications" is the *Journal*'s way of making sure that readers are alerted to errors, typographical or otherwise. All staff members are kept keenly aware that even innocuous "typos" can have serious repercussions, and the column serves as an ongoing reminder of the need for accuracy. It is a great tribute to the newspaper that "Corrections and Amplifications" doesn't appear very often. Every day a clearly marked column carries from one to four corrections.

Quite often corrections are printed weeks or months after the original articles and are apt to be overlooked by readers, including those who have already made a judgment based on erroneous information. Yet, more often than not, the subjects of the errors believe the *Journal* has made amends. Here is a sample of some corrections and the responses they elicited from the parties concerned:

May 1, 1980—Corrections and Amplifications

CITIES SERVICE CO.'S first quarter net income of $170.1 million includes $33 million from oil-supply transactions that are the subject of litigation between Cities Service and the Energy Department. The $33 million is part of $100 million in net, applicable to periods prior to today, that Cities Service could lose if the courts rule against the company. The amount of first quarter net that the company could lose was misstated in an earlier edition.

On May 22, 1980, Robert E. Spann, manager of corporate communication for Cities Service Company, wrote:

The correction with respect to Cities Service was requested by me and was a reasonable solution to the problem created by a slight misstatement in the original article appearing April 30. . . . As far as we can ascertain, Cities Service suffered no negative impact as a result of the misstatement.

April 22, 1980—Corrections and Amplifications:

AMERICAN MOTORS CORP.'S wholesale shipments of regular passenger cars rose 14% in the second quarter, ended March 31. In an earlier edition, it was incorrectly reported that those shipments declined, contributing to a 96% drop in profit for the quarter that was brought on largely by plunging utility-vehicle sales.

On June 13, 1980, George F. Thompson, director of financial communication for American Motors Corporation, said:

We were, of course, aware of the error made by *The Wall Street Journal* and its subsequent retraction. . . . While we regret any error in reporting about the company's affairs, we were most gratified by the *Journal*'s prompt correction. We have no evidence that this error had any negative impact on the company.

April 29, 1980—Corrections and Amplifications:

MUNSINGWEAR INC.'S South Robeson Mills Inc. subsidiary continues to operate at a loss. It was incorrectly reported in an earlier edition that the unit is operating at a profit.

On May 22, 1980, Raymond F. Good of Munsingwear, Inc., said:

The error and retraction really did not have any negative impact in terms of our business results, but it did cause some problems. It prompted the question in the minds of certain customers as to whether we were going to shut down the operation, and several days of contacts and correspondence were required to resolve that issue. The article upset the people of South Robeson Mills, and it caused some problems with a union who had been told by us that we were not making money at the facility. It also caused me personally some minor degree of discomfort because some people felt that I either did not know what was going on or deliberately misinformed the press. In short, there was some temporary and relatively minor irritation, and it did take some time to correct them.

Three Mile Island

The Wall Street Journal's coverage of the accident at Pennsylvania's Three Mile Island nuclear power plant in March, 1979, provided a textbook illustration of the paper's ability to coordinate the efforts of dozens of newspeople in bureaus around the country and the world to handle a major story, and provide in-depth reporting on its many facets and implications. The following report was filed by Jack Cooper, then a reporter.

The accident on Three Mile Island instantly created doubts about the safety of the 70 other operating nuclear power plants, in every part of the nation, so it wasn't surprising that nearly every one of the *Journal*'s bureaus quickly became involved in the reporting activity.

In less than a month's time the nuclear crisis generated seven page one features and about 45 inside stories. John Emshwiller (New York) and Walt

Mossberg (Washington) were involved in the story from the first day and provided many of the ideas for our follow-up coverage.

But the extent to which everyone pitched in is indicated by the fact that five other reporters had page one bylines—Jonathan Spivak (London), Vasil Pappas and Rich Hudson (Philadelphia), George Getschow (Pittsburgh) and Tim Metz (New York)—and eight others had inside bylines—Dan Machalba (Philadelphia), Priscilla Meyer (New York), Earl Gottschalk (Los Angeles), Gail Bronson (New York), Gene Marcial (New York), Byron Klapper (New York), Tom Petzinger (Pittsburgh) and John Moore (Philadelphia). Nearly every bureau also was asked to check its local utilities on the status of nearby nuclear power plants and this reporting was inserted into roundup stories or used in the nightly spot stories.

The timing of the accident couldn't have been worse for the *Journal*'s manpower availability, coming as it did at the onset of the annual meeting season when both the Philadelphia and New York bureaus have to cover dozens of stockholder meetings every day. If we had our druthers, we would prefer mid-July or possibly late November for major stories to break.

As it was, the Philadelphia bureau manager and the New York editor had to do some fast shuffling.

In Washington, Walt Mossberg found himself covering two major stories at once—the Nuclear Regulatory Commission's daily announcements and Congressional hearings on the Harrisburg situation, and the mounting speculation about President Carter's energy program that was to be announced April 5. Affairs came to a head of sorts on Sunday, April 1, when Walt finished three takes [rewrites] of his page one feature on the outlook for nuclear power and then had to dash off for a 12:30 television appearance on NBC's "Meet the Press" before coming back to his office, still in TV makeup, and finishing his feature for that night's paper. The following Sunday, Walt went through a similar exercise, appearing on CBS's "Face the Nation" and then coming back to the office to add a few touches to a story he and John Emshwiller had written on past breakdowns at nuclear plants—but by then he had become an old hand at these split-second role changes.

Our spot newsmen in Harrisburg [technically Middletown, Pa.], first Emshwiller and then Hudson, had plenty of problems, too, trying to sort out the conflicting reports coming from Metropolitan Edison [operator of the damaged nuclear plant], Pennsylvania Governor Thornburgh, and officials of the Nuclear Regulatory Commission and then dictating a coherent daily story—often of 1,000 words or more—to *Journal* stenographer Janet Scudder in New York in time for the first edition.

Later, the NRC took over as the official spokesmen for developments at the plant, but the agency began holding its daily press briefings later and later in the afternoon, which hardly helped matters for Assistant National News Editor Pete Keller and his assistant, Mary Schenker, who had the responsibility for assembling all the various nuclear inside stories that came during the Three Mile Island crisis.

This "roundup" story is an example of speed, dedication, and thoroughness. The *Journal* scooped most other national dailies on this one and followed a story that had implications for society far beyond those of an economic nature. It clearly illustrates the virtue of being able to draw on a multitude of talent in bureaus around the globe.

A Lot of Business News

Journal reporters are fully aware that being assigned to a particular bureau in a particular section of the nation, or the world, will not stop them from seeing their columns printed and read in just about every corner of the country.

From Seattle to Atlanta to New York City *The Wall Street Journal* travelers pick up at airport, hotel, or newsstand is virtually identical in news content to the one they receive at home. On any given day 99—or more—percent of the news content is the same all over the country.

What is the 1 percent difference? Because of variations in the amount and nature of the advertising, mainly among the four regional editions, small news "fillers" may be added to fill out a column. Some news may appear on different pages in different editions, but for reader convenience an effort is made to see that stories are grouped by subject as much as possible.

The reward for reporters is knowing that several million people may be reading their columns. Collectively the paper's 400 writers produce an incredible amount of copy. In a single issue of the *Journal* there are a minimum of 90 columns of news. With an average of 55 words per column inch, that means the *Journal*'s news staff produces (after editing) a minimum of 103,950 words a day, 519,750 words a week, and 25,987,500 words a year. That's a lot of business news!

CHAPTER

11

The Second Front

The Wall Street Journal today begins an expansion of its news coverage. To accommodate this, the paper is being divided into two sections.

WARREN PHILLIPS,
Dow Jones chairman

THAT NOTICE TO READERS, which appeared on the front page of the *Journal*'s June 23, 1980, issue, heralded the most sweeping physical change in the history of the *Journal:* the debut of its second section.

The smooth introduction of a two-section newspaper was the result of more than a year of meticulous planning and a coordinated effort on the part of the news and production departments. There were many discussions among news executives, meetings with nearly all *Journal* reporters, "focus group" interviews with *Journal* readers, changes in printing and production systems, and five weeks of dry runs.

Detailed planning began in April, 1979, when Fred Zimmerman agreed to come to New York from Atlanta and serve as an editor of the second front. Four key questions had to be answered right away: What would the second front page look like? What kind of stories would go on it? Who would edit them? How would production of a two-section *Journal* be handled?

Zimmerman and executive editor Fred Taylor, who had overall charge of the project, spent hours and hours finding answers to them. By the time final decisions were made, all bureau chiefs had been brought into the talks. Eventually fifteen writers and editors were added to the *Journal*'s news department to build a second front staff.

By September an early phase of dry runs began, with news bureaus being asked to submit the kinds of stories—such as corporate and executive profiles—that might be run on the second front.

A second week-long dry run of a two-section *Journal* began on March 24, 1980. After some fine tuning of design and content, a third, two-week, dry run began in late April.

Meanwhile, as the day for launching the second front drew closer, it became clear that the production units were not ready for the shift. Some changes had to be made at Dow Jones's printing facilities across the country; many of them were not geared up to produce what would in effect be almost twice as many pages of newsprint. At some of the older plants, equipment had to be "dusted off" and put in smooth running order. Production managers were told to make as many test runs of a two-section paper as they needed "to feel comfortable," without unduly depleting newsprint supplies.

The final dry run began on June 9; the second section was introduced two weeks later. Reader reaction was instantaneous and ranged from:

I hate your new format.

Joseph B. Ahearn

Lexington, Mass.

to

The Wall Street Journal has expanded to two sections: My cup runneth over!

William M. Clark

New York

Page one of *The Wall Street Journal*—perhaps the most distinctive front page in the world—had been confronted, after more than ninety years, by a new member of the family with a personality of its own.

As family dynamics normally operate, the arrival of a second front page could have resulted in some serious sibling rivalry. But Dow Jones and the *Journal* editors were aware of the possibility and went to considerable lengths to avoid it.

173

Once the decision to expand the paper to two sections had been made, the next step was to decide on the format of the second front and its underlying concept. The options were varied. It could be devoted to an ad or a series of ads; it could be simply more of the same *Journal*—a regular spot news page or a more prominent position for such back-of-the-book features as "Your Money Matters," "Abreast of the Market," and "Heard on the Street"; it could present something entirely different from the traditional editorial product.

A quick glance at the second front immediately demonstrates how vigorously the last course was pursued. The first page of the second section is a marked departure in format and content from its older sister, yet there is a strong family resemblance.

One of the primary aims of the second front was to focus on areas where space limitations had made the *Journal* either weak or inconsistent in its coverage. According to Fred Zimmerman:

There was a consensus around here that, considering the large percentage of our readers who are small businessmen, we weren't writing enough about small business. Similarly, there was a general feeling that we weren't doing enough on advertising, technological developments, real estate, and regional issues—that our readers wanted more than we were giving.

The *Journal* now offers five rotating columns—one on each of these subjects—each week, and none is duplicated by coverage in the first section. In Zimmerman's view the second front has been given something of a mandate to break new ground, in terms of both the way stories are told and the subject matter. The five rotating columns help set this innovative tone, and the second front leaders keep pace by approaching business news quite differently from their first-section counterparts.

Second front stories steer clear of straight political events, international affairs, and worldwide economic matters. Instead, most of the coverage is domestic, related to business and the economy and—more pointedly—to the players rather than the game.

This emphasis on people, according to Zimmerman, spotlights one of the chief fascinations of business journalism: the personalities involved. "After all," he points out, "there is inherent conflict and drama in the marketplace, in the workplace. People are trying to get ahead of the next guy, trying to make ends meet. Money involves conflict. And power makes exciting reading.''

Take, for example, the fascinating scenario of Jane Pfeiffer's dismissal from NBC, which fueled not one but two second front leaders. By its very nature the subject aroused a plethora of passions. Was NBC president Fred Silverman a difficult taskmaster, jealous of a female subordinate and apparent rival? Or did an uppity Ms. Pfeiffer get what she so richly deserved? Clearly, only a brutal conflict could have moved the most public of companies to air its dirty linen in the most public of arenas.

Subsequent coverage of the drama, particularly in a roundup of reactions from prominent people, was a natural. More important, claims Zimmerman, the event sparked entertaining and insightful reporting that simply could not have appeared in a one-section *Journal*.

The second front stresses the human consequences of business as much as business itself. What happens on the job affects people's opinions and attitudes on everyday life. The extent to which these beliefs are shared by the business community underscores perhaps the most "human" of second front features: *The Wall Street Journal*/Gallup polls.

These jointly sponsored polls, which appear from time to time on the second front, investigate both professional and personal attitudes, ranging from assessing presidential leadership on business issues to identifying retirement problems among top executives. As Zimmerman sees it:

Nobody polls Fortune 500 executive officers about how many hours they work each week and the personal sacrifices involved. Nobody asks consumers what they think about the quality of goods and services they buy. That's the area we're going to try and carve out.

Filling the two pages just behind the *Journal*'s second front was initially the responsibility of Neil Ulman and his staff. The six columns each day provide a lot more space than the paper has previously been able to devote to foreign events. Ulman recalls:

When I became foreign editor in January, 1979, I realized that to do the kind of job I wanted to do, I needed more space in the paper. One of my first moves was to propose that we start an international section. But because space was so limited, I wasn't at all sure of getting it until the second front came along.

The international pages carry five bylined columns, none of them on a regular basis. "We run them only when they have something especially good to say," says Ulman. Frank Ching, the *Journal*'s reporter in Peking, writes "China Notes," a collection of revealing glimpses of life and business in China that are too small to rate full-scale stories. In "Foreign Policy Perspective" Karen House, the newspaper's diplomatic correspondent in Washington, takes a look at impending developments for the benefit of readers with international interests.

"Trends Abroad," usually written by Skip Martin, assembles news on economic events or statistics from several countries to produce a composite picture of what's happening worldwide. "Foreign Insight" gives the *Journal*'s overseas-based reporters a chance to look at interesting subjects in a more subjective or interpretive way. "Credit Lines" examines the people and motives behind developments in international banking—particularly the large syndicated loans made by groups of banks to countries or major companies. The one thing Ulman never has to worry about is running out of news to fill his pages.

The *Journal* has some three dozen reporters assigned full time to cover events in foreign countries. Most work out of six overseas bureaus (London, Paris, Bonn, Mexico City, Tokyo, and Singapore) and four Canadian bureaus (Toronto, Montreal, Ottawa, and Vancouver), but several are based in one of the paper's domestic news offices, and from ten to fifteen other reporters are traveling abroad at any one time, as part of their regular news assignments.

Reports from several of these globe-trotting news staffers suggest that the career of the foreign correspondent is not quite the glamorous, intrigue-filled life that the movies and television depict. On the contrary, it's an often arduous existence made more unpleasant—and sometimes dangerous—by such things as jet lag, the wrong clothing for the season, interminable waits at airports, contaminated food, and polluted water. There may also be violent official reactions when a reporter files an uncomplimentary story about the regime in power.

Everett Martin, a *Journal* reporter in South America, considers his beat one of the world's last frontiers. "I'm kind of an underdeveloped expert,'' says Martin. ''I always get sent to places with bad toilets.'' Usually Martin finds his stories in major cities, where the lodgings are adequate, if expensive. It's when he ventures into the hinterlands that he occasionally encounters conditions that would give a less determined traveler pause.

I don't worry too much about the food. I guess my stomach's pretty strong. But I do remember one place in northern Peru where, after eating, I went around back and saw them washing the dishes under a cold, dripping faucet. They were just moving the grease around on the plates. After seeing that, I got a hepatitis shot as soon as I got back to Lima.

Some of Martin's best stories come from personal contacts—and after ten years of roaming around South America he has a lot of them.

I work with a theory of concentric circles. Each trip I try to spread out another ring. The technique is to talk to someone and then ask him to introduce you to someone else. Particularly in Latin American countries, where people tend to be a little formal, you get a much better reception if a local man calls up and introduces you first.

It's very difficult to get straight information on anything in Latin America, because everything is so ideological. Everyone's either left wing or right wing, and they interpret your stories that way. For example, if you say Chile's economy is picking up, that means you support torture. If you say Chile's economy is in trouble, that means you favor Cuba. It's very hard to deal with.

Martin has filed a number of odd-ball stories picked up in the course of his regular reporting on the economics and politics of the countries on his beat. He can spin tales of a miraculous village in Ecuador where you can live an extraordinarily long life—if you can stand the place; of wonderous jungle plants that will stop bad cuts from bleeding and heal wounds in a day or two; of restaurant tables decorated with goldfish bowls inhabited by piranhas; and of a place where dolphins have been held responsible for impregnating wayward girls.

From a few visits to the Caravel, a sidewalk cafe in Aquitos, Peru, a village at the headwaters of the Amazon River, the correspondent was able to learn about a Norwegian naturalist who is trying to save animals and about an outfit called the Amazon Natural Drug Company, which takes biologists on river trips in search of new drugs derived from the amazing variety of herbs and other jungle growth. Martin also discovered the story behind the plaque honoring Peru's heroes of the War of the Pacific, which was fought against Chile in 1879; the bronze plaque was ordered from an Italian craftsman who misread the instructions. As a result the plaque shows the Peruvians standing off a charge of Chinese warriors, complete with slanted eyes and coolie caps.

Martin originally went to Aquitos to check out the story of a big oil strike. The reports proved to be highly exaggerated, but he came away with an A-hed based on the bizarre things he learned during his vigil at the Caravel.

"The humorous stories aren't just throwaways," Martin is quick to point out, "because they often tell you more about the real cultural life of a country than any amount of writing on the balance of payments or the gross national product."

Foreign affairs being what they are, the news from abroad is often disquieting. But working around his South American beat, Everett Martin has recently come up with at least two bits of encouraging news. The first is that Brazil's infamous killer bees are becoming tamer as they move north. Intermingling with local bees has made them less aggressive than they used to be. "South American bee-keepers like that," reports Martin, "but they don't want the killer bees to change too much, because being aggressive also makes them produce more honey."

Martin's second piece of good news concerns airline travel. After flying around South America he has concluded that U.S. air travelers are in incredibly safe hands. "In a given year," he says, "half of all the airplanes in Bolivia have an accident claim." Martin had one air trip that he'll never forget.

I was on an old surplus C-47, flying a load of butchered cattle into La Paz. We were at 18,000 feet, there was only one bottle of oxygen, and I figured I'd better let the pilot have most of it. I suffered severe oxygen starvation and almost blacked out. It felt like being drunk.

When I got back to the States, they told me I had some brain damage, but that it would probably clear up in a few weeks. I was dizzy for nearly a month—but the funny thing was, during that month I wrote some of my best stories!

Ray and Margaret Vicker are undoubtedly *The Wall Street Journal*'s most unusual news-gathering team. For one thing, they've covered stories all over the world together; for another, Margaret doesn't officially work for the *Journal*. As Ray says, with tongue-in-cheek chauvinism:

I believe if you have a woman with you, you should put her to work. So, I've put her to work, and she's been very useful to me. Sometimes we've been places where there's considerable trouble; shooting in the streets and things like that. Well, then I need somebody to run errands, so I send Margaret while I stay at the hotel.

Ray Vicker came to the *Journal* in 1951 after Dow Jones acquired the Chicago *Journal of Commerce* and turned it into the Midwest edition of the *Journal*. Vicker started at the *Journal of Commerce* as a reporter in 1946, two years after he and Margaret were married. He operated out of Chicago and New York for nine years, serving successively as reporter, automobile editor, and news editor. He became the *Journal*'s European news editor in 1960 and, based in London, traveled widely, particularly in the Middle East. Named senior international editor in 1975, he set up shop in Beirut, Lebanon, and became the *Journal*'s first full-time correspondent in the area. Later he moved his base to Nicosia, Cyprus.

A three-time winner of the Overseas Press Club Award, among others, Vicker has written six books dealing with topics ranging from British politics to the world food shortage. He has filed more than 500 page-one stories during his *Journal* career, a performance he doubts he could have achieved without Margaret's help. She is not only his wife, but his friend, traveling companion, teammate, and copyreader.

Looking back, I would say she's been working with me almost throughout my career, but even more so in the last ten years. Now if I have an interview with King Hussein [of Jordan], for example, she goes with me, takes a pad. She's my backstop. I have my notes, her notes, and a tape.

179

At a meeting of the OPEC heads of state in Algiers early in 1975, Margaret Vicker passed herself off as a delegate to one credulous male secretary and obtained a copy of the minutes of the closed-session meeting that had just ended. When her husband sat down to work, the volume was resting beside his typewriter. In those minutes, written in English, he had the entire story—the position being taken at the meeting and its likely outcome. The story ran in the *Journal* on January 27, 1975, under the head, "OPEC Puts Off Formulating Dialogue to be Held With Importing Countries."

According to the *Journal*'s former foreign editor, Neil Ulman, this is typical of the kind of support Margaret Vicker gives her husband. It goes beyond keeping her eyes and ears open for useful information. Ulman recalls working on a story with Vicker in Geneva; they were covering a shareholders' meeting of Investors Overseas Services, Ltd., a now-defunct mutual fund company:

Ray and I were putting it together in a room of the Intercontinental Hotel. Every time we'd finish a take Ray would hand it to Margaret, who would dash off about a mile or so to the Telex office at the United Nations to file the story.

Having his wife along sometimes means trouble, Vicker confesses. Following an interview with the pair, the Sultan of Oman asked if they'd been to his province of Dhofar. "And Margaret, always looking for news, pops up, 'Oh, no, we've never been,'" says Vicker. "And he says, 'Well, you must see Dhofar; I will arrange for you to see Dhofar.'"

When they got outside, Ray Vicker snarled at his wife, "Do you know that Dhofar is a place where a rebellion is under way? They've been battling there for years. There's no reason for us to go to Dhofar."

"Well, we're going there now," was her cool reply.

They were soon aboard a military helicopter, Ray in front with a colonel, Margaret behind with about twelve Omani soldiers. "Armed to the teeth. Rifles, bayonets, and everything," Vicker recalls. High on a mountain in Dhofar, crouching behind a ridge, Ray and Margaret got their chance to see the front line and a close-up view of the enemy troops and their rockets.

One encounter the Vickers recall with particular affection was with the Ayatollah Shariat Madari, an Iranian religious leader. It was in August, 1978, at the peak of the frenzied demonstrations calling for the Shah's ouster. For the trip, which would take them to the holy city of Qum, ninety miles south of Teheran, Margaret would have to wear a *chador,* a large square shawl worn by Islamic women to cover their faces. She rushed out, bought a piece of heavy black fabric, and made herself a *chador* that very afternoon.

The ministry of information had agreed to arrange the trip, but they couldn't promise that Vicker would be granted an interview. Nor could they provide an interpreter or driver to take the Vickers to the riot-torn city. Ray and Margaret hired their own driver/guide, who, once there, deposited them near the gate of the mullah's monastery-like residence and sped off to safer ground down the street.

Despite the 120-degree heat, Margaret donned her *chador.* Her husband's knock brought to the gate an awesome individual who didn't speak a word of English. After several frustrating attempts at communication, the porter scurried off and returned with a mullah, or holy man. The mullah's beard hung to his waist, and he was wearing a long heavy robe. He addressed the visitors in French. Identifying himself as a reporter, Vicker explained that he was there for an interview with Shariat Madari.

"Which newspaper?" the mullah asked, still speaking in French.

"One you probably never heard of," Vicker replied, assuming that Iran's holy men led a secluded life, *"The Wall Street Journal,"*

"The Wall Street Journal!" exclaimed the mullah in perfect English. "I took an economics course at Columbia University, and that was compulsory; it was good reading. I read *The Wall Street Journal* every day for two years."

Ray was promptly invited into an intricately decorated, lavishly carpeted audience hall packed with mullahs who had come from all over the country to pay their *zakaz,* or religious tax, to Shariat Madari. The tax (amounting to about $40 million that particular year) is paid annually to Iran's ayatollahs, who supposedly use it to help the poor.

Following the *zakaz* ceremony, Ray returned to Margaret, who had been sitting alone outside. Shortly thereafter Shariat Madari and five of his aides joined them, and while they all squatted on the floor, Vicker got his interview.

Another far-flung news source—and one of the oldest and least known of all Dow Jones's operations—is the Canadian news service. It began in 1927, two years before the Pacific Coast edition of the *Journal* was established. At the outset the service was available only in Montreal. Toronto and other Canadian cities came later.

Then, as now, the Canadian ticker carried U.S. and international news of interest to Canadian subscribers. In the early days the ticker was operated locally, not nationally as it is today. Copy was sent from New York to Montreal on a Morse wire. Boston was on the same wire, and the news services in both cities were dependent on both the sending operator in New York and the receiving operators at their ends of the line. The ticker of that era was the "metallic" type and had a speed of around thirty words a minute. The Morse wire was replaced by an automatic printer around 1935.

About this time a national wire system that would permit the use of a new high-speed ticker was being developed. The new tickers were first put into service in New York in 1931. The metallic-type tickers in other cities were gradually replaced, and wire service was completed in 1937, when Canada joined the network. That same year the Canadian operation was reorganized. It became Canadian Dow Jones Ltd., a wholly owned subsidiary with its own officers and directors.

The high-speed news service started in both Montreal and Toronto in May, 1937, and gradually expanded throughout Canada. At the outbreak of World War II, however, the Canadian economy tightened under harsh wartime measures. The number of customers declined sharply, and serious consideration was given to discontinuing the service. The low point was reached in December, 1942, when there were only eight subscribers in all of Canada.

Canadian Dow Jones hung on, though, and as the tide of the war reversed in 1943–44, so it was with the fortunes of the news service. The number of customers began to increase, and the trend has been upward ever since.

The news that appears on the Canadian ticker is not a carbon copy of the U.S. product; it is selected and edited with the needs of Canadian subscribers in mind. Likewise, Canadian Dow Jones reporters are responsible for feeding news from north of the border to the Dow Jones News Service and *The Wall Street Journal* in New York.

The *Journal* moved its Canadian news operation's headquarters to Toronto from Montreal in 1979, following the dramatic corporate shift out of French-speaking Quebec Province. The paper continues to maintain a Montreal bureau, but its management staff and copy desk are in Toronto.

Jan Bouchek, news editor in Toronto, estimates that from 200–300 Canadian firms are of interest to Americans. A good part of his job is covering stories on companies listed on the Toronto Stock Exchange.

Pat Wallace, managing editor, has full responsibility for the country's operations. Although there is no Canadian edition of *The Wall Street Journal* today, numerous columns in the paper come from Canadian bureaus, a situation that was almost the reverse in the past.

No other U.S. newspaper has as many reporters in Canada as *The Wall Street Journal*. John Urquhart, bureau chief in Ottawa, has his office across from Parliament. He spends most of his time at government committee meetings, listening to press releases over a PA system, and keeping in touch with regulatory agencies—a routine similar to that of a Washington reporter. One difference is that Urquhart sometimes skis to work and goes skating on the Rideau Canal during his lunch hour.

Len Anderson, the Montreal bureau chief, was with Dow Jones in New York and London before being transferred to Canadian Dow Jones. Noting that about two-thirds of all U.S. newsprint comes from Canada, Anderson and his staff emphasize the pulp and paper business, although the country's other industries are by no means neglected.

The Wall Street Journal has a staunch following among Canadian businessmen. Their ranks have been increasing ever since the creation of the second section, which allows for even greater coverage of Canadian affairs.

Five columns alternate in the space on the left side of the *Journal*'s second front. Three of them—"Small Business," "Regions," and

"Technology"—explore subjects that had not been covered regularly in the one-section *Journal*. The other two—"Marketing" and "Real Estate"—allow for more comprehensive coverage than was previously permitted because of limited space. According to second front columns editor Roger May, the five are "a dividend for *Journal* readers, providing them with a wider range of useful information in areas we felt were not being served well enough by the *Journal*."

Like the five rotating columns on page one, those on the second front are based on the principle that readers want information and want it quickly. Although often devoted to a single subject, the columns may also contain a number of shorter items. In either case the emphasis is on concise writing and careful attention to detail.

Monday's "Small Business" column is written by Sanford Jacobs. In his new assignment Jacobs explores topics of particular interest to small businessmen, emphasizing problems and how some entrepreneurs handle them. The column regularly examines conflicts between smaller companies and government and alerts readers to present and proposed government regulations. Since not all small business owners want to stay small, Jacobs also profiles companies that have developed into larger firms.

Tuesday's "Regions" column, presided over by Sam Allis, keeps readers informed on regional business developments, social trends, and attitudes.

We want to tell them of the variations in housing costs between Los Angeles and Houston, of the attitude toward governments in South Dakota versus New York City, to follow important demographic shifts, and punch holes in the mistaken belief that there are no regional differences left.

Allis and his contributing writers seek to identify trends and issues that may be prevalent in only parts of the nation but are nevertheless significant enough to warrant everyone's attention. One "Regions" column, for example, described the headaches airline deregulation is causing in medium-sized cities located near large ones.

Covering the regions requires combing the country for source material. Allis himself travels widely, seeking local color and human-interest stories; he relies on *Journal* bureaus across the country for additional ideas. Government agencies, large regional banks, insurance companies, and utilities are also important story sources.

In Wednesday's "Real Estate" column, reporters serve up a potpourri of information far broader than the column's title implies.

We present the standard fare of interest to anybody who owns a home or may buy one: mortgage news, financing trends, property prices. But we also cover such topics as architecture, real estate business trends, and new construction methods.

Rout's columns frequently deal with large issues such as the urban renaissance in Kansas City or the nationwide trend in housing starts. Of equal importance are such personal topics as "timesharing" vacation homes and innovative mortgage arrangements. For pessimistic readers the column once examined survival homes that could resist bullets, earthquakes, and small explosions.

Ideas for the column come from a variety of sources, but for the most part Rout relies on standard reportorial techniques: talking to people, reading extensively, being alert for ideas. "Wherever people own homes, put up buildings, or invest in property," he says, "there's a real estate story."

In Thursday's "Marketing" column Bill Abrams covers the consumer and industrial products and services that touch everyone's daily life. Advertising, promotion, packaging, pricing, and distribution are explored; the column consistently goes beyond surface news and gossip to analyze the strategy behind marketing decisions.

"Marketing" columns may examine industrywide activities such as the success/failure ratio of new product introductions (nineteen out of twenty fail), delve into marketing efforts by specific companies, or examine product repositioning with stories such as the "rejelling of Jell-O," an eighty-three-year-old product that was recently born again.

Sources for the column are varied. Abrams plows through a mountain of reading material every week—trade magazines, industry newsletters, ad agency reports, and speeches. His routine also includes talks with marketers, consultants, advertising and public relations people. "But some stories suggest themselves during interviews I'm doing for other stories," says Abrams. "In fact, it's rare that I do a story without coming up with at least one idea for another."

185

In Friday's "Technology" column Dick Shaffer and his contributing writers explore "discoveries and ideas from applied science which are likely to produce new commercial products sometime in the future." The focus is not on what to expect in the year 2000. Rather, Shaffer looks for technical solutions to current problems which may emerge in the next five years or less.

This column covers a lot of territory, from innovations in the field of health and medicine, such as the use of electrical stimulators to heal injured bones, to developments in energy conservation, like the continuing effort to build a practical turbine-engine car.

To scout this broad terrain Shaffer voraciously reads everything from scientific journals to press releases. He also relies on his personal contacts among scientists, engineers, technicians, and university professors. The results of his research efforts are carefully translated into layman's terms, to provide *Journal* readers with insights into which products to buy or invest in over the next few years.

In a newspaper as serious-minded as the *Journal* there's no place for gossip and rumor . . . or at least there wasn't until the coming of the second front. Now the lively "Shop Talk" appears in its third column once a week, offering a pinch of gossip, a sprinkling of rumors, and a soupçon of serious business, all gently stirred together.

"Shop Talk" gives *Wall Street Journal* reporters the opportunity to make use of juicy morsels of information that otherwise would never see print. In submitting items for the column they have a chance to zero in on the bits of human interest behind the business news.

Although "Shop Talk" admits to publishing rumors, it insists that they be well founded. Says Don Moffitt, who edits the columns:

A rumor can be news, too—but I always make sure an unsupported assertion has been backed up by more than one source. You have to be very careful about taking a story at face value from just one disgruntled executive. We apply the same standards of accuracy to our gossipy items that we would to a major news story.

The Wall Street Journal's financial heart lies in its final twelve pages (excluding the back page). There is enough commentary, analysis, and statistical material there to keep a professional investor busy for hours.

The *Journal*'s national news production manager, Dan Hinson, is responsible for all these facts and figures, which include the complete transaction listings of the New York and American Stock Exchanges.

We also carry the New York and American bond quotations, regional exchange quotes, government securities, and the options quotations—but we don't get them directly from the various exchange floors ourselves. The Associated Press supplies the ones I've just mentioned, as well as some of the regular market features such as the daily percentage leaders and the lists of highs and lows on the New York Stock Exchange. But United Press International supplies two tables, the mutual fund quotations, and both over-the-counter lists.

By using two wire services—Associated Press and United Press International—and through special arrangements with them, the *Journal* is assured of coverage in case of mechanical or computer failure at either one.

Edward P. Foldessy and Peter B. Roche write the daily "Credit Markets" column, a lively feature that is the outgrowth of a fairly sedate column called "Bond Markets." Roche writes about long-term securities—those that mature in more than one year—while Foldessy concentrates on short-term notes. Between the two of them they cover a number of investments that have recently been enjoying a wealth of investor attention—such as short-term U.S. Treasury certificates, tax-free municipal bonds, and corporate bonds.

"The markets involved have become very volatile, and have to be watched closely," says Foldessy. "Interest rates used to remain stable for years on end—but now, as everyone knows, they tend to fluctuate violently."

Foldessy is an experienced Federal Reserve watcher and scrutinizes the Fed's monetary policies on a day-to-day basis. "What they do eventually will determine what the economy will do and how the market will perform."

His partner concurs. Says Roche:

We're doing essentially what Wall Street has done for years—combining the money and capital markets, which after all don't exist by themselves, but act in concert. We write the column with the needs of the professional investor in mind—but at the same time, we try to explain things well enough so that any consumer can read the column, understand what's happening, and make his or her own decisions.

Formerly a subject with limited appeal, commodities (soybeans, sugar, and the like) now have a wide following among corporations that produce or use them, homemakers who buy them, and investors considering alternatives to the stock market.

Former commodity news editor Bob Prinsky observes:

Public interest in commodity markets has grown substantially in recent years, and so has the *Journal*'s coverage of them. Few people have been ignorant of the rise of gold, the rise and fall of silver, and the embargo on grain sales to the Soviet Union—to name a few headline-grabbing developments.

The *Journal*'s commodity page (which sometimes runs to two pages) generally carries at least two major articles. One is a feature on a commodity in the news or an industry development. Occasionally some arcane but important aspect of the field is explained for the uninitiated. The second daily (except Mondays) item is a summary of significant developments in individual futures markets on the previous day. In addition there are tables of futures and cash commodity prices. Important commodity stories may also appear on the front page and in the main news section of the paper.

To compile this information the *Journal* relies on its staff of specialized reporters in New York and Chicago—the main market centers—as well as correspondents in Washington and London. Reporters in other bureaus occasionally write commodity stories, too. All are aimed at meeting not only the sophisticated needs of commodity professionals, but the simpler needs of new investors anxious to find answers to their basic questions.

In April, 1981, the second front expanded its statistical coverage in several domestic and international areas. The Wilshire 5000 Equity was added to the list of market indicators. The index is based on closing prices of all domestic common stocks listed on the New York Stock Exchange and the American Stock Exchange, plus about 2,500 over-the-counter stocks, for a total of about 5,000 issues.

The statistical pages also began to carry prices of selected new issues in the over-the-counter market. This enables readers to remain abreast of issues that don't initially qualify for inclusion in the regular

OTC lists. The prices are collected by the National Association of Securities Dealers.

In keeping with growing investor interest in the Pacific region, the daily foreign markets lists were expanded to include selected issues traded on the Hong Kong and Sydney stock markets. Also on the international side, the dollar conversion rate of special drawing rights appears along with the foreign-exchange table. The SDR-dollar rates, provided by the International Monetary Fund each day, follow the format of the exchange rates of various national currencies. The first two columns show the latest and previous day's dollar-and-cents value of one SDR. The next two columns show the proportion of an SDR equaling one dollar.

The Wall Street Journal carries a total of more than 6,000 stock and bond quotations in its financial section every day. If a company's stock is quoted, it's the paper's policy to report its dividend announcements and earnings statements as well.

The earnings department works directly with the companies in the greater New York area; the *Journal*'s news bureaus around the country tend to those outside the city

National news production manager, Dan Hinson, reports:

We try to be consistent in the way we present such information following generally accepted accounting principles. If a company won't supply the information we need or feel is pertinent, we won't run the table. It's too easy to play games with numbers.

The same principle holds true for dividend notices. Stocks are bought and sold on such announcements, and the *Journal*'s dividend department tries to be absolutely accurate, particularly if a change in the size of a dividend is involved.

The decision on whether a company's report of earnings or dividends will be included in a standard table of such listings or merit a separate "lead" depends on the size of the company and the number of its shareholders. The rule is: the more people likely to be affected, the more prominent the story. However, the significance of the announcement is also taken into account. If a company declares a dividend beyond its regular quarterly one, or if it raises or lowers its dividend, that would be an important story.

Both "Corporate Dividend News" and the "Digest of Corporate Earnings Reports" tabulate companies' statements alphabetically, enabling readers to scan the columns quickly and check the firms in which they have an interest. Companies are also grouped according to the action taken, so readers can easily spot those that have increased or decreased their dividends.

During the usual quarterly reporting periods an entire page may be given over to such tabulations. The *Journal* carries the reports as they're issued, provided they meet the publication's standards. Hinson states:

While the people who scrutinize the quarterly and annual reports are not themselves professional accountants they are well trained and experienced in statistics, and very familiar with the accounting principles we follow.

The mobility of management is chronicled daily in the *Journal*'s "Who's News" column, enabling the business and financial communities to keep track of executive moves. Since the success of any corporation depends in large part on the quality of its leadership, "Who's News" serves a vital role for securities analysts, private investors, and others who must evaluate the strength and direction of companies. The column is useful to the sales forces of supplier companies and to individuals who keep tabs on the progress of their peers; it is often used as an early-warning system by corporate leaders who like to keep an eye on their competitors.

Guy Riotto of the national news desk compiles "Who's News." There are strict regulations on who qualifies for coverage in the column, with different guidelines for various groups or companies. Riotto is frequently bombarded by public relations people and individuals who complain of being excluded from the column. Some of them resort to pressure tactics ranging from demands to speak with his boss to offers of lunches at fine restaurants, with or without female companionship. Riotto stands firm, invoking the company rules when necessary. To wit: For companies included in the Fortune 500, "Who's News" covers management changes from the vice presidential level up (which unfortunately excludes those who hold the positions of secretary, treasurer, and comptroller). Subsidiaries and divisions of Fortune 500 companies are covered from director up, including presidents, chairmen of the board, vice chairmen, chairmen of the executive committee, chief operating officers, but excluding vice presidents.

There are, however, two exceptions to these rules for the 500. For companies such as insurance firms and banks, where there is often a plethora of vice presidents, the cutoff for inclusion is the senior vice presidential level. For subsidiaries of Fortune 500 companies that are large enough to make the list on their own (the New York Telephone Division of AT&T, for example), the rules for parent ''500'' firms apply.

If a company is not included in the Fortune 500 but its stock is traded on any stock exchange listed daily in the *Journal,* coverage of personnel news goes from director on up.

Guy Riotto also keeps track of the ''Foreign 500'' and of privately held companies with annual sales exceeding $100,000,000, which appear on a list compiled by *Forbes* magazine.

Possible—and rare—exceptions to those basic guidelines might include an internationally or nationally renowned person (a U.S. senator, for example) who had been in the news recently, but such exceptions must be okayed by the national news editor.

Once a week, on Mondays, *The Wall Street Journal* turns personal financial counselor with its back-page feature, ''Your Money Matters.'' The column looks at a broad array of personal financial problems—among them the costs of car ownership, health care, life insurance, obstacles in planning for retirement, and new wrinkles in home mortgage financing.

Journal copy editor Don Moffitt, who originated the column, tells how it came to be:

Most of the material inside the paper is written from a corporate viewpoint, and treats our reader either as an executive or shareholder. In this column we have a chance to deal with things that directly affect people's own pocketbooks, as opposed to having an effect on a corporate treasury.

''Your Money Matters'' aims to be, above all, useful. ''Our objective,'' says Moffitt, ''is to make it possible for readers to learn something new every week that's likely to have a direct influence on their financial situation.''

The column enjoys enthusiastic responses from readers. After one column on estate planning Moffitt received some forty phone calls, including several from tax accountants who were unfamiliar with a few of the finer points made in the article.

Moffitt's oddest experience came when he wrote a column outlining the investment possibilities of Eurodollar certificates of deposit, which he said were being sold by a major brokerage house. Several readers called Moffitt to complain that they had called their branch offices and the brokers there had never heard of the investment.

It turned out that Eurodollar CDs were so new and so infrequently bought, many people at the brokerage house itself were unfamiliar with them. I had to give the callers specific instructions on what to ask for. I also had to reassure them that I wasn't playing a trick on them—that this new kind of CD really did exist!

Ideas for the column come from members of the *Journal* staff and from readers. From time to time the column has been turned over to a *Journal* reporter or editor with expertise in a particular area. "We have an enormous pool of talent around here," Moffitt observes, "people who not only know a subject, but can write about it clearly."

Interestingly, one feature of the column has developed its own following, according to Moffitt.

In the beginning we decided to include a little box with some figures readers might want to have handy—bond yields, Federal Reserve rates, mortgage interest rates, things like that.

Of course, a lot of holidays fall on Mondays now, and a holiday meant no column and no box. We were quite surprised to get calls from a large number of readers who really missed those figures. So now, even when there's a holiday on Monday and there's no column that week, we'll run the box on Tuesday.

I've been a journalist long enough that it comes as no surprise to recognize that some of the simplest things you do can be so well received. That little box is probably as popular as the column itself.

For the last eighteen months, "Your Money Matters" has been written by Jill Bettner.

To subscribers a day's reading is never complete without turning to the next-to-the-last page of the *Journal* for two widely respected and popular columns, "Abreast of the Market" and "Heard on the Street."

The former, usually written by Victor J. Hillery, tells of the previous day's activities and moods of the stock markets in New York. The column includes quotes by financial experts, and Monday's edition carries a creative "Stock Market Appraisal."

Victor J. Hillery has been writing the column since 1963. Sounding much like Charles Dow, he sees the stock market "as a battleground . . . a contest where the negative factors are opposed by the positive. The direction of the market depends on the strength of either side at any one time, much like a tug-of-war."

According to Hillery, the three main categories on which market movements depend are "economic, political, and psychological."

Economic factors include corporate profits, sales, unemployment, and credit policy. Political factors include the policies of the administration and Congress, their tax views, and what value they put on employment versus inflation. Under the psychological category come such things as people's confidence in the country generally, whether they're frightened or optimistic, and the extremes to which these feelings are carried.

In "Abreast of the Market" Hillery tries to tackle all three elements each day, using them to explain why the market is moving as it is.

No description of "Abreast of the Market" would be complete without mentioning Oliver J. Gingold, who started editing it in 1933. A staff member of the *Journal* for more than sixty-five years, Gingold joined Dow Jones—at $4 a week—in 1900 and never left. He received many offers, some at salaries far above what he later earned, but he turned them all down, explaining almost apologetically that he had stayed with the paper this long, he guessed he wouldn't make a change.

The *Journal* felt the same way about him. "Oliver Gingold will never be retired," Barney Kilgore told his associates. "He will be a member of the *Journal* news staff until the day of his death."

Gingold—a cousin of the actress, Hermione—coined the expression "blue-chip stocks" more than fifty years ago, but his memories of Wall Street went back even further. He wrote in an article that appeared in the April, 1951, issue of the *New York Stock Exchange* magazine:

I roamed amid a ferment of panics and booms. I knew them all, all the big stock operators of the last 50 years. All are gone, the old familiar faces, and they can have no successors. They were a product of their times and such times they were.

About everything went in those days of 50 years ago. Wall Street and its captains ran the stock market, and they and their friends either owned or controlled the pools and often whole great corporations through stock ownership and manipulations. The speculative public hardly had a chance.

In the early 1950s Gingold was stricken with polio, and the disease eventually confined him to a wheelchair. He remained cheerful in spite of his affliction and was always one of the first in the office each morning.

Gingold became a sort of "schoolmaster of financial journalism." More than 100 writers and editors broke into what he called "the game" under his direction. He could also entertain them with stories of the old days. One of his favorites was about an early managing editor of the *Journal* who abandoned his family to elope with Dow Jones's only telephone operator. Said Gingold: "We didn't miss the managing editor at all, but it was chaos without anyone to run the switchboard."

Gingold was in his sixty-sixth year of unbroken service with Dow Jones when he died in 1966, at the age of eighty. He never did finish his memoirs, which were to be titled *I Survived 37 Managing Editors*. The *Journal* paid final tribute to Oliver Gingold with a touching editorial:

When the end comes for an old friend like Oliver Gingold the sadness comes in two ways.

One part is personal and cannot be shared except with those who, like ourselves, knew him for some part of his eighty years.

The other part can be shared, whether they know it or not, by all who read this newspaper. He gave them much more than his name at the top of the "Abreast of the Market" column.

The newsroom is populated by those who learned some part of their trade from Oliver Gingold. His pupils include the present editor and the newest reporters; he was the connective link between the newspaper today and the newspaper of Charles Dow, six decades ago.

But Oliver taught something more than the journalist's trade. In the years since 1900, when he first came to this country, he saw two World Wars and a score of smaller ones, wild booms, deep panics, great growth and the great depression. You could hardly encounter an experience he hadn't met at least once before.

But his own encounters never shook one conviction. At a party last year celebrating his 65th year with this newspaper, he remarked to his friends that looking back over it all the whole six decades had really been "one long bull market" for his adopted land.

In times when everywhere the troubles mount, you can't help but miss a man like that.

Immediately below "Abreast of the Market" is "Heard on the Street." Until a few years ago it was written by Dan Dorfman, then by Charles J. Elia. It is now done by several *Journal* specialists. Elia said:

"Heard on the Street" can sometimes look in great depth at what has happened to the trading activity in one stock, and why it's happening, and it can also get into developing trends that might affect stocks, before they actually affect them. . . . I talk to as many people as I can during the course of the day, and try to see as much research as possible—so I'm sometimes able to pull together, from many different sources, analyses of what's happening that any single source may not have.

Elia was among the first to spot the major shift in the stock market away from small investors to dominance by a few giant ones. He believes that one of his main functions is to spread information about securities and companies to the general public, instead of leaving it in the hands of large financial institutions that have the resources to do research and analyses.

"Heard on the Street" is filled with interesting glimpses of people and companies; perhaps more than any other newspaper feature, it convinces the public that finance and business are moved by individual motives and needs.

Regrettably, there are a few areas that touch on business that haven't yet made the second front. If the *Journal* were published six days a week, readers probably would have seen a sixth rotating column devoted to "The Law." The subject is a useful one, and staff writers are encouraged to pursue it in leaders.

Similarly, the health and medical field was viewed as an area of growing importance. It, too, received serious consideration as a subject for a rotating column. It was abandoned for lack of space, but health and medicine are regularly covered in Friday's "Technology" column.

A proposed humor column was scuttled in the early stages of second front planning. The prime difficulty, according to Fred Zimmerman, was finding someone "with a strong, universal sense of humor to do the writing."

As the second front gathers momentum, some features will survive, and others may be dropped. According to vice president/associate publisher Peter R. Kann the creation of the second section, important as it is, represents simply one more event in an ongoing process of development.

The desire to do better, to meet reader needs and to satisfy our own standards of excellence, is both tradition and mission at the *Journal*. In that sense, the change to two sections is thoroughly evolutionary. It's by no means the first news expansion or physical change the *Journal* has undertaken in its ninety-one-year history—and it surely won't be the last.

Bartley's Editorial Page

History has moved to the point where the Journal's ideas will have their time.
ROBERT BARTLEY,
editor of *The Wall Street Journal*

IN EARLY 1979 Robert L. Bartley, editor of the *Journal*'s editorial page since 1972, was named editor of the newspaper. In making the appointment chairman Warren Phillips said:

The editor's title has not been used since Vermont Royster retired from that post in 1971. Mr. Bartley has earned it by his distinguished work in further developing the paper's editorial and op-ed page. He also has earned it by the force of his writing, which clearly puts him in the company of the most distinguished past *Journal* editors.

Robert L. Bartley was born in Marshall, Minnesota, but grew up in Iowa. He graduated from Iowa State University and, after a tour of duty in the army, went on to earn a master's degree in political science from the University of Wisconsin.

Bartley joined the *Journal* in 1962 and worked as a reporter in both the Chicago and Philadelphia news bureaus. Vermont Royster claims that he and associate editor Joe Evans discovered Bartley as a kid in the Philadelphia bureau. "We gave him some books to review and were so pleased with his performance that we invited him to come to New York."

In 1964 Bartley joined the editorial page staff in New York, where he also took to lecturing his bosses, Evans and Royster, on how conservative they were. Says Royster, "He had a brashness and brightness that appealed to me." In addition to being a good reporter Bartley is also a serious thinker. According to Royster, "A lot of good reporters have been lost by asking them to think." This would never be a problem with Bob Bartley.

Bartley was sent to Vietnam and Japan to introduce him to the "wide, wide world." From there he went to the *Journal*'s news bureau in Washington, where he wrote editorials and commentary. Then it was back to New York, where the brashness—which came through in his writing—was more likely to be appreciated.

That was in 1971. Vermont Royster had recently retired and Joe Evans, who was slated to succeed him as editor, died abruptly of a heart attack.

In desperation Warren Phillips called Royster for advice. "Get Bartley up there," was the response. Not without hesitation Phillips offered Bartley the title of associate editor. For the time being the *Journal* would function without an editor and its associate editor would report to Phillips.

Within a year Bartley assumed overall direction of the editorial page. (Royster later said that one of the best contributions he ever made to the *Journal* was finding Bartley.)

Tom Bray, the manager of the *Journal*'s Philadelphia news bureau before joining the editorial page in 1976, and Daniel Henninger, who came to the editorial page from the *National Observer* when that paper closed in 1977, have daily charge of the *Journal*'s editorial page and op-ed feature columns.

The editorial page carries several columns on a rotating basis. In addition, the editors draw on a board of contributors, established in 1972, to present a broad range of viewpoints on current topics.

The board is currently composed of seven distinguished academics, five of whom have also been active in government: Walter H. Heller, Regents' Professor of Economics at the University of Minnesota and former chairman of the Council of Economic Advisors under Presidents Kennedy and Johnson; Irving Kristol, Professor of Social Thought at New York University and coeditor of the quarterly, *The*

Public Interest; Paul W. McCracken, Edmund Ezra Day University Professor of Business Administration at the University of Michigan and former chairman of the Council of Economic Advisors; Arthur Schlesinger, Jr., Albert Schweitzer Professor of Humanities at the City University of New York and winner of Pulitzer Prizes in history and biography; Herbert Stein, the A. Willis Robertson Professor of Economics at the University of Virginia and former chairman of the Council of Economic Advisors under Presidents Nixon and Ford; Martin Feldstein, Professor of Economics at Harvard University and president of the National Bureau of Economic Research; and Charles L. Schultze, a senior fellow of the Brookings Institution, chairman of the Council of Economic Advisors in the Carter administration.

The members of the board of contributors are invited to contribute regular monthly articles to the editorial page, and agree to write eight to twelve columns per year. Bray says:

> We deliberately have tried to maintain a philosophic balance on the board, ranging from Arthur Schlesinger and Walter Heller on the left to Messrs. Kristol, Stein, and McCracken on the right. Though each achieved his reputation in a particular discipline . . . all are broad-gauged enough to address a wide range of issues.

Contributions from other non-*Journal* writers appear on a regular basis. Peter F. Drucker, for example, Clarke Professor of Social Science at the Claremont Graduate School, regularly writes on management.

George Melloan, deputy editor of the editorial page, says the procedures that are followed in producing it "are simple in structure but sometimes complex in the thought processes and idea exchanges that go into the formulation of editorial policy."

> Our week usually begins with a staff meeting on Monday morning, which is about the closest we come to a structured process. At that meeting Tom Bray tells us what feature articles he has on tap for the coming week, and we consider whether any subject might come up that would suggest a separate editorial comment. The remainder of the meeting is devoted to members of the staff telling what they have heard, read, or seen over the past several days that might have possibilities for discussion on the editorial page. This usually leads to a discussion of one particular idea, or perhaps several ideas,

and very often to the suggestion by Bob Bartley that the originator of the idea write an editorial based on the discussion, quite possibly for that night's paper. Discussions, arguments, debates of editorial ideas continue around the office during the rest of the week on a less structured basis.

The staff often goes outside the office to gather material and get ideas; they can also count on frequent visits from federal policy makers and other authorities on important issues.

The editorial page is rounded out by "Letters to the Editor" and the "Leisure and Arts" page. The latter, started in 1968 and edited by Daniel Henninger, features reviews by the *Journal*'s regular critics, as well as essays—many of them written by reporters in the *Journal*'s domestic and foreign bureaus—on trends in both the high arts and popular culture. These pieces present distinctive and wide-ranging points of view trying, says Bartley, "to show the broader social significance of intellectual and cultural events as they occur."

Adds deputy editor Melloan, "Our reviewers enrich the page, broaden our scope and help provide insight into currents in our popular culture."

Edwin Wilson, chairman of the Theater and Film Department at Hunter College, is the *Journal*'s theater reviewer; Joy Gould Boyum, former president of the New York Film Critics Society, reviews movies; Manuela Hoelterhoff, editor of *Art and Auction* magazine, writes the art and opera criticism; and Peter Rosenwald, an advertising executive who commutes between New York and London, contributes articles on dance. General interest and business book reviews also appear on the editorial page in addition to Edmund Fuller's regular Monday column.

Despite the dominance of New York City as a cultural center *Journal* reviewers attempt to cover events nationwide. If a choice must be made between reviewing two dance companies, for example, the company making a national tour is apt to be given preference.

In May, 1980, *Wall Street Journal* editor Robert Bartley won a Pulitzer Prize for "distinguished editorial writing, the test of excellence being clearness of style, moral purpose, sound reasoning and power to influence public opinion in what the writer conceives to be the right direction." Bartley was the third consecutive editor of the

Journal to have won the Pulitzer, after William Grimes in 1947 and Vermont Royster in 1953.

Although there are any number of journalism awards, the Pulitzers always have been the most highly regarded. The awards, which started in 1917, were created under the will of Joseph Pulitzer, the wealthy newspaper publisher. Pulitzer also bequeathed funds to create the Columbia School of Journalism, which opened in 1913. There are twelve Pulitzer Prizes in journalism: four for reporting, two for photography, and one each for public service, editorials, cartooning, criticism, commentary, and feature writing.

The *Journal* was originally excluded from the competition. Pulitzer's son, Joseph Pulitzer II, did not consider it a general-circulation newspaper, and thus it was not eligible for an award. By 1947, however, the *Journal* had changed to such an extent that Pulitzer's views were overruled, and William Grimes was awarded the *Journal*'s first Pulitzer Prize for his editorial writing.

Bob Bartley describes the paper's present editorial policy as "pragmatically conservative." He is quick to confess that he is not exactly sure what that means but feels there is a distinct difference between his editorial approach and that of other newspapers. The *Journal,* he says, regards "reasoning" as more important than "position."

Bartley's Pulitzer Prize-winning editorials have dealt with a variety of topics—the impact of the Chappaquiddick accident on Ted Kennedy's presidential campaign, the leadership qualities of the presidential aspirants, the strategic arms limitation treaty, General Motors' support of wage-price controls, the threatened Chrysler bankruptcy, and the situation in Iran.

In a dramatic departure from the normal *Journal* policy of not running news photographs—associate publisher Peter Kann likes to remind critics that the *Journal* "has always believed that one word is worth a thousand pictures"—an editorial raising questions about Senator Kennedy's version of Chappaquiddick was accompanied by three pictures of the accident site.

The editorial concluded, "Voters will have to ask themselves whether they can believe his account of the major crisis in his life, and whether they could believe what he would tell them about any crisis of his Presidency."

The *Journal*'s editorial page is frequently controversial. "We're pro free enterprise" says Bartley, "but often the business community isn't." Bartley has excoriated Chrysler Corporation for seeking a government bailout, scolded the steel manufacturers for demanding protectionism, and blasted General Motors for pressuring its suppliers to live within the wage and price guidelines. He also wrote an editorial disclosing that the United States had made a secret nine-point agreement with the former Shah of Iran in December 1979.

Newsweek magazine once reported on some inside gossip about the *Journal*'s editor:

While staffers generally praise the editorial page for its clear prose and well-reasoned arguments, many blanch at its ideological bent. Some Washington reporters have particularly bitter feelings toward Bartley who, they say, resists staff-written op-ed pieces that disagree with his conservative views. At a contentious dinner in Washington [April 1980], Bartley said he did not want to run too many pieces that his sources consider "ridiculous."

Outside the *Journal*'s office Bartley also has his share of supporters and detractors. Of his suggestions for dealing with the economy, Mike Evans of Chase Econometrics, Chase Manhattan's economic financial arm, says, "Congress obviously isn't listening to them but there really is some very clear thinking there."

At the opposite end of the scale financial expert Eliot Janeway says: "I don't have the physiological resources to get beyond the second line of their editorials. That page is an intellectual ghetto, and what they're saying has nothing to do with the real world."

Bartley is philosophical about it all:

History has moved to the point where the *Journal*'s ideas will have their time. Now that a majority of the respondents in polls classify themselves as conservatives, whatever that may mean, there is a sense that somewhere there really are some basics. . . . Time to get back to basic realities.

Bartley is well aware that his corporate readers are interested in the things that are good for corporations, and he feels that such things more or less coincide with the national interest. Nevertheless, says Bartley, "We would depart from the interests of our constituency on some questions. We'd say no to the bailing out of Lockheed. We would let Pan Am go under. If the citizens of Belgium want to subsidize people flying the Atlantic, let them do it.''

As for government handouts, Bartley is vehement on the subjects of food stamps, welfare, Medicaid, and Social Security:

These transfer payments are rising at a rate of 9 percent a year in real terms. Transfer payments have failed. . . . They don't help the poor. We should, by all accounts, be taking care of our poor and our helpless much better than we ever have before. But you don't see any evidence of that in the body politic. After all this expense, you have the same worries of fifteen years ago.

A supporter of unemployment compensation, Bartley explains, "that's self-liquidating when people go back to work." Essentially he believes that hard work and the Protestant ethic remain the nation's best solution to its economic problems.

Doing what we recommend would not only be to the benefit of big business, but to everyone else. It would create jobs, economic growth, and we would be able to afford clean air and clear water without paying for it with a lower standard of living, the burden of which would fall on the poor.

The *Journal*'s editorials are direct and filled with prescriptions. During a three-month period the following solutions were put forward:

[*Keynes is dead*]: You cannot fight inflation and recession simultaneously with the traditional Keynesian remedies. . . . [The] only way to fight both at once is to concentrate not on demand but on supply, relying on lower tax rates to increase incentives.
[*Markets*]: There must be a restoration of real, useful production that will generate real capital, which will in turn be employed efficiently by market forces.
[*Tax cuts*]: The most straightforward way to cut taxes on capital is to cut the rate on corporate profits, which after all are not spent on champagne and wenches but as capital.
[*Money*]: Monetary policy is by far the government's most powerful weapon in fighting inflation. . . . Unless money creation can be held in some balance with the growth of real goods, there is absolutely no hope of avoiding another round of inflation.
[*Energy*]: The only solution to our energy problems is to decontrol petro-

leum and natural-gas prices, allowing decentralized market forces to distribute supplies to the most efficient uses.

Some experts maintain that Bartley's editorials, although hard-hitting, often miss their mark. One outsider who surveyed readers reported: "The readership of the editorial page ranks it a low sixth in their priorities, 29.4 percent citing it as their main interest, compared with nearly 70 percent for the business news. The two-column news digest on page one seems to hit the button with *Journal* readers."

These statistics hardly faze Bartley. "If you put out a newspaper—or, in my case, one page of a paper—you put out what interests you. . . . If your interests parallel those of the people out there, you'll be successful. But I think it's a mistake to worry too much about your influence."

Economist Dr. Albert Wojnilower of First Boston Corporation remains skeptical of the *Journal*'s impact: "I detect a tendency that if someone of more moderate views agrees with their position, they move farther to the right. They want to be seen as the sole depository of the revelations."

Another critic maintains: "Bartley reveres willpower with a Teutonic enthusiasm. If economics yielded to willpower alone, he would be a prophet."

Bob Bartley has many fixed ideas about the future of the American economy. He will rigidly defend a point of view and argue with intelligence and skill for a cause he is supporting. When he errs, which is not too often, he will swallow his mistake. In April, 1981, for example, his "Review and Outlook" editorial titled "John Maynard Domenici" attacked the Senate Budget Committee's chairman Pete Domenici for his insistence on using economic projections that assumed President Reagan's budget programs would fail: "Surely this is not what the voters thought they were buying by electing Mr. Reagan, giving Republicans control of the Senate and making Pete Domenici chairman of the Budget Committee."

Senator Domenici's angry reply was published a few days later. ". . . your reference to me as a Keynesian—when I have argued against Keynesian economics all across this country and just last week in my own state—is not only highly inaccurate, but truly insulting.''

Soon other letters to the editor came pouring in, including one from budget director David Stockman and another from Senator Rudy Boschwitz. All of them protested Bartley's attack on Domenici. Bartley thereupon offered an apology entitled ''For Pete's Sake.'' Acknowledging that he had erred in his earlier headline, ''John Maynard Domenici,'' and conceding that Domenici is a self-described anti-Keynesian, Bartley wrote: ''We accept that self-description and if our headline writing was overly playful, we beg forgiveness.''

Nevertheless, Bartley had the final word:

Whatever the Budget Committee Republicans may have thought about the mumbo-jumbo of long-range projections, they should have voted for the Reagan program and their chairman should have been careful to give them no reason for doing otherwise. The Reagan tax cuts are not ''too big a deal'' for this Congress but the Republicans had better stick together if they want to prove it.

Ben Bagdikian, former assistant managing editor of the *Washington Post,* is an outspoken critic of the *Journal*'s editorial page.

Its staff is so split over ideology of business and journalistic judgment that it is a regular occurrence that a phenomenon reported on page one as a fact will be written on the editorial page as a non-fact. What reporters in the field document as a proved deception will be praised by the editorial writers as The Truth.

Bagdikian, who also is on the faculty of the Graduate School of Journalism at the University of California at Berkeley, believes that in a world full of conservative and doctrinaire newspaper editorial pages, the *Journal*'s editorial page may be the most conservative and doctrinaire of them all. Moreover, Bagdikian finds the editorials predictable. In a randomly selected period he found that 8o percent of them were devoted to five condemnations: government regulation of business, spending for social benefits, taxes, any government budget other than defense, and official programs that favor ''special interest groups.''

In recent decades the *Journal* has had a number of internal wars between editor and reporters over editorials that seem to repudiate regular columns. For example, in 1969, when New York City's telephone services began to deteriorate, *Journal* stories placed the blame on AT&T's decision to expand profits by reducing costs and curtailing already planned service expansions. The newspaper's editorial, in this pre-Bartley era, took a contrary position by apologizing for the telephone company for having been forced to hire slum dwellers "who by ordinary standards lack the education or skill to hold a job." The editorial ended with a plea that AT&T should be "relying less heavily on its newly trained employees."

Fifty *Journal* reporters protested the editorial's apparent racism to top management. The only response they received was an angry reprimand because news of the protest had been leaked to other papers.

More recently, during the 1980 convention of the American Society of Newspaper Editors in Washington, D.C., while Dow Jones chairman Warren Phillips was hosting a dinner for his capital reporters, the journalists proceeded to attack the paper's editorial page. They complained that their columns and those of fellow writers in other bureaus had been significantly cut because of ideological censorship by Robert Bartley. They also noted that the editorials "often flew in the face of the paper's best reporting."

In an attempt to placate his staff Bartley agreed to be less dogmatic in the future. But a month later another episode occurred. Several California oil firms were protesting a proposed state tax that they claimed would cost $100 million to administer. A *Journal* reporter, after considerable research, found the oil companies' figure to be highly exaggerated. Two days after his story appeared, an editorial stated that "according to one estimate, enforcement of the tax would cost taxpayers $100 million, and this figure could balloon."

Ben Bagdikian, writing in the *Washington Journalism Review,* attempts to explain the balancing act played out at the *Journal.*

Disparities between editorials and news columns are not new. Editorials are seen as rendering unto Caesar, letting owners see flattering treatment of their personal economic and political views in return for which news would be left to reporters. But at the *Journal* there may be a further rationale. . . . Executives and stockholders really do want to know the unpleasant truth about corporate life when it affects their careers or incomes. At the same

time, however, most of them are true believers in the rhetoric of free enterprise whose imperfections and contradictions are standard content in *The
Wall Street Journal*. By reporting critical stories about realities in particular
industries in the news columns, but singing the grand old hymns of unfet-
tered laissez-faire on the editorial pages, the *Journal* has it both ways.

Bagdikian refers to this phenomenon as a "split personality," with
each side serving a useful purpose in making the *Journal* appear to
be the conscience of society.

Editorials reassure the captains of industry that unlike all those other milk-
and-water defenders of all things corporate, *The Wall Street Journal* is the
Rock of the Only True Faith. So these captains are more likely to open up
to *Journal* reporters who may or may not be pursuing the Only True Faith
but who, thanks perhaps to the prophets on the editorial page, enjoy privileged access to corporate executives.

Bob Bartley, of course, doesn't see himself in that light. "I never
set out to be a prophet," he says. "I just have a great curiosity. I
seek understanding, not prophecy."

Several years ago Bartley wrote two editorials a week; now it's
more likely to be one, although he contributes ideas for many others.
He works with a twenty-member staff, but the three prime architects
of the *Journal*'s editorial thinking are Bartley himself, deputy editor
George Melloan, and Thomas Bray, who is an associate editor of the
editorial page.

Bartley is fully aware of the impact of the paper's editorials and is
quick to defend his point of view. "I'm not trying to kill the Great
Society, but instead create social mobility," he says. ". . . we've
won the War on Poverty. . . . I wish the liberals would take the
credit for it, but they won't for they've got to have a cause."

Column three on the *Journal*'s editorial page is set aside for three
distinct voices, talking on the subjects of management, money, philosophy, and politics. Lindley Clark, Vermont Royster, and Susan
Garment aren't exactly household names, but *Journal* readers know
them well. Their bylines appear on the rotating columns.

Tom Bray describes the columnists' role this way: "They are the
heart of the feature side of the editorial page—each with long expe-

rience in his field. Together they are our 'touchstones,' if you will—our best people talking about what they know best, dealing with subjects that concern our readers generally."

The week begins with the column "Manager's Journal," written by guests or staff members and edited by Adam Meyerson of the editorial page staff. The Monday column reprints, in complete or condensed form, articles or speeches that Meyerson feels will be of interest to managers in both the private and public sectors. "They look for variety," says Bray. "The point of view can be anything at all, as long as it's well presented and seems to have practical value to managers."

If someone has recently made a challenging statement, either verbally or in print, Meyerson may ask him to restate it for the column. Other contributions arrive unsolicited, but they are carefully considered just the same. The column has addressed a broad range of subjects, including the discharge provision of American labor laws; the problems of the expatriate executive; the efficiency of Japanese industry; and the fetish for overplanning evinced by some managers.

Lindley Clark, economic news editor of the *Journal,* writes Tuesday's column, "Speaking of Business," in addition to his daily coordination of the economic news and his monthly contribution to the "Outlook" column on the front page.

" 'Speaking of Business' is an opinion column," Clark explains, "much more likely to be editorial in nature than the 'Outlook' piece I do. This one has a much more definite point of view. It's very freewheeling and can cover almost anything."

In a typical month the column included a biting critique of the treasury secretary's views on financing the federal deficit; an examination of the plight of professional economists; a discussion of underspending by the federal government; musings on the current state of international trade; and a look at the past, present, and future of credit unions.

"Thinkings Things Over" is Wednesday's regular column. It is written by Vermont Royster, former editor of the *Journal,* a director of Dow Jones, and professor of journalism and public affairs at the University of North Carolina. The column is often philosophic in nature. Since Royster is a man of wide-ranging interests, it covers a wide range of subjects. The column also reflects its author's informal style.

Vermont Royster keeps a little notebook for jotting down column ideas, most of which he claims are never written. He is influenced by big items in the news, but if nothing major catches his attention, he may write a review of a book he's read recently, ponder some aspect of economics, politics, or human nature, or talk about one of his personal experiences.

In a single month "Thinking Things Over" included a discourse on the difference between inflation and price increases; a discussion of the ethics of American citizens (journalists or otherwise) sharing knowledge of foreign countries with government agencies; a piece on procrastination, with a recommendation that the President try it; a tongue-in-cheek lecture on liberation linguistics; and an exercise in the futility and frustration involved in the spring ritual of filing one's income tax returns.

In discussing his weekly column Royster notes that it originated with *Journal* editor Thomas Woodlock in 1920. "It lapsed after his death," says Royster, "and was resurrected by my predecessor, William H. Grimes, who wrote it for a number of years. Then it lapsed again, until I retired as editor and started it up again."

The fourth weekly column is "Capital Chronicle," written for the Friday page by Susan Garment. "Suzi," as she is called by her friends, is also an associate editor of the editorial page, but she's based in Washington. Married to Leonard Garment, a Washington lawyer who once served in the Nixon White House, she has been a United Nations aide to former Ambassador Patrick Moynihan, a Yale professor, and has authored or co-authored several books. Her columns attempt to provide insight into the Washington community, telling readers how the business of government and politics is conducted through both formal and informal channels of high-level communication.

A less frequent editorial page column, "Perspective on Politics," is written by Norman Miller, chief of the *Journal*'s Washington bureau. The column appears about once a month. Says Miller:

The column is a nice change of pace from my supervisory duties, although it flows naturally out of my work as bureau chief, which brings me into contact with a wide range of political subjects and people. Finding ideas isn't difficult; finding the time to research and write the column sometimes is.

Miller believes readers are often overwhelmed by avalanches of detailed information on major issues. He tries to step back and write about what he sees as the essence of things, without too fixed a philosophical position.

The nice thing about a column is that when I think a politician is talking baloney, I can call him on it. The more provocative the column, the more feedback I get from readers—which often provides thoughts for future columns. I thoroughly enjoy the whole thing.

If the editorial page is a forum of opinion where the discussion of public issues is created and stimulated, the "Letters to the Editor" column is the soapbox from which readers contribute their side of the dialogue.

"Letters serve as a corrective to our own occasional excesses," says features editor Tom Bray. "They often offer ideas or viewpoints that our contributors hadn't thought of, and that keep the *Journal* and its readers in touch with each other."

The letters columns originally appeared on Mondays and occasionally on other days if a particular subject aroused a great deal of controversy. Because of space limitations only about fifteen letters were printed each week.

As 1981 began, however, and a daily op-ed page was inaugurated to provide more diversity of political and economic commentary, letters were included in every issue. They share the page with new columns from Europe and Asia and articles by both liberal and conservative writers.

The contents of the *Journal*'s op-ed page can range from erudite expositions on highly technical subjects to whimsical matters, like commercial interruptions during the Olympic games. One letter to the editor on this subject said:

Dow Jones News Service: Joseph Guilfoyle (center), then managing editor.

Alan Abelson (left), presently editor of *Barron's*; Lawrence Armour (center), formerly associate editor, now director of corporate relations at Dow Jones & Company; and Robert L. Bleiberg, now editorial director of *Barron's*.

A sample of Ottaway newspapers, owned by **Dow Jones & Company.**

George Flynn, senior vice-president at Dow Jones and president, Affiliated Companies Group.

Some of *The Wall Street Journal*'s Pulitzer Prize winners (from left to right): Stanley Penn, Ed Cony, Lou Kohlmeier, Peter Kann, Vermont Royster, and Robert Bartley.

Print mill, Rivière du Loup, Quebec, Canada.

Composing room, Chicopee, Massachusetts.

Donald Macdonald, vice-chairman, Dow Jones & Company.

Ed Cony, vice president, News, and Peter Kann, associate publisher of *The Wall Street Journal*, celebrating the publication of the first issue of *The Asian Wall Street Journal* in 1976.

Robert L. Bartley, editor of the editorial page of *The Wall Street Journal* since 1972 and editor of the paper since 1979.

William L. Dunn, vice president and general manager, Dow Jones & Company.

Ray Shaw (left), president and director of Dow Jones & Company, as well as chief operating officer. Warren Phillips, chairman and chief executive officer of Dow Jones & Company.

Fifteen-foot-high antenna dishes used in Dow Jones printing facilities to receive coded information from a satellite 22,300 miles above the equator.

On the West Coast, when the U.S. hockey team scored the tying goal (2–2) against Finland, ABC which had promised us live coverage was showing a Royal Crown ad of a girl falling on her fanny.

After the ad, they then showed us in instant replay the tying goal. It was frustrating to say the least.

Imagine getting up at 7:30 a.m. PCT to watch a live game only to have it botched up. Especially when they had 20 minutes between periods to run the ad.

It was dumb, and I'll never buy another Royal Crown again.

Steve Priskie

North Hollywood, California

Soon after that the paper published another letter, this one from the vice president of Royal Crown Company.

We have to call foul! Mr. Steve Priskie's letter (which appeared in your March 10 issue) complaining about a Royal Crown ad interfering with the American Olympic hockey team game versus Finland on TV is a misdirected slapshot. The ad referred to is a Tab commercial . . . a product of Coca-Cola.

It's hard enough scoring against big Coke . . . although we're pleased that he thinks of Royal Crown's product, Diet Rite, when he sees a sugar free cola commercial.

Come on back to RC, Mr. Priskie . . . don't buy the other guy's product.

Arnold Belasco

Atlanta, Georgia

The signatures on the *Journal*'s mail are often familiar ones—senators and congressmen, heads of foundations, corporate leaders, distinguished academics, and high-ranking military officials. Dissent may emanate from readers as diverse as IBM chairman Frank Cary and liberal activist Tom Hayden.

The editorial page staff eschews preferential treatment. Letters are published because they're informative or interesting, and a fair share of the writers are not well known.

George Melloan, deputy editor of the editorial page, regards reader mail as an important source of information.

We certainly don't think we have all the answers on the editorial page. We value readers' contributions because they give us the benefit of their expertise on the subjects we're discussing. When readers are as knowledgeable as ours, it's foolish not to listen to them.

On December 26, 1980, the "Review & Outlook" column directed readers to an accompanying letter to the editor written by Lee A. Iacocca, chairman of the Chrysler Corporation. In response to a December 11 editorial titled "They Shoot Horses, Don't They?" Iacocca said in part:

You chose to print that editorial without the facts and before you saw our plan to respond to today's economic recession. You chose to impose our death sentence when we were only halfway through the recovery program agreed to by Congress. And you chose to be mean about it. Your readers deserve better.

Two columns away Bob Bartley ran another editorial "On Shooting Horses." He concluded by saying:

No one wants Chrysler to die. The new administration should move quickly to get the Department of Transportation out of the hair of the auto makers, so they can start making competitive decisions again. The UAW should be told to bargain with the auto makers, not Washington. The Nader crowd should be invited to go pick on the Japanese. Energy policy, the cover for some of the worst depredations against the auto industry, should be focused on restoring competition in the energy industry by getting the government out. As to Chrysler, it is not a question of shooting horses, but of disconnecting a life support system we can ill afford.

For sixty years, through bad times and good, the *Journal* has supplied readers with a daily ration of humor through the cartoons and quips of "Pepper and Salt," which appears on its editorial page.

Charles Preston, a Dow Jones contributing editor for many years, has supervised the column since 1960. "There are two postures available to the comic commentator," he says. "You can chastise the erring by focusing on and often exaggerating their behavior. Or you can recognize—and empathize with—human fallibility."

Preston prefers the latter course, and editor Bob Bartley lets him do it his way. Bartley cites the story of the baby bird, ready to dive from the edge of the nest, that turns to its mother and asks, "Any instructions, or shall I just wing it?"

"Nowhere is 'winging it' more necessary than in humor," says Bartley. "Either it's funny or it isn't. There is no instruction manual. Nothing can kill humor more quickly than trying to sort, classify, and analyze it. Half the game is the surprise, the what-will-they-do-next."

An incurable punster, Charles Preston likes to strike when the irony is hot. When the energy crisis first loomed, "Pepper and Salt" issued lighthearted warnings about acting fuelish. Preston also publishes "daffynitions," which include such gems as:

Income Tax—the hauls of Congress
Recession—lapse of luxury
Bores—the criminally inane
Writer's Block—blankruptcy
Puns—cornography.

"Pepper and Salt" cartoons tend to reflect news events and world affairs, but the anecdotes, epigrams, and verse cover all sorts of subjects. Over 1,000 contributions arrive each week from readers all over the world. Only a few are chosen for the column, but those that are printed invariably crop up again, enlivening the speeches of business executives and public officials.

A Technological Newspaper

Facsimile Edition—Transmitted by Satellite
Logo, *The Wall Street Journal*

NEW YORK, CHICAGO, DALLAS, AND SAN FRANCISCO all had Dow
Jones printing plants, but it was not until 1952 that Joseph Ackell,
business manager and research director for the *Journal,* invented
equipment that made possible the publication of multiple editions with
identical news and statistical content.

Pursuing new advances in automatic typesetting, Ackell evolved his
own remote-control electronic method, a vast improvement over the
teletypesetter, which Ackell called "a clumsy substitution of sole-
noids for printers' fingers . . . it doesn't set type fast enough to be
worthwhile."

One morning Ackell escorted William Kerby to his machine shop
on New York's lower Sixth Avenue and showed him a working model
of a machine he called "Mary Ann." The new system worked with
a paper tape punched out with a typewriterlike keyboard using a code
of six electrical impulses.

The beaming Ackell announced that his newly created Electro-
Typesetter could set the entire news and editorial content of *The Wall
Street Journal* in twenty-six hours—half the time it took with manual
operation. By the end of 1955 presses producing identical editions
started rolling at the four Dow Jones printing plants and at a new one

in Silver Spring, Maryland, near Washington. They started at about the same hour in each city, and although deadlines varied because of mail schedules and time zone differences, the mailrooms and delivery crews were able to dispatch over 400,000 copies of the paper each night to readers in every state in the union.

Joseph J. Ackell became known as the father of newspaper automation, but oddly enough he never formally trained for a career in technology. He started out as an insurance adjustor and later became an accounting clerk. Even more remarkable, for years he worked on his own, hiring a technical assistant for the first time in 1951.

In mid-1959, with the *Journal*'s new technology performing well, Barney Kilgore announced plans to build two new publishing plants at a cost of about $6 million. A Cleveland, Ohio, center would produce part of the *Journal*'s Midwest edition, serving its 80,000 subscribers in Ohio, Indiana, Michigan, and the province of Ontario, Canada. The Springfield, Massachusetts, facility (actually an eleven-and-one-half-acre site in Chicopee, five miles from downtown Springfield) would be a branch of the Eastern edition, serving readers in the New England states, western New York, and portions of eastern Canada. This included some 60,000 subscribers at the time. The Chicopee plant also housed the *Journal*'s central circulation records. Between subscriptions and newsstand sales, the paper could now count some 645,000 buyers a day.

In 1961 somebody noticed that California had more subscribers than any other state, a goodly number of them in the vicinity of Los Angeles. Their copies had to be air expressed from San Francisco, where the Pacific Coast edition serving seven western states had set up shop in 1929.

Deciding that a more efficient system was in order, Barney Kilgore authorized the construction of a publishing plant in Riverside, sixty miles east of Los Angeles. When it opened on May 28, 1962, 50,000 subscribers in southern California and Arizona read the first facsimile newspaper to be regularly and commercially printed in the United States.

The *Journal*s printed at Riverside were exact duplicates of the Pacific Coast editions prepared by conventional methods at the *Journal*'s San Francisco plant.

The entire facsimile function in both cities was operated by a staff of electrical engineers and other technicians. As each page of the newspaper was set in type in San Francisco, a special proof was made and an exact picture of the page transmitted to the plant in southern California, 392 miles away.

Each page took approximately four and one-half minutes to transmit over a complex of coaxial cable and microwave circuits installed by the Pacific Telephone & Telegraph Company. The images received in Riverside were reproduced on photographic film. After developing and processing, the film was etched onto zinc printing plates, which were then used to print the *Journal* on a conventional press.

By the time its eighth publishing center went into operation *The Wall Street Journal* had a circulation of 824,835. California still led with sales of 111,852 while New York was second with just under 100,000. Within a few years the *Journal* could boast that its circulation was exceeded only by the *New York Daily News* and the *Chicago Tribune*.

Dow Jones management soon realized that its highly efficient new plants were being underutilized. There was only one thing to do. On April 2, 1963, the company announced that after seventy-four years of publishing in New York's financial district, it would shut down its printing operations there. *The Wall Street Journal* would still be edited in New York, but readers in the city's metropolitan area would receive copies printed at plants in Massachusetts and Maryland.

On the eve of Dow Jones's seventy-fifth anniversary, the company registered 110,000 shares of common stock for public sale. The first offering of common brought in more than $11.5 million; an additional amount of stock worth almost $700,000 was offered to the employees. According to *Value Line,* "Insiders control about 70 percent of the stock."

Most of the revenue raised was set aside for expansion, and the company lost no time in doing just that. A skyscraper at 30 Broad Street became Dow Jones's new headquarters. With the addition of a data-transmission system the *Journal* now had a single communications circuit instead of the eight that had previously been necessary.

The circuits were used to send the electric impulses that activated tape-perforators at the various printing plants. This new equipment was faster primarily because it used a telephone line, which had a wider communications channel than the telegraph circuits it replaced. A single telephone line can carry almost as much data as fifteen telegraph lines.

The computers and teletype at DowCom headquarters in South Brunswick, New Jersey, make it possible for more than 95 percent of *Journal* subscribers around the nation to receive their papers on the day of publication. Dow Jones's new printing facility at South Brunswick, which opened in the fall of 1969, took five years to complete. It was designed to share production of the Eastern edition of the paper with facilities in Massachusetts and Maryland.

The South Brunswick center was to be more than printing plant number nine. Costing more than $2.5 million, it was the country's first facility designed exclusively for production of a major daily newspaper using facsimile transmission and offset printing in one continuous operation. (The point of origin for the transmission was Chicopee.)

At the New Jersey plant today an advanced IBM computer, the 360 model, receives copy throughout the day and early evening and sends it on to the right place at the right time. This data-processing complex, the center of the DowCom network, is critical to the smooth operation of the national newspaper, so another IBM 360 is kept hooked up in case of emergency. When not in use, the backup computer processes advertising insertion orders, newsdealer draw changes, and accounting information. A two-way line connects the IBM computer in South Brunswick to Dow Jones's other plants.

Working journalists use the computer, too. Normally a reporter in any part of the country who has completed a story relays it to the New York newsroom via telephone or with a teletype machine. If the lines there are busy with other communications traffic, the copy is detoured to South Brunswick, where the 360 computer retains it until a line is free, then automatically speeds it along to headquarters.

Once the story has arrived and been scanned by a rewrite editor, the DowCom network sends out requests from bureaus for local commentary. The proposed story is reviewed by several pairs of editorial eyes for accuracy, possibility of reporter bias, and, thanks to the nationwide hookup, additional input from around the country.

When the final copy is completed, senior editors take over. If it's newsworthy enough to be a "leader" or an "A-hed," the article goes directly to the managing editor; otherwise it's sent to the front-page editor or to the appropriate inside editor.

Once a story has been assigned a specific newspaper location, it is placed page by page on the facsimile transmitter. An exact copy, including all editorial alterations, is then reproduced over wire at either the Chicopee or Silver Spring tape-punching departments. The choice of either Massachusetts or Maryland is flexible, depending on the availability of circuit time.

Now the article moves to production. The copy is passed to a technician who enters it onto paper tape with typed punched holes. The resulting tape, which contains structured symbols instead of letters, is fed into an 1130 computer, which arranges it in lines, hyphenating words when necessary, to make it fit the newspaper's space requirements.

The finished product is examined for accuracy before being prepared for the automatic typesetters. At this point the symbols from the tape are forwarded to the 360 computer in South Brunswick.

The copy, with programmed instructions specifying its type face and priority ranking, is then stored in the computer's memory bank, ready for retrieval by printing plants across the country.

Once the layout of an issue has been determined, page plates are set and proofreaders seek out the inevitable typographical errors. The punched tape signals from the computer are then fed into the photocomposition equipment, yielding a picture of the text set in columns. After another check by a proofreader, photographs are made of the layout strips bearing the columns. The negatives are developed onto a metallic printing plate that is sturdy enough to withstand the pounding it will get from the heavy presses.

Once Chicopee has prepared its page proofs, the copy for each page is relayed by facsimile over radio microwave to South Brunswick. The proofs are placed around a drum, and as the drum spins around rapidly, an electronic scanner passes over each line, reading the page at the rate of 800 lines to the inch. Equipment located in immense poles then transmits these impulses from the scanner in Chicopee down to South Brunswick. The coded signals are duplicated on another revolving drum that spins at the same speed as the Chicopee unit, absorbing the impulses on a negative film that is then processed into a ready-for-print page.

The DowCom network of the early 1970s could transmit more than 160 miles at the rate of one page every 3.8 minutes. The envy of newspaper publishers around the world, the network soon became the model for other publications which sought Dow Jones's assistance in modernizing their own facilities. But the management of Dow Jones did not sit back and let the competition catch up to them; they were already hatching plans for an even better way to disseminate their copy to plants across the United States. Transmitting by satellite would be the next step.

No reader noticed it was different. And that made page five of the *Journal*'s August 30, 1974, Eastern edition a success. For the first time a communications satellite system had been used for plant-to-plant transmission of a high-resolution facsimile of a newspaper page.

The dispatch of the August 30 page was part of an experiment by Dow Jones and the Communications Satellite Corporation (COMSAT) to gather information on the practicalities of newspaper production via satellite facsimile. Transmission, speeds, effects of climate conditions, and error rates were studied to determine the specifications necessary to design a permanent installation.

Page five, a sheet of news copy and ads, was composed in the Chicopee plant in the same manner as other *Journal* pages. But instead of using a proof of the page to send a facsimile via microwave to the South Brunswick plant, this page left Chicopee via a COMSAT earth station, sped 22,300 miles to Intelsat IV hovering in a stationary orbit over the Atlantic, turned around, and came down in the South Brunswick printing plant ready for plating. It was the first time that the entire process for a single page, from composition to printing, was completed between plants during the normal production process.

The facsimile process, transmitted by satellite, can be summarized as follows:

1. Composition: Stories and headlines are set in type and, along with advertising, assembled in full pages at Dow Jones's production facility in Chicopee, Massachusetts.
2. Proofing: After type corrections and copy inserts are complete, full-size reproduction proofs are made of each page.
3. Facsimile: The reproduction proofs are individually wrapped around a transmitting drum which "reads" the page at 800 lines per inch, converting the print to electronic impulses.
4. Transmission: The impulses are transmitted at the rate of 150,000 bit/sec to Westar, 22,300 miles over the equator, which relays the impulses to the receiving unit in Dow Jones's production facilities.
5. Reception: The receiving unit reconverts the impulses back into light, which exposes the image on page-size sheets of film in an average time of three minutes.
6. Processing: Each sheet of film containing one complete page of the next day's *Journal* is developed and checked for clarity of transmission.
7. Plating: The developed film is laid over a page-size sheet of treated aluminum, and the image is transferred. The result is a lithographic plate.
8. Press: Plates are attached to the press, which has a maximum printing capability of 70,000 newspapers per hour.

In less than two years Western Union's Westar I was launched as the first U.S. domestic communications satellite designed for commercial use. This satellite had a life expectancy of more than seven years and a capacity of more than 7,000 telephone circuits or twelve simultaneous color television channels. The April, 1974, Westar I was followed in October by Westar II, to serve one of Western Union's chief clients, *The Wall Street Journal*. With the new satellite Dow Jones now spends $2,000 a month to transmit its pages to regional printing plants, compared to the $72,000 it spent on conventional land communications.

Dow Jones pioneered in the use of a communications satellite system for daily newspaper publishing. To implement the new system the company opened a new production plant—its tenth—in Orlando, Florida.

Bill Satterfield, a fourteen-year veteran of the *Journal,* is manager of the printing facility, which has no editors, no copy desks, no reporters. Nevertheless, the Southeastern edition gets printed on time and is as complete and up-to-date as the editions circulated elsewhere in the country.

The secret of the *Journal*'s distribution success, which makes it a truly national publication, is its ability to get the same edition of the paper out to subscribers and newsstands without having to use long-distance planes or over-the-road trucks—as is usually the case with other great dailies, including the *New York Times* and the *Washington Post.*

The night sky over the Orlando plant is brightened by a searchlight beam striking against a giant-sized cup, behind which rests a small bunker containing highly sensitive equipment.

Around 5:00 P.M. every night except Saturday satellite transmission commences. Twenty men, some working the presses, others operating the satellite receiver, will use up nearly fifty tons of paper. Some 160,000 copies of the *Journal* will be printed and prepared for shipment within three hours. Using DowCom, it takes about four minutes to reproduce an exact copy of one page from Chicopee, and a full fifty-six-page edition is turned out in two hours.

Thanks to laser technology a negative can be processed in thirty seconds from developer, fixer, water, and dryer tanks. Before the negative is reproduced on the metal hard copy needed for final printing, the Orlando team cuts away the sections of the New York edition that are not considered appropriate. The daily box giving the Orlando address and subscription information must be inserted; "chasers" (including updates), corrections of errors, and advertising for the Southeastern edition must also be added. Decisions regarding advertising copy are made in New York and forwarded to Orlando. Only rarely will a story that is considered regional, but not national, appear. The general rule is that if it's of interest to a Georgia reader, it should be of interest to a California reader. If it isn't, leave it out.

Beginning in January, 1978, facsimile images of the *Journal*'s Western edition, composed in the Palo Alto, California, plant, were transmitted by Westar II and returned to receiving dishes at the Riverside, Tacoma, and Denver plants.

Three more printing facilities opened in 1981, at Bowling Green, Ohio; Sharon, Pennsylvania; and Des Moines, Iowa. These are connected by satellite to a plant outside of Chicago at Naperville, Illinois, which opened in 1980. Full-page images are transmitted from Naperville to the three new Midwest locations and to an existing plant at Highland, Illinois, eliminating the heavy cost involved in composing pages at each plant. The Sharon facility prints a portion of the *Journal*'s Eastern edition and is connected by satellite to a transmitting plant in Chicopee. Work also began in 1981 on new plants in Beaumont, Texas; LaGrange, Georgia; and Charlotte, North Carolina. When these are completed in 1982, the *Journal* will have seventeen printing facilities.

In 1981 Dow Jones announced that it would share ownership with Western Union of Westar V, a communications satellite launched in 1982. Dow Jones will then own two of Westar V's twenty-four transponders, the devices that receive, amplify, and retransmit signals to earth stations.

Aside from being the first publishing plant to operate via satellite transmission, Dow Jones's Orlando, Florida, facility is distinguished by another first: daily updated labeling done entirely by machine.

Unlike most daily newspapers, the *Journal* distributes the majority of its copies through the U.S. Postal Service. In Orlando 85 percent of the plant's circulation must be individually labeled, sorted according to zip codes, and bundled off to sectional centers in time for next-day delivery.

Working in conjunction with the Avery International Corporation, Dow Jones developed an on-line addressing system that labels subscriber copies as they come off the presses at high speeds at the rate of up to 70,000 per hour. The labeler, working in tandem with a compensating stacking machine and a mailroom control unit (MCU), applies pressure-sensitive, preaddressed labels to papers on the press stream. As the stream passes over the label head, the forward edge of each paper triggers a sensor that emits a pulse to the labeler, telling it to dispense a label.

After a number of papers have been labeled, a mark on the label list will tell the automatic stacker whether to compensate the bundle being formed or eject it. If ejected, the bundle is either of maximum size or is the end of a zip code. The bundle is then wrapped in plastic, wire-tied, transported through a heat tunnel to shrink the plastic wrapping to size, and delivered to a waiting Post Office truck—all without the touch of human hands.

In 1978 Dow Jones announced an agreement to participate in a three-company limited partnership that would build and operate a newsprint mill near Richmond, Virginia. Cost of the mill was estimated at approximately $100 million. Through a wholly owned subsidiary, Dow Jones Virginia Co., Inc., Dow Jones invested about $12 million as a limited partner and held a 30-percent interest in the mill.

The other partners in the venture were a subsidiary of the Washington Post Company, which also was a percent limited partner, and Brant-Allen Industries, an affiliate of Bato, a private company based in Greenwich, Connecticut. Brant-Allen as general partner held a 40 percent interest in the venture in addition to managing and operating the mill.

Through another subsidiary, Bato manages and operates a Canadian newsprint mill at Rivière du Loup, Quebec, the Dow Jones Newsprint Company, in which Dow Jones holds a 39.9 percent interest. About 33 percent of the mill's total output is purchased by Dow Jones for its publications; the remainder is sold on the open market.

About a third of the capital for the Richmond mill was contributed by the partners; the remainder was raised through loans. The agreement provided Dow Jones and the Washington Post Company with contracts for a portion of the mill's newsprint production.

Located in Hanover County, about twenty-five miles north of Richmond, the mill uses a pollution-free, thermomechanical refiner process and a twin-wire paper machine. It began production in 1980 (nearly three months ahead of schedule), with an annual newsprint capacity of about 175,000 tons.

No one could be happier about this development than George Flynn, senior vice president of Dow Jones and primary decision-maker on the purchase of newsprint. Years earlier he had taken the necessary steps to get Dow Jones in on the ground floor and beat out the competition for the decreasing and progressively more expensive supply of newsprint.

Being far-sighted is a Dow Jones trait. The company has taken *Wall Street Journal* subscribers a step into the future with its alternate delivery system, National Delivery Service (NDS).

Delivering newspapers by hand is hardly a new idea. The original *Wall Street Journal* was delivered entirely by hand to subscribers in New York's financial district. By 1912 Dow Jones had fifty-six carriers, most of whom rode bicycles. Seven decades later hand delivery still makes sense. Although the *Journal*'s two million U.S. subscribers live in every state in the union, there is a high enough concentration of them in certain areas to make personal delivery faster and more economical than postal delivery.

Some 380,000 subscribers in more than 103 cities from coast to coast (nearly 22 percent of the *Journal*'s subscribers) now receive their papers each weekday from NDS carriers. That figure is expected to grow to a half-million by the end of 1982.

The reason is simple: Between 1971 and 1975 unprecedented postal rate hikes doubled the cost of delivering the *Journal* by mail. Spurred on by this costly development, Dow Jones began to explore the feasibility of alternate delivery, and test-marketed hand-carrier service in Boston, Los Angeles, Washington, and other major cities.

By late 1975 the verdict was in. Hand delivery had not only proven itself economically sound, it actually provided subscribers with better service than postal delivery. The alternate delivery department was formed, and by January, 1979, the National Delivery Service (a wholly owned Dow Jones subsidiary) was in full operation.

It now costs roughly eleven cents to deliver a copy of the *Journal* using an NDS carrier, against almost fourteen cents to send it by U.S. mail. Multiplying the three cents saved by 315,000 copies a day, five days a week, and fifty-two weeks a year, the economies are substantial—almost $2.5 million annually. In addition, the service is better.

Early in the day copies of the newspaper are transported to the NDS area and left at an established drop point. NDS carriers converge on the drop, pick up their allotted supply, and go off to cover their designated routes. Deliveries are usually completed by 7:00 A.M.

National Delivery Service started out delivering only the *Journal*—but with 1,350 part-time carriers and 200 full-time employees, it's well on its way to becoming a private postal system on a grand scale. In addition to the *Journal,* NDS also delivers *Barron's* in Boston, Los Angeles, and lower Manhattan. In Washington, D.C., carriers take along *Time* magazine and the *Congressional Monitor,* a daily newsletter.

How does the U.S. Post Office feel about its upstart competitor? Officially they're not wild about the idea—but their personal reaction is something else. Kurt Olson, vice president for operating services, knows of some postal officials in Washington who didn't like to wait for the mail to arrive to read the *Journal,* so they'd buy it at a newsstand on their way to work. "When NDS was expanded to include the postal headquarters area, they immediately ordered subscriptions," says Olson, "because now they could be sure the paper would reach their desks before they did."

At the present time Dow Jones is the second largest deliverer of what would be second-class mail in the nation, but corporate vice president Bill Dunn predicts that eventually the *Journal* will be hand-delivered to 50 percent of its subscribers.

Printing *The Wall Street Journal* is an amazing accomplishment. The paper begins its daily manufacturing process with no finished goods in inventory at noon, and, within 12 hours, creates, processes, packages, and distributes—from 14 different plants—a product to more than 2 million consumers spread over 3.5 million square miles, insuring that over 95 percent of them receive their newspaper the next morning whether they live in a large city or small hamlet.

14

The Dow Jones News Service

The fiercest competition in American journalism at the moment is the one raging between the Dow Jones News Service and RUR, the financial reporting arm of Reuters News Service . . .

WILLIAM J. SLATTERY,
Esquire Magazine

THE FOUNDERS OF DOW JONES didn't start out as newspaper publishers in 1882. Their first products were news bulletins—hand-written sheets that brought their Wall Street customers important business and financial news. And while those early "flimsies" expanded into newsletters (and ultimately became *The Wall Street Journal*), their initial enterprise—delivering the news as soon as it was reported—still flourishes as the Dow Jones News Service.

The service began in 1897 with the development of a machine that could transmit news stories by wire, a full page at a time, directly into the offices of subscribers.

Today's News Service is a direct descendant of the original Dow Jones venture; it also retains one of its earliest nicknames, the "broadtape"—so called because Dow Jones chose a printing machine using extrawide paper.

Those early machines, known as news tickers, were a variation of the stock tickers that carried news of prices on the New York Stock

Exchange. They were cumbersome clockwork devices that had to be wound by hand every half-hour. By the mid-1920s Dow Jones's engineering department had developed a "high-speed" electric version capable of printing sixty words per minute. At the same time the news ticker service was expanded beyond the boundaries of New York City, reaching the West Coast by 1928.

The firm's founders would undoubtedly be astounded by the current DJ300, a variable-speed electronic newsprinter capable of processing copy at 300 words per minute. But one suspects they wouldn't be at all surprised by the tumult that still characterizes the Dow Jones News Service copy desk or by the conscientious service it provides to its thousands of subscribers nationwide.

Banks, brokerage houses, financial institutions, newspapers, and a growing roster of large corporations now subscribe to the News Service. The quiet hum of the DJ300 as it prints out the news they need is in sharp contrast to the orchestrated chaos that goes into delivering that news accurately, concisely, and—above all—quickly.

The News Service newsroom is dominated by a horseshoe-shaped desk manned by a small army of copyreaders. Each has a twenty-three-button call-director telephone, a typewriter, and other tools of the news-editing trade. The inside of the horseshoe—the "slot"—accommodates three editors: the desk slot editor, the back slot editor, and the control editor.

A few yards away is the wire room, where a bewildering assortment of teletypewriters, Telex machines, and TWX printers are constantly monitored. These machines link the News Service with all the Dow Jones bureaus in the U.S., Canada, Europe, and the Far East as well as with the Associated Press, United Press International, and various specialized business wires.

Within arm's reach of the control editor a group of operators presides over an L-shaped bank of six News Service Teletype machines. But that's only the beginning; there is also the stock market news writer, a Dow Jones printer, tape machines connected with the New York and American exchanges, computer readout terminals, and telephones, not to mention a bunch of cathode ray tube terminals (CRTs) scattered around the office.

The control editor's desk is equipped with a CRT that describes the current status of the News Service operations. A glance at the screen tells the editor which stories remain on the waiting list, their position, and the time it will take to run them. The stories are also assigned reference numbers so they can be called up on any of the CRTs should developments necessitate changes. By touching a few keys the control editor can quickly reposition any story on the waiting list.

The control editor's desk is also equipped with a DowVue screen, which shows each word as it moves on the broadtape, and a down-counter, which tells exactly how many seconds it will take to complete the item currently being sent to subscribers.

Another key piece of equipment on the control editor's desk is the backup system, which can be put on-line instantly if the primary computer malfunctions.

A team of expert news analysts brings order out of this chaos. It is their job to decide which news is important, to write it in remarkably few words, and to get it onto the broadtape, speeding on its computerized way.

When one of those twenty-three buttons lights up on a copyreader's phone, signaling a call from a Dow Jones reporter, the copyreader records the reporter's name on a piece of paper already positioned in the typewriter and prepares to take a headline. If the headline as dictated seems sufficiently important, the copyreader passes it along to the control editor; if it doesn't, the copyreader continues to take the story from the reporter, tearing each line from the typewriter as it's completed and passing it to the desk slot editor.

If the story warrants immediate attention, the control editor must decide whether to "break" the story currently moving on the broadtape or to hold the new item until the current story is finished. If the decision is to hold, the desk slot editor retrieves it from the control editor for editing.

If a "break" is decided on, a number of alternatives may be followed. By pushing one of the many buttons on a typewriterlike keyboard at his desk, the control editor can order the computer to stop sending the current story—either instantly, at the end of the sentence being transmitted, or at the end of the paragraph. If the new story is deemed more important than the one currently being transmitted but not so important as to demand an immediate "break," the control editor can glance at the down-counter to see how much time is needed to complete the current item. If it's only a matter of seconds, he may wait for the end, but if quite a bit of time remains, he may decide to break in at once.

In any case, the new headline is given to one of the Teletype operators, who will transmit it "live," directly onto the broadtape. As copy for the story continues to come across the control desk a line at a time, it is quickly read, edited if necessary, and passed on to the Teletype operator for transmission.

When a story has been interrupted, it is transmitted to the screen of a nearby CRT for "repair." A copyreader immediately sets to work, deleting the part that has already moved across the tape, putting an identifying line on the remainder, and typing in whatever information is necessary so the item, even though it begins at the "break" point, will still have all the pertinent details. Once the revision is completed, the control editor decides where the story should be replaced on the broadtape waiting line.

Not all news comes from Dow Jones reporters, and an item from any other source must be verified before it's transmitted. If a company sends a news release, for example, one of the copyreaders will call back to ensure authenticity while another is taking the story over the phone. Once an item has been verified, the copyreader immediately writes a headline, and the cycle begins again. A good bit of editing is usually necessary on material from outside sources, since they rarely adhere to the same standards of brevity as Dow Jones reporters.

Many news dispatches are brought to the desk by New York-based reporters or arrive on the Teletype from one of the Dow Jones bureaus. These items are given to the back slot editor, who rates each for importance. "Hot" stories are given a headline and immediately passed along to the control editor. The story continues to be edited in small pieces, or "takes," as it's torn from the Teletype or excerpted from the reporter's copy. From there it goes to the control editor, who keeps it moving across the broadtape.

On a busy day as many as twelve or thirteen stories may be handled at one time. They are funneled almost simultaneously to the desk slot editor, who passes them in turn to the control editor to be moved onto the broadtape in rapid succession.

Subscribers have received as much as 13,000 lines of News Service copy in a single busy day. That translates into approximately 130,000 words—a far cry from the era when a whole day's worth of flimsies seldom totaled more than 800 words.

The guiding lights of the Dow Jones News Service—executive editor Joe Guilfoyle and managing editor Everett Groseclose—are long-time employees of the company. Guilfoyle oversees the radio and television activities of DJNS, while Groseclose is responsible for the print side.

Guilfoyle has been with Dow Jones for fifty-three years, longer than any other current employee. He started as a copy messenger for *The Wall Street Journal* in 1927, joined the news staff in 1934, and performed various assignments, including a hitch as Latin-American correspondent, until his appointment as news editor in 1957. He was named assistant managing editor of the News Service in 1965, then managing editor, and executive editor in 1980.

Groseclose, who was born in 1938 on a cattle ranch near Childress, Texas, majored in journalism at Texas Technological University. After graduation he devoted a week to reading newspapers to decide which one he wanted to work for. The *Journal* won out, and after a stint of military service he wrote to Ray Shaw, who was then chief of the Dallas bureau. Shaw hired Groseclose as a reporter. He went on to become a page-one rewriter in New York, a writer on general assignment (often referred to as a "Green Beret"), and, in 1970, assistant managing editor of the *Journal*'s news operations in Cleveland. He became Dow Jones's director of public affairs in 1976 and succeeded Joe Guilfoyle as managing editor of the News Service in 1980.

DJNS's chief competitor is RUR, the financial reporting arm of Reuters News Service, the largest and oldest wire service in the world. Both agencies gather news that may alter stock prices and flash it to subscribers at lightning speed from eight in the morning until six in the evening every business day.

Clients include corporations, banks, multinational organizations, and brokerage firms. Some brokerage houses, notably Merrill Lynch, keep tickers from both Reuters and Dow Jones, but only a few can afford this luxury.

The battle for dominance in the financial news service field heated up in 1968, when Reuters invaded the U.S. and Dow Jones's eighty-year monopoly came to an end. According to a former Reuters reporter the European news agency figured that if they could beat Dow Jones on a story three times a month, then brokerage houses would have to take Reuters as well as Dow Jones. And if they could beat Dow Jones ten times a month, maybe the brokerage house would take Reuters and forget about Dow Jones altogether.

Dow Jones knew its own vulnerability. Its broadtape was technologically behind the times, capable of printing out data at the rate of only sixty words per minute. Moreover, the cost of the service had become outrageously expensive. The fee for the ticker alone was $80 per month, with an added fee of $127 a month for each branch office of the brokerage house, whether it had its own ticker or not. Thus, a firm with one branch office paid $207 a month to receive the service, and a mammoth operation with 200 branch units would be billed for nearly $21,000 each month. At that time, Reuters claimed as a selling point that Dow Jones had no employees reporting the news; that they depended on *Wall Street Journal* reporters, who regarded the ticker service as a secondary responsibility. One former *Journal* reporter claimed:

The only advantage in having a story appear on the news service was that if you made an error some subscriber was sure to spot it and so you could correct it before it appeared in the paper. In effect, that turned the subscribers to the service into proofreaders.

One-time *Journal* reporter Dan Dorfman had a love-hate relationship with the ticker. He loved it because it gave him an opportunity to scoop the competition on a regular basis, but he also hated it because it sometimes forced him to scoop himself. When Dorfman uncovered a significant piece of news, he had to decide whether to keep it to himself until he broke it in his next morning's column, or hand it over for ticker consumption and general dissemination to the entire financial community, including Reuters.

Dorfman is not alone in his feelings. Most *Journal* reporters resent the ticker, often with a passion. Alan Otten, Washington bureau chief, put it bluntly. "For some Washington reporters the ticker is a considerable added burden," he said. "For some it's also a first-class pain in the ass."

Not surprisingly, although *Journal* writers were instructed to telephone the ticker immediately with "hot news," they often failed to do so. Most of them would write up their stories for the newspaper first and drop copies off at the ticker room later. In most cases this didn't really matter, but when news of a tremendous ore find near Ontario in 1965 took forty minutes to get on the ticker, Dow Jones subscribers and executives were furious.

Capitalizing on Dow Jones's weaknesses, Reuters went after the U.S. market with a vengeance. At the British news service's behest New Jersey's Ultronic Systems Corporation introduced a new teletype, RUR—Reuter-Ultronic-Report—that could spew out 100 words a minute. Subscribers were assured that reporters would service the financial wire exclusively, and charges were made only for tickers actually installed. The latter announcement prompted one brokerage house, Eastman Dillon, to drop Dow Jones in favor of RUR at once, not because Reuters was a superior organization, but because its pricing was more reasonable.

Another blow to Dow Jones was the loss of its monopoly position with the New York Stock Exchange. Originally the Big Board had required all listed corporations to notify Dow Jones whenever important data was to be made available to the public. Under pressure from Reuters, and over the protests of Dow Jones, the exchange's notification list was extended to include AP, UPI, and Reuters.

The Wall Street Journal may produce the most income for its parent organization, but the ticker has always played a major role in the company's success. Warren Phillips, Dow Jones president at the time, recognized the challenge his company faced and announced that he had no intention of allowing Reuters to become number one.

Dow Jones retained its pricing policy but fought back on technological ground by developing its own 100-words-a-minute ticker. Joe Guilfoyle was brought in as managing editor of the Dow Jones News Service with orders to beef it up. One of his first moves was to eliminate regular coverage of over-the-counter firms. This gave way to increased coverage of whatever firms were making news at the moment. The traditional "Dow Jonesers"—two- or three-paragraph interviews with government and corporate officials—were also cut.

Guilfoyle became a fanatic on the subject of Reuters. Dow Jones deskmen reportedly were afraid to go out for lunch lest they miss a call and Reuters score a beat. Reporters around the country were called on the carpet whenever Reuters beat them out with even the smallest tidbit of news. The reporters in turn would berate their sources for not telling them first.

Dow Jones even went so far as to use a spy, an old friend at Reuters who would call Guilfoyle when he spotted a story that Dow Jones didn't have. Guilfoyle never apologized for this tactic. "The news business is competitive, and my object is to win," he insisted. "I'm willing to take my lumps, but I think it would appall any red-blooded newsman to settle for a tie."

By mid-1970 Dow Jones was ahead of its rival with 1,200 installations; Reuters could claim only half that number. Dow Jones retained its lead into the 1980s. One reason may be that many subscribers, although preferring the Reuters technology, subscribe to the Dow Jones ticker in hopes of finding their way into a *Wall Street Journal* article.

Another factor may be Dow Jones's skill at ingratiating itself with its news sources. "I'd have to be an idiot to call Reuters with a story first," admits one public relations man. "They won't even send me a copy as it appeared on the wire so I can show my boss that I'm doing my job."

While battling with each other, both agencies also have to be on the alert for con artists who might use the ticker to manipulate stock prices. Writers are ordered to double-check their sources before putting any information on the wire. This can be a nuisance, especially when time is a factor, but it is vital. As Reuters staffer Margaret Klein points out, "We've even had press releases come in under phony General Motors letterheads. It's one of the hazards of the game."

The heart of the battle between Dow Jones and RUR—and the place where it may ultimately be won or lost—is in technology. Ticker capacity has long since passed both the 100-words-a-minute and the 300-words-a-minute marks—1,000-words-a-minute capability is now feasible. If that capability is used, the major difficulty may be finding enough news that is both accurate and useful to keep the ticker going.

CHAPTER

15

Covering Asia

We think the next twenty-five years belong to Asia—and we want to be there when it happens.

PETER KANN, first publisher of
The Asian Wall Street Journal

A FEW YEARS BEFORE the Dow Jones News Service found its territory invaded by Reuters, Dow Jones had been thinking of extending its own operations to Europe. Ironically, they began by setting up a series of exploratory talks with Reuters.

At first it appeared that the two agencies could work out a joint venture to market Dow Jones news on the continent. Then, at a meeting in London in 1966, Reuters abruptly backed out. The reason became apparent not long after, when the European agency launched its bid for the American market.

By coincidence another wire service, United Press International, approached Dow Jones for a joint venture around this time. Warren Phillips, who was in charge of the negotiations, declined. UPI appeared to be having financial problems, and he was afraid it would become a weak sister to Dow Jones.

Phillips's next candidate was the Associated Press, and before long an agreement for a fifty-fifty venture was signed. The Associated Press would handle the business and sales aspects as well as the communications network, and Dow Jones would furnish the news. Thus was born AP-Dow Jones, which now offers business news services to clients in forty nations around the globe.

The Wall Street Journal has yet to enter the European market. It came close in the early 1970s, when Bill Kerby became interested in printing local-language business newspapers and contacted Axel Springer, the West German publisher, about the project.

Springer was enthusiastic about a partnership, and in December, 1974, Dow Jones's board of directors voted to give Kerby a free hand in negotiating a deal. "I won't give away the shop," he promised them.

The negotiations were left to Springer's confidential aides, but differences soon began to surface, and several proved to be irreconcilable. The American-West German publishing alliance reached a dead end, becoming, in Kerby's words, "another might-have-been."

Bill Kerby refused to be dismayed. The arrangement with the Associated Press gave Dow Jones a toehold in Europe. A full-scale attack with a European edition of *The Wall Street Journal* would have to wait for some other time. In early 1983 *The Wall Street Journal* plans to publish a new international edition in Europe, to be edited and published in Brussels. Meanwhile a far more novel idea was in the works.

The year was 1972. The Nixon administration had just carried off one of its major triumphs—the establishment of a working relationship between the U.S. and Red China. Fresh on the heels of this important event a select group of Western newspapers was invited to send representatives to tour China.

Among the visitors were Warren Phillips and Robert Keatley from *The Wall Street Journal*. They toured the Far East for a solid month, studying the people and the economy and sending back reports that made fascinating reading in the paper.

In the course of his travels Phillips got a firsthand glimpse of Asia's incredible economic boom. It struck him that the Asian business community could use a reliable daily source of business news and information. Why shouldn't Dow Jones be the one to provide it?

On December 22, 1975, *The Wall Street Journal* announced that it would start publishing an Asian edition in Hong Kong the following year. To do it they would have the help of four on-the-scene partners and an investment of $1 million.

In making the announcement, Warren Phillips said: "Our aim is to be as useful to Asian businessmen as we are to their counterparts in the United States. We will draw heavily on the advice and talents of our Asian partners, all of whom are outstanding publishers with long experience in Asia."

Each of the four copublishers was in a different part of the Orient. The *South China Morning Post* would print and distribute the paper in Hong Kong; the *Nihon Keizai Shimbun* would distribute the paper in Japan; while the two branches of the *Strait Times* organization would handle Malaysia and Singapore. The publications all became partners with Dow Jones in the *Asian Journal*.

An intensive direct mail campaign for the new publication yielded 6,000 subscribers, who paid from $45 to $187 a year depending on where they lived. Another 4,000 in newsstand sales was projected. Even more encouraging, 65 percent of the subscribers were Asians. "We are happy about those subscribers," said the paper's first publisher and editor, Peter Kann. "We do not see this paper as being produced only for expatriate businessmen."

The new venture involved enormous risks. Although *The Asian Wall Street Journal* maintained a backup news transmission system, there were many hazards—from an airline strike to a typhoon—that could disrupt its distribution. On top of that there was the question of success. Would the newspaper be able to find a market in the area? Did such a market even exist? What if the *Asian Journal* failed to come up with the right mix of stories or, worse yet, failed to deliver them to readers in time to be useful?

It was up to Peter Kann to meet these challenges. He had to provide the most thorough, accurate, timely, and unbiased information possible; he had to tailor the *Asian Journal*'s content to the specific business and economic interests of its readers; and, perhaps most difficult of all, he had to ignore arbitrary geographical boundaries to serve the larger community of industry and government leaders throughout Asia.

Kann was undaunted by the challenge. Formerly the *Journal*'s correspondent in Hong Kong, the new publisher was not unfamiliar with his territory. Dow Jones's four Asian partners were equally well chosen.

The *South China Morning Post* is Hong Kong's leading English-language newspaper with a daily circulation of about 50,000. It owns a 51-percent interest in the *Far Eastern Economic Review,* a highly respected weekly of about 25,000 circulation that is read throughout Asia. Dow Jones owns the other 49 percent.

The *Nihon Keizai Shimbun* has the largest circulation of any economic and financial daily in the world. Its morning and evening editions sell a total of 2,760,000 copies a day.

The *Straits Times* of Singapore is the dominant English-language paper in Singapore with a daily circulation of 150,000. The *New Straits Times Press Berhad* is the leading newspaper publisher in Malaysia. Its principal paper, *The New Straits Times,* has a daily circulation of more than 155,000.

By arrangement with its four partners the *Asian Journal* was allowed to use any of their stories or editorials that were of regional interest. The paper also had access to wire services and guest contributors from countries throughout Asia.

To be truly viable, however, the Asian edition had to transmit more than 40,000 words and headlines from New York to Hong Kong in about six hours. Stories had to be selected, reedited, and printed in time to make the midday flights to other Asian cities.

With a satellite-assisted leap across the Pacific, the *Journal* launched its Asian edition, covering a sixteen-country, 6,000-square-mile business beat from Manila to Karachi. The five-day-a-week paper went into partial competition with its sister publication, the *Far Eastern Economic Review,* as well as with *Newsweek International* and with *Time*'s Asian edition.

Ed Cony, then Dow Jones executive editor (now vice president/news), had overall responsibility for the *Journal*'s fifth edition. He was on hand when the first copies of Vol. I, No. 1 of *The Asian Wall Street Journal* came off the *South China Morning Post*'s offset press on Wednesday, September 1, 1976.

Things went fairly smoothly that morning despite the fact that they were producing a thirty-page paper—two and a half times the size of the dummy editions that had been turned out in the preceding two weeks.

There were some tense moments as deadline approached. AP was having computer problems back in the U.S. As Cony recalled:

Up until about thirty minutes before deadline, it looked as if we would not be able to give our readers the final stock quotes from the U.S. markets— despite our repeated public promises to do so.

But AP came through with the quotes, and we had all thirty pages locked up at ten o'clock, right on deadline. Perhaps not the smoothest cold-type composition ever witnessed west of Chicopee. Nevertheless the job got done.

The presses started at 10:27, three minutes before deadline. Before long the distribution team was loading trucks bound for the airport and for the central business district of Hong Kong. *The Asian Wall Street Journal* was on the streets of Hong Kong by lunch hour—right on schedule—and made every flight out of Kai Tak airport to the major cities of Asia. Back in the newsroom Peter Kann was serving champagne to his triumphant staff.

Kann, who was born in New York City and grew up in Princeton, New Jersey, joined *The Wall Street Journal* after graduating from Harvard in 1964. His first assignment was Pittsburgh, where he covered business and labor news. The following year he moved to Los Angeles, where he handled the entertainment industry and made forays into Nevada to report on the gambling casinos. He also spent several weeks in Mexico, writing about opium growing in the Sierra Madre mountains.

Kann was sent to Vietnam in 1967. A year later he settled in Hong Kong as the *Journal*'s Asia correspondent. The most dramatic of his adventures in that part of the world occurred in December, 1971, when he set off for Dacca, East Pakistan, and found himself in the midst of a war between India and Pakistan. It was impossible to transmit dispatches to the New York news desk, but Kann kept a vivid diary that was published in the *Journal* as soon as the lines were open.

In New York Mike Gartner, page-one editor at the time, compiled an imaginary chronology detailing Kann's movements in the meantime:

Wednesday, December 1: Peter Kann cables New York editors from Hong Kong: "Heading for Dacca, East Pakistan. Staying Hotel Intercontinental. Believe war imminent. Regards, Kann."

Thursday, December 2: One New York editor asks how come Peter Kann going to war. "In Los Angeles bureau, he was such a pacifist he couldn't kill the ants who invaded his apartment. Ants made steady line each night from a crack in wall to refrigerator; he made guests step over them. He's a weirdo, that Kann."

Friday, December 3: Peter Kann arrives in Dacca. War breaks out same day. Events believed unrelated. No cables arrive in New York. Editors unsure of his whereabouts. Peter's mother calls New York office, worried about son. "Peter is fine and safe," she is assured. Debate rages among editors on ethics of lying to reporter's mother.

Monday, December 6: Managing editor Fred Taylor cables Peter: "Your stories unarriving here. Situation looks dangerous. Suggest you depart immediately."

Tuesday, December 7: Kann cables back: "What? Regards, Kann, Dacca."

Wednesday, December 8: Taylor cables Kann: "Get out of Dacca before it's too late." [Kann muses they never sent him cable like that when in Pittsburgh bureau, when he really needed it.]

Thursday, December 9: Kann cables Taylor: "Cable urging me to leave Dacca unarrived. Sorry. Regards, Kann."

Friday, December 10: Taylor cables Kann: "Depart Dacca at once. Regards, Taylor-Cony-Phillips-Kerby, New York."

Monday, December 13: Kann cables Gartner: "Who Taylor-Cony-Phillips-Kerby? Guy has funny name. Cheers, Kann-Kann-Kann-Kann."

Tuesday, December 14: Taylor cables Kann: "Catch plane out immediately. I am serious. Your life perhaps not in jeopardy, but job is. Regards, Taylor."

Wednesday, December 15: Kann cables Taylor: "Will catch plane out. Which way Dacca airport, please?"

Thursday, December 16: State Department correspondent Bob Keatley advises New York editors that last relief plane has left Dacca, with empty seats but without Peter Kann. Kann cables Taylor: "Missed plane. Never got cable advising where airport is. Regards, Kann." Taylor calls Kann a dirty word. A very, very dirty word.

Friday, December 17: Taylor tries again: "Kann. Get out of town. No regards, Taylor, Your Boss." Staff tells Peter Kann stories to each other. Turns out: Peter, in Los Angeles, did not pay phone bill so (a) phone company would take phone out, so (b) ticker would never be able to call him at 6:00 A.M. to ask stupid questions. It worked. Peter once had ivy plant growing out of crumpled right front fender of old Ford Falcon. Car died; plant lived. Peter once announced he would win Pulitzer Prize; passed out shortly thereafter.

Monday, December 20: Kann cables Taylor: "Your cables arriving. Get feeling you perhaps want me to depart Dacca. Will do immediately. Incidentally, war ended over weekend. Kann."

Monday, May 1: Peter Kann wins Pulitzer Prize for reporting from Dacca during war. Taylor modestly accepts accolades for being great editor.

There is some debate about how much truth Mike Gartner's opus contains, but one thing is certain: in May of 1972 Peter Kann won a Pulitzer Prize for distinguished reporting on international affairs. Four years later Kann was named publisher and editor of the new *Asian Wall Street Journal* and alternate director of the *Far Eastern Economic Review* and the *South China Morning Post*. (He is presently associate publisher of *The Wall Street Journal*.)

After little more than a year of existence *The Asian Wall Street Journal* had a circulation of about 12,000. (It has since jumped to 26,000.) A survey showed that it was read by key executives in manufacturing, finance, and government and that the average household income of subscribers was $61,800. The paper has firmly established itself as the first regional business daily in Asia. It carries advertising for more than 550 Asian and international companies and is sold in every noncommunist country in Asia and one communist country, the People's Republic of China.

Many people wonder how the Asian edition manages to get distributed in a part of the world where the press isn't really free. Surprisingly enough, it does, although it has occasionally been banned—or specific stories clipped or blacked out—in a number of countries including South Korea, Taiwan, Indonesia, and Malaysia.

The staff of the Asian edition is fortunate in having excellent sources to draw on for news. There are news bureaus in Hong Kong, Tokyo, Singapore, Kuala Lumpur, Jakarta, Manila, and Bangkok, with part-time correspondents in such cities as Seoul, Taipei, New Delhi, and Islamabad.

The Asian editors also have access to news provided by reporters from other Dow Jones publications, principally *The Wall Street Journal* and the AP-Dow Jones News Service.

A high-speed, computerized communications link allows the Asian edition to cull the same day's issue of *The Wall Street Journal* for additional material—breaking news, stock market and financial news, even editorial page features if they are relevant or interesting.

This vast quantity of business and economic news is selected, edited, and rewritten from the point of view of the Asian business community by a select group of editors based in Hong Kong. If the news is important to Asians, no matter what its origin, *The Asian Wall Street Journal* puts it in its proper regional perspective.

On a number of occasions stories put together by the *Asian Journal* proved to be important to readers outside of Asia.

One day in November, 1978, the phone rang on the desk of Seth Lipsky, who was involved with *The Asian Wall Street Journal* from its founding, most recently as managing editor in Hong Kong. (He is presently foreign editor of *The Wall Street Journal*'s editorial page.) It was Raphael Pura, their correspondent in Jakarta, Indonesia, calling to say he'd heard something ominous. A big boat was being tracked in the South China Sea; according to local gossip it was carrying as many as 2,500 refugees from Vietnam.

Pura planned to recheck his own sources, but he suggested that Lipsky contact Barry Wain, *The Asian Wall Street Journal*'s correspondent in Kuala Lumpur, Malaysia, where the office of the United Nations High Commissioner for Refugees is located. Two days later Pura and Wain landed the story of the incredible and harrowing voyage of the *Hai Hong,* the opening chapter in the massive flight from Indochina. Within a few days the Vietnam exodus was on the front pages of most of the important newspapers and magazines in the world; it dominated the TV news for weeks.

Another important story was the end of Maoism in China and the opening of the country to Western business. The first hint came in a three-inch-long dispatch in the *Asian Journal*—a brief account of a speech given by a Red Chinese official to a group of Hong Kong newspaper editors who were sympathetic to Peking. The official said that if little countries like Taiwan and South Korea could build strong economic bases, there was no reason why a big country like the People's Republic of China couldn't become an industrial nation by the year 2000.

The speech was given in mid-1977, a year after Mao's death. It prompted Frank Ching and other Asian edition reporters to start tracking down stories about China's business plans. By the time the rest of the world woke up to just how far down the capitalist road China's post-Mao leadership was prepared to go, the story was old news to the readers of *The Asian Wall Street Journal*.

In the fall of 1979 Ching left the Asian edition to set up the parent *Journal*'s first bureau in Peking. *The Wall Street Journal* was one of four American newspapers, including the *New York Times*, the *Washington Post*, and the *Los Angeles Times*, invited by the Chinese government to do so.

The following June the *Journal* beat out the other three papers and became the first major U.S. publication to run a section of advertising from China. It included ads for such Chinese goods as watches, vodka, arts and crafts, porcelain, and silver objects. By the end of 1980 the *Journal* carried more ads—often as many as nineteen pages—from the People's Republic than any other important Western publication.

Getting news out of Red China was one breakthrough; getting news in was another. As the post-Maoist government gradually softened its policies, magazines like *Time, Newsweek, Far Eastern Economic Review,* and *Reader's Digest* began appearing on newsstands for the benefit of visiting businessmen. *The Asian Wall Street Journal* soon joined them, becoming the first foreign English-language daily newspaper to be regularly distributed in the People's Republic.

Dow Jones & Company's interests in Asia extend beyond *The Asian Wall Street Journal*. As previously mentioned, it is a co-owner, with the South China Morning Post, Ltd., of the *Far Eastern Economic Review,* which for more than twenty-seven years has been reporting on business, economic, and political events from Islamabad to Taipei.

To most people *F.E.E.R.* is the least familiar of Dow Jones's publishing ventures. Its style and language have a British "flavour," but its format is similar to *Time* and *Newsweek*. The *Review* has correspondents and contributors in more than thirty capitals throughout the

Far East. It is distributed from Hong Kong each Friday to over 50,000 subscribers in all parts of Asia.

Dow Jones also owns a 20-percent equity interest in a Japanese advertising agency, Nikkei International. It is patterned after another arm of the company, Dow Jones International Marketing Services; both companies sell advertising in Japan on behalf of Dow Jones publications.

On June 17, 1981, *The Asian Wall Street Journal* began using satellite-communications technology for simultaneous production in Hong Kong and Singapore. Page images of the newspaper are transmitted from Hong Kong via the Intelsat IV satellite 22,300 miles over the Pacific Ocean at the equator. Satellite transmission enables the *Asian Journal* to distribute the paper in Singapore at noon on day of publication; previously it was not available until the following day. The *Asian Journal* now boasts of being the only morning newspaper in Singapore with closing New York Stock Exchange quotations and up-to-the-minute news and financial information from North America.

Some months after *The Asian Wall Street Journal* was successfully launched, Bill Kerby visited Hong Kong and threw a party on board a rented cutter. Friends, spouses, and family accompanied the staff on a cruise around Hong Kong harbor. During the festivities a Chinese clerk turned to Kerby and said: "I could work for fifty years for British or Chinese Hong Kong company and never see the chairman. . . . Here I have drink with him. May you and your *Journal* live a thousand years."

The Asian Wall Street Journal was the inspiration for Dow Jones's newest publication, the tabloid-size *Asian Wall Street Journal Weekly*. It appeared in April, 1979, and is available in the U.S., Canada, and Europe. Warren Phillips described it as "a natural adjunct" of the daily Asian edition. "We see the weekly as filling the need of American and European business executives for more comprehensive information on Asia's striking growth and the new opportunities being created there," he said.

Advertised as "a new publication for a new year of unmatched opportunity in the Asian marketplace,'' the paper provides U.S. readers with a comprehensive report and analysis of the week's business, economic, and political news from Asia. In particular it emphasizes emerging trends of interest to businessmen who trade in Asia or have investments or affiliates there.

The *Weekly* draws heavily on *The Asian Wall Street Journal*'s news staff reporting from key Asian capitals. Two pages are devoted to news from the *Japan Economic Journal,* the English-language weekly of *Nihon Keizai Shimbun.*

The inside pages utilize a four-column format. News is indexed according to country, subject matter, and company, allowing easy, quick selection of stories of greatest interest to the reader.

The *Weekly* normally runs twenty-four pages, but if advertising and news are especially heavy, it's expanded to twenty-eight pages. Advertising averaged seven pages per issue early in 1980, exceeding expectations.

The bulk of the *Weekly*'s news content, of course, comes from its daily counterpart in Hong Kong. However, a steadily increasing number of news stories, features, and commentary originate with the *Weekly*'s New York staff. One September issue, for example, contained a page-one story about Sri Lanka's attempts to attract American investors, a commodity-page lead about Indonesia's attempts to halt the current slide in U.S. rubber purchases, and a commentary-page review of *The Money King,* a new novel about life in Hong Kong. These as well as all other New York-originated stories were relayed to the daily in Hong Kong. Several were later used by the U.S. *Wall Street Journal* and AP-Dow Jones.

Like the famous Tinker to Evers to Chance triple play in baseball, Dow Jones stories tend to go from ticker to news columns to feature stories. Packaging and repackaging news has been an important part of Dow Jones's operations since the company's inception. In those days bulletins that appeared early in the day were originally recapped in the *Customers' Afternoon Letter* and later in *The Wall Street Journal.* Today the recycling process is carried even further.

A corporate earnings report, for instance, will arrive at the office and be put on the Dow Jones News Service ticker. The story will then be filed for the inside of the paper. If a reporter senses something significant about it, however, it may emerge as page-one "leader" material.

If the company is a multinational corporation and the leader brings out something about its dealings in the Orient, *The Asian Wall Street Journal* might pick up the story and reedit it for regional interests. *The Asian Wall Street Journal Weekly* might also use it, edited again for non-Asian readers. At the same time a rewriter on the page-one staff may wonder whether other corporations are having similar experiences and, after querying news bureaus around the country, may produce a roundup article or series on the subject.

At the end of 1980 *The Asian Wall Street Journal Weekly* had a circulation of about 4,000. By design it is not sold in Asia; but in early 1979, just a few weeks after its birth, the *Weekly* was spotted on some Hong Kong newsstands. The mystery was quickly solved. A Hong Kong entrepreneur, perhaps a member of the Kai Tak Airport cleaning crew, was collecting the papers left behind by passengers, meticulously ironing each copy, and selling them to local newsdealers.

16

Investigative Reporting at the *Journal*

The "conscience of business."

HENRY GEMMILL, former
managing editor

JOURNAL REPORTERS HAVE BEEN among the first to reveal wrong doing in high government places, in overseas financial dealings, in guarded palaces, corporate boardrooms, and union halls. Their names may not be as familiar as Woodward or Bernstein, but they command equal respect as investigative reporters on the financial scene. They deal with the frailties of human nature and the motives that prompt some people to contribute to, and others to defraud, society.

In the mid-1970s, two years after the disappearance of former Teamsters' Union boss Jimmy Hoffa, the *Journal* detailed the alleged "sweetheart" deals in which firms were paying Tony Provenzano's union men wages far below those set forth in the National Motor Freight Agreement. The article revealed that Hoffa had been unhappy with the "sweetheart" arrangement and might have fought to overturn the deal. His disappearance, the *Journal* surmised, may have been linked to the threat posed by Hoffa's possible return to power as president of the Teamsters.

The Wall Street Journal's reputation for investigative reporting stems chiefly from its dogged inquiries into corporate corruption. The paper has been responsible for dozens of exposés. This chapter highlights a few of them.

A Decade Covering Iowa Beef Processors

On January 10, 1981, Robert L. Peterson, the forty-eight-year-old president and chief executive officer of Iowa Beef Processors Inc., was also named cochairman of the company, the nation's largest meat processor.

In two decades Iowa Beef had acquired a 17 percent share of the American beef market by building cost-efficient meat-packing plants. Peterson had started as a cattle buyer when the company was founded in 1961. Eight years later he had become vice president-beef operations. He then left to become executive vice president of another meat packer, Spencer Foods, Inc., and in 1971 became an owner of Madison Foods, Inc. When Madison was purchased by Iowa Beef in 1976, Peterson returned to his original employer, becoming a group vice president that year and president and chief operating officer a year later.

"This business does have its up and downs," he said at the time, "but I'm not an emotional type of person with highs and lows, I'm just looking forward to building better pork and beef products than we have in the past."

The "ups and downs" of Iowa Beef have been closely followed by *The Wall Street Journal* for almost a decade. As a result Robert L. Peterson spends a great deal of his time condemning the *Journal*, its executives, and its reporters.

On March 14, 1973, the paper ran a page-seven story titled: *Iowa Beef Officer indicted by U.S., New York Juries:*

Federal and state grand juries indicted Currier J. Holman, co-chairman of Iowa Beef Processors, Inc., on charges of conspiring to bribe labor union officials and supermarket meat buyers in New York. "Iowa Beef, Dakota City, Nebraska" is named as a defendant in the state indictment but isn't in the federal indictment. Named with Mr. Holman in the federal indictment and in a second state indictment are Moe Steinman, director of labor relations for Daitch-Shopwell, a New York supermarket chain, and C. P. Sales, Inc., a New York meat brokerage firm the federal grand jury described as the "vehicle" for the alleged conspiracy. The federal and state indictments were returned in New York City yesterday.

New York State Supreme Court Justice Burton B. Roberts contended that the bribe was intended to facilitate the retail sale in New York City of IBP's boxed beef, a revolutionary procedure for packaging and distributing meat.

Journal reporter Jonathan Kwitny, who later wrote a book about the case, *Vicious Circles,* described the proceedings:

On the first day of trial, the defense lawyers, Richard Wynn and Jeffry Atlas, made a tactical blunder that may well have cost them the case. They waived a trial by jury, and asked Judge Roberts to try the case himself. They reasoned that consumers were so angry over high meat prices, a jury would want to hang any meat producer it could get its hands on, and that no housewife could give Currier Holman a fair shake. What they ignored was that Holman's only hope for acquittal was the flexibility by which juries can depart occasionally from the legal straight and narrow to allow for moral right and wrong. A jury might be persuaded that Holman had no real choice but to break the law and pay Moe Steinman, that any other man might have done the same thing.

Judge Roberts had no such flexibility. His only real option was to rule that Holman had broken the law, and was therefore guilty.

And that's exactly what happened.

The decision kicked off a series of claims and counterclaims that lasted for the next eight years. On June 5, 1974, William Heubaum, IBP general counsel, said,

Mr. Steinman has never at any time admitted—and indeed he has at all times specifically denied—that he ever received any moneys from IBP for the purpose of paying bribes to anyone and that he has also denied that he ever paid any bribe moneys from whatever sources to anyone on behalf of IBP.

Jonathan Kwitny wrote two page-one articles for the *Journal;* on September 10, 1974, the headline was: *The Kingpin: If Meat's Your Game, Moe Steinman is Man to See in New York;* the following day's headline was: *Boxed In: To Sell in New York, Iowa Beef had to Deal*

249

with Broker Steinman. Both articles were reprinted in an advertisement in the September 13, 1974, issue of the *New York Times*. The ad asked in bold type: **Is New York for sale? What every meat eater should know about graft and food prices.**

The stories and the ad produced an instant reaction from IBP. Their New York attorneys sent off a letter to William F. Kerby, then board chairman of Dow Jones & Company: "We must strongly protest the publication of the two articles and advertisement . . ." it said. Calling Dow Jones's actions ill-conceived while the court case was still in session, the attorneys declared:

We need only note in closing that the excesses of the press in recent years have substantially interfered with the speedy processes of the law, with the ability of counsel to select fair and impartial juries, with the ability of the State to punish real offenders and with the ability of the innocent to live free of scorn that such publications engender.

Three weeks later, on October 7, 1974, Justice Roberts completed the trial of *The People of the State of New York* vs. *Currier J. Holman and Iowa Beef Processors, Inc.* IBP and its cochairman, Currier J. Holman, were convicted of conspiring with Moe Steinman to bribe supermarket executives and union leaders. Mr. Holman received an unconditional discharge, and Iowa Beef, its name smeared, was fined a total of $7,000.

Referring to Holman, Judge Roberts wrote in his decision:

He knew that payoffs had to be made on behalf of [Iowa Beef] to sell its meat in other areas. He was also very much aware that payoffs were considered a necessary cost of doing business in the New York City retail meat trade. He had been in the meat business too long and had come too far not to have seen the handwriting on the wall. It is naive to think that he would allow the fate of the company he built, but which was now so perilously close to ruin, to hinge on the possible success of an honest-to-goodness salesman who had to pound the pavement and knock on doors in hopes of finding a meat buyer who was not already "on the take" and convincing him of the merits of boxed beef. [Iowa Beef's] survival depended on someone to sell their meat who was capable of satisfying the "crooks," as he called them, in the New York market. The tribute the unions and buyers were apparently receiving from everyone else would have to be paid by [Iowa Beef] as well . . . Somewhat to his credit, it was not until the com-

pany was on the brink of fiscal disaster that he agreed to pay the price. . . .
Sadly, like a modern day Dr. Faustus, Currier J. Holman sold his soul to
Moe Steinman.

In mid-1975 Jonathan Kwitny asked to come to company headquarters in Dakota City to interview Mr. Holman and view IBP beef
slaughter and processing operations. The firm's general counsel
replied:

While we are interested in setting the record straight (and in this regard
much remains to be done following a series of articles you wrote last Fall),
we nevertheless conclude that, during the pendancy of the appeal in *People
v. Iowa Beef Processors, Inc., and Currier J. Holman* it remains inappro-
priate for either client or attorney to discuss with the press the evidentiary
matter involved in the case.

Kwitny's columns in the *Journal* persisted, much to the chagrin of
IBP executives. On November 19, 1975, a year after Holman's conviction for conspiring to commit bribery in connection with millions
of dollars in phony "commissions" paid to C. P. Sales, Inc., with
Steinman in prison and Holman's attorneys seeking yet another appeal, Iowa Beef hired Steinman's son-in-law, Walter Bodenstein. He
replaced its chief operating officer and executive vice president, who
had resigned rather suddenly.

According to a Justice Department indictment that was later
dropped, Bodenstein, a lawyer, played a significant role in some of
his father-in-law's crooked meat dealings. Bodenstein had taken over
the chairmanship of C. P. Sales after Moe Steinman stepped down in
1971, just prior to the federal-state investigation into meat racketeer-
ing. Kwitny reported:

Mr. Bodenstein himself was indicted in 1973 along with his father-in-law
and two other associates. A federal grand jury charged them with filing false
employer quarterly income tax returns. Allegedly, the tax returns listed sa-
laries paid by several Steinman meat brokerages to 22 persons, including relatives of supermarket chain executives, who weren't "bona fide
employees."

In the wake of its startling shakeup in management, officials of the
New York Stock Exchange immediately stopped trading in IBP. The
appointment of Bodenstein was a clear signal that the Steinman influ-

ence would continue. "You couldn't miss the implication of the Mafia connection," said Richard Edgar, a member of the exchange's listing department. "It put a tremendous selling pressure on the stock."

At the same time the American Credit Indemnity Company suspended IBP's credit insurance. Bankers, fearing that IBP was coming under Mafia control, were loath to increase its credit line.

On November 25 the *Journal* reported that only one week after his appointment Bodenstein had quit under pressure and that the U.S. Department of Agriculture was auditing IBP's books.

Executives of the meat-packing firm now turned around and accused the press, especially *The Wall Street Journal,* of "distorted" reporting that was "calculated to cause harm." Currier J. Holman took out full-page ads in several newspapers defending Bodenstein and accusing the press, in particular the *Journal,* of unfairly riding Bodenstein out of IBP. *The Wall Street Journal* stood by its stories.

On August 4, 1976, the *Journal* reported that IBP had chosen Dale C. Tinstman as president and chief executive officer, noting, "It's the second time in less than a year that the company had named to a high post a man accused by the government of improprieties." (Dale Tinstman subsequently became cochairman with Robert Peterson.)

That same year, in the book *Swindled! Classic Business Frauds of the Seventies,* edited by Donald Moffitt and published by Dow Jones Books, Kwitny wrote a brief essay titled, " 'Necessary' Payoffs— But Who Really Pays?"

He stated that Moe Steinman had received from Holman fifty cents per 100 pounds of IBP meat entering the New York City area, and that in one year Steinman had collected $1 million, all of which was hidden and undeclared. Aside from the legal aspects, Kwitny reminded readers that attempts to dilute the difference between a commission and a bribe are less important than determining how the consumer is affected by these manipulative tactics. Concluding his essay in *Swindled!* Kwitny said: "The difference, according to some estimates, amounts to retail meat prices five cents or more per pound higher—it's the person at the supermarket checkout counter who pays."

IBP counsel wrote to Dow Jones & Company protesting a discrepancy in wording between Donald Moffitt's introduction to the book and Kwitny's essay. As it turned out, Moffitt was incorrect. William F. Kerby, chairman of Dow Jones, wrote back:

As you requested, I have advised Mr. Moffitt of this and in the future he will only refer to the matter, if at all, as a "conspiracy." Mr. Moffitt also regrets this unintentional inaccuracy. As we highly value our reputation for accuracy and integrity, we intend to make a correction in the book.

The following erratum was placed in all future copies of *Swindled!:*

On Page VIII of the book's Introduction, the sentence beginning on line 6 should read: "By contrast, a New York judge fined Iowa Beef Processors, Inc., just $7,000 for conspiracy to pay bribes of $1 million a year to a New York meat broker.

The following month Currier J. Holman, still IBP's chairman, wrote a letter to Kerby that said in part:

What Mr. Kwitny will learn during a visit to Iowa Beef may directly conflict with his current beliefs, but surely that is not his fear. His fear, if anything, should be that his suspicions are groundless. No corporate Watergate sits here astride the Missouri's bank, nor any other kind of coverup.

Kwitny's columns continued. One article in December, 1976, began by quoting Currier J. Holman. "Business as we pursue it here at IBP is very much like waging war." Another article was headed: *Troubled Packer, Iowa Beef's history of shady characters far outruns '74 Case.* It reminded readers of the firm's brief history of spectacular growth, which had been laced with "criminals, gangland figures, civil wrongdoers, brazen conflicts of interest and possible violation of anti-trust and labor law. Floating in and out of the scenes are people engaged in vicious beatings, shootings, and fire bombings."

IBP counsel, William Heubaum, fired off a reply: "In view of the true facts of the matter, that statement is probably the most distorted and unfair characterization of a company, its history, and its officials that has ever been printed."

In a speech given on January 18, 1977, Heubaum raised some critical questions regarding the *Journal*'s long-standing coverage of IBP.

Why does Mr. Kwitny continue to write articles in this fashion? We can't tell you for sure, but we don't think it is mere coincidence that our labor agreement at Dakota City is once again due to expire in a few days and that the Amalgamated Meat Cutters Union is doing everything in its power to cast the company in a bad light, apparently with the active cooperation of some members of the press.

Charles Harness, IBP's manager of media relations, tried another approach:

As a former news reporter, I have been appalled at the *Journal*'s apparent reluctance to give IBP any opportunity to respond to some of Mr. Kwitny's stories. I am hopeful you will see fit to use your good offices to correct what I personally feel is an injustice not just to IBP, but to *Journal* readers who turn to your distinguished paper for objective reports on various segments of the American business community.

On February 18, 1977, the *Journal* reported that Currier J. Holman had died of a heart attack at the age of sixty-four.

His death prompted the following letter addressed to Bill Kerby from IBP counsel William Heubaum:

Mr. Holman was a giant of American agriculture who devoted his life to bringing efficiency to the beef industry and less expensive protein to people everywhere. Your newspaper and Jonathan Kwitny are largely responsible for hounding this great man into an early grave. I wonder if you are proud of yourselves for this "accomplishment." For my part, I pity you for the burden you must bear for all the rest of your days.

The saga of IBP continued despite Holman's death. The *Journal* covered the firm's battle with government officials to get back some documents that might spell trouble for the company. Again, on November 1, 1979, the *Journal* claimed that officials of Iowa Beef had traded cattle futures for their "personal accounts while they were involved in setting prices paid and charged by the big packer."

The company was in print once more on July 17, 1980, in a column by the *Journal*'s then Chicago-based reporter Paul Ingrassia: *As Iowa Beef Builds a Huge Kansas Plant, Area Packers Get Set for a Battle for Cattle*. Counsel Heubaum immediately protested the story, insisting that it failed to cover the subject in a fair and complete manner. The feud persists, but the *Journal* seems to be winning.

In June, 1981, Iowa Beef Processors, Inc., and Waldbaum, Inc., were found guilty of price-fixing in a suit filed by Bohack Corporation. The *Journal* told how a federal jury in Brooklyn had decided that Iowa Beef had given, and Waldbaum had received, preferential treatment in beef prices. The *Journal* went on to remind its readers:

In 1974, Iowa Beef and its co-chairman, Currier Holman, were convicted in state court in New York on two counts each of conspiring to bribe butchers' union officials and supermarket chain executives to get Iowa Beef's boxed beef products into the New York area market. A judge in that case gave Mr. Holman an unconditional discharge without a sentence, and imposed $7,000 in fines on Iowa Beef.

More than eight years have passed since the *Journal*'s original story. Obviously the newspaper will not soon forget the mysterious doings of Iowa Beef as it purports to protect the interests of the consumer.

And what of the reporter who kept after the story?

Jonathan Kwitny was born in Indianapolis in 1941. As a teenager he served as editor of the *Shortridge Daily Echo,* the oldest and largest high school daily in the country. He graduated from the University of Missouri, earned a master's degree in history at New York University, and went on to serve in the Peace Corps.

After working briefly for a small paper in Perth Amboy, New Jersey, and quitting to take a round-the-world, hitchhiking trip with his wife, Kwitny joined the *Journal*.

I had never wanted to work for *The Wall Street Journal* because I assumed—a lot of people still assume—that it was just this long, gray mass of financial data. Luckily, we spent a week or ten days at my parents' house in Indianapolis. The *Journal* came every morning, and I began to realize that it was the exact stuff I wanted to write.

The *Journal*'s management told Kwitny to poke around for possible stories while waiting for a bureau assignment. Within four weeks he had uncovered his first big swindle, which he reported in a series of articles, "The Fountain Pen Conspiracy." After more than ten years of investigating, Kwitny still has no beat or bureau base. He goes and comes as he pleases, when he pleases.

Fellow reporter David Warsh, writing in the *Boston Globe,* said, "If the phone rings and it is Jonathan Kwitny of *The Wall Street*

Journal, watch out. If you've got anything to hide, that is. If you don't, sit back and enjoy the work of perhaps the most engaging and consistently interesting investigative reporter in business journalism." Closer to home, the *Journal*'s executive editor Fred Taylor once remarked: "He's been involved in more potentially libelous situations than any other *Journal* reporter. We've never lost a nickel on him. Our lawyer, however, has built the Jonathan Kwitny wing on his house."

Jonathan Kwitny was awarded a 1982 Missouri Medal for distinguished service in journalism. The University of Missouri-Columbia said Kwitny's "citation recognizes the reputation he has earned as a respected investigative reporter."

GeoTek and Otis Chandler

Otis Chandler, publisher of the *Los Angeles Times,* is an extremely wealthy man. He is also extremely gregarious, maintaining friendships with scores of people including his old Stanford University classmate, Jack Burke.

In 1964 Burke organized GeoTek, an oil exploration and drilling firm financed with funds raised through investments by wealthy friends and associates. In addition to big profits, the firm promised investors a tax shelter under the Internal Revenue Service's regulation (later amended) that permitted an oil-depletion allowance of 22 percent of all revenues from oil activities. GeoTek's brochure gave the details: "A person whose taxable income is $50,000 will find that a $10,000 investment . . . will have an after tax cost of only $4,950 . . . In other words, 51 cents on the dollar is actual tax savings."

Otis Chandler invested some of his own funds and brought other wealthy clients to Burke, for which he received finder's fees totaling $109,000. Chandler also received $373,000 worth of promotional securities, bringing his overall profit from GeoTek to between $700,000 and $1.5 million, although his own investment had been only $248,000.

As a member of the company's board of directors, Chandler was instrumental in arranging to have the firm's stock go public in 1971. Plans were also under way to merge GeoTek and the Pacific Oil and

Gas Corporation, which was already listed on the Pacific Coast Stock Exchange. Then in November, 1971, the Securities and Exchange Commission issued an investigation order; formal proceedings would begin in January. Burke, realizing that the SEC could charge him with setting up a dummy corporation—which is exactly what GeoTek was—resigned from the firm. Chandler and the other senior officers were left to fend for themselves during the regulatory agency's hearings.

After a month-long investigation *The Wall Street Journal* printed a front-page headline on August 11, 1972: *Wealthy Acquaintances of California Publisher Evidently Lost Bundle; Otis Chandler 'Opened Doors' for College Pal Who Ran Oil Fund, SEC Now Probes.* Other papers across the country were soon running the same story of oil reserves estimated to be worth $25 million or more that were at best worth $5 million.

On May 17, 1973, the SEC presented indictments in the GeoTek case. Charges were brought against Jack Burke and his brother, Bob, on various counts of fraud and conspiracy to commit fraud, and against the firm's treasurer and lawyers, Arthur Young (GeoTek's audit firm), and Otis Chandler. The last was charged with violations of government securities laws, primarily his failure to inform and file with the SEC data under the agency's disclosure rules. No criminal charges were filed; all the indictments were on civil charges.

In early 1974 the *Journal* covered the emerging evidence of Chandler's involvement in the alleged GeoTek fraud as well as the fact that he would probably get off rather easily. Appearing before a grand jury, the publisher was not once asked about his finder's fees, promotional stock, or about any of his other activities that might smack of criminal wrongdoing. He testified solely as a witness for the prosecution.

The investigators from the SEC were upset that the Justice Department never brought forward criminal charges parallel to the civil accusations. Clearly, GeoTek had violated Section 17A of the Federal Securities Law by failing to inform purchasers of the existence of any finder's fee.

Jack Burke's trial ended in November, when he pleaded guilty. The prosecutor agreed to drop all but one of the sixteen counts against him if Burke would accept the charge of filing false documents with the SEC. In early 1975 he was sentenced to ten to thirty months in federal prison and fined $5,000.

Now it was Chandler's turn, and the *Journal* continued to follow the proceedings closely. In the end the SEC agreed to drop all charges against Otis Chandler brought in the May, 1973, civil fraud suit. Chandler, in turn, agreed to drop all counterclaims against the SEC; basically this involved his allegation that the commission had acted in bad faith by including him among the defendants. In March, 1975, the Los Angeles publisher received a statement from the SEC declaring ". . . it did not and does not claim that Otis Chandler intentionally violated any securities law."

Otis Chandler had, in effect, been exonerated, but the prestige of the *Los Angeles Times* was badly tarnished. *The Wall Street Journal* had proven that it would not hesitate to report allegations of fraud even when they involved a member of the publishing fraternity.

Exposing the Home-Stake Swindle

Robert S. Trippet had started the Home-Stake Production Company in Tulsa, Oklahoma, in April, 1955. His brother-in-law, O. Strother Simpson, was president, but Trippet, whose title was executive vice president, was actually in charge. For more than eighteen years he succeeded in attracting and bilking wealthy investors with the greatest tax-shelter fraud in U.S. history. He promised his clients an astounding 400-percent profit on their investments and enormous tax savings in the bargain.

"It was well known that more than three dozen high-ranking General Electric officers, including board chairman Fred J. Borch, had invested in Home-Stake's drilling programs," wrote the *Journal*'s David McClintick. "So had top people at the First National City Bank of New York, the Western Union Corporation, the United States Trust Company of New York, the Procter & Gamble Company, and some of Wall Street's most prestigious law firms."

The investors also included a long list of show business personalities, among them: Alan Alda, Candice Bergen, Diahann Carroll, Sandy Dennis, Phyllis Diller, Faye Dunaway, Mia Farrow, Buddy

Hackett, Walter Matthau, Liza Minelli, Mike Nichols, and Barbra Streisand.

The following figures reveal the enormity of the swindle:

Between 1955–1972, Home-Stake
collected from investors . . . . $140 million

Home-Stake's projected return
to investors . . . . $420 million

Home-Stake's actual return
to investors . . . . $ 50 million

Difference between projected
and actual return . . . . $370 million

Six weeks after Home-Stake released its 1970 prospectus, the SEC decided to take a closer look at the firm. The following January the assistant director of the agency's division of corporate finance announced that there was evidence Home-Stake had "willfully" violated the securities laws in soliciting 1970 investments. Disbursements of approximately $23 million already collected would "compound the willful violations." On February 11 the SEC filed its lawsuit against Home-Stake in the U.S. District Court for the District of Columbia.

Three years went by, and the public learned little of Home-Stake's ventures. The SEC investigation was dormant; multimillion-dollar lawsuits—by now some thirty had been filed—raised few eyebrows; the firm's bankruptcy proceedings were virtually ignored.

Then *Journal* reporter David McClintick heard about the case from a New York lawyer and set out on a three-month investigatory journey. The paper broke the silence as soon as it became aware of the full dimensions of the scandal. On June 26, 1974, a major story appeared in a front-page column under the headline: *The Big Write-Off; Rich Investors' Losses in New 'Ponzi Scheme' Could Hit $100 Million.** The story described the swindle and provided a list of the peo-

---

*Charles Ponzi was a swindler who flourished in Boston in 1919–20. He promised investors huge returns from dealing in international postal-reply coupons but actually paid them off with money from member investors. Eventually his pyramid scheme collapsed, and he was imprisoned.

ple who had been defrauded along with the amount of their investments.

That very day Stanley Sporkin, chief of the SEC's division of enforcement in the District of Columbia, asked Robert Watson, the agency's regional administrator in Fort Worth, about the status of the criminal investigation. Watson had planned to present the Home-Stake case to the Justice Department in early September, but he was urged by Sporkin to do so sooner.

The *Journal* had identified Robert Trippet as the mastermind of the swindle. He reacted by hiring Jay H. Topkis, a prominent New York attorney who had recently played a significant role in keeping former vice president Spiro Agnew out of prison. The *Journal* also described Trippet's modus operandi. The investment money he received was used to pay off complainers, provide high living for himself and his executives, and buy lavish gifts to impress present and prospective investors.

By the week of July 4 David McClintick's first Home-Stake story had become a source of front-page material for newspapers such as the *New York Times,* the *New York Post,* and the *Washington Post.* Articles quoting McClintick appeared in *Time, Newsweek* and the *Financial Times* of England.

This was not McClintick's first article on tax and securities frauds. He has written other *Journal* stories on such frauds and on the Internal Revenue Service. He reported on how former House Ways and Means Committee Chairman Wilbur Mills pressured the IRS into approving a $100 million tax concession to large shoe firms; how the Hartford Fire Insurance Company acquisition by ITT was made possible by an IRS ruling obtained by questionable means; and how the IRS can apply federal tax laws inconsistently, unfairly, and unconstitutionally.

A first-rate investigative reporter, McClintick tracked down General Electric's former chairman, Fred J. Borch, who had invested $440,920 in Home-Stake, to get his reaction to the swindle. The reporter tells how he did it:

He [Borch] had recently retired, and no one at the company would give me his phone number. I learned that he had homes in Naples, Florida, and New Canaan, Connecticut. The Florida number had been disconnected. The Connecticut number was unlisted. Finally I looked up Borch in *Who's Who in America* and phoned each of his private clubs listed there. An attendant at one gave me his Connecticut phone number. I dialed it and Borch answered. His first words, after I identified myself and gave my reason for calling, were: "How did you get my number?" I said a mutual acquaintance had given it to me. He said he had nothing to say and hung up.

The Home-Stake case took a long time to come to trial. The Los Angeles indictment was superseded by a new indictment in Tulsa, Oklahoma. There were countless delays and postponements and lengthy disputes between the Justice Department and the federal judiciary. After nineteen months of legal maneuvering the trial was set for July 6, 1976; the following day it was again postponed.

On July 22 a former Home-Stake aide filed a plea of no contest to a misdemeanor charge connected with the case and began to testify against Trippet and the officers of the firm. Five weeks later Trippet pleaded no contest to conspiracy and to mail fraud charges that the now defunct Home-Stake had bilked investors of millions of dollars.

After negotiating the no-contest plea for Trippet, his lawyer and long-time confidant Pat Malloy attacked the *Journal* for printing "falsehoods":

A lack of serious investigation and a flare for sensationalism and the dramatic all led to the appearance in *The Wall Street Journal* of a feature article that catapulted the California prosecutors into the hurried and irresponsible indictments—"Ponzi scheme," "pink pipes," "fraud of poor investors," "missing money stashed in Swiss bank accounts," catch-phrases, movie stuff, Arthur Haley novel material but not evidence. Fortunately, your honor, still in this country newspapers do not convict when the judges involved are guided by the evidence, not headlines, and by facts, not pressure. . . .

The *Journal* had not initiated action or printed falsehoods in the Home-Stake case. The paper had merely reported on the SEC documents that had been filed and on the numerous lawsuits charging the firm with the operation of a mammoth Ponzi game, offering strong evidence to support these allegations.

Just before Christmas the *Journal* reported that a federal judge had given Robert S. Trippet three years' probation and ordered him to pay a fine of $19,000. Around the same time Congress tightened its laws on tax shelters.

Julie Andrews summed up the attitude of some of the celebrities who had been defrauded by Home-Stake: "It makes you wonder whether you shouldn't put all you have into a nice Van Gogh painting, so you can hang it on the wall and say, 'There. It's all there.'"

The Journal *Meets Equity Funding*

The Equity Funding Corporation of America fraud is sometimes referred to as the Watergate of American business. Drawing from a *Barron's* article, *The Wall Street Journal* revealed the story on April 2, 1973. It had an immediate impact; that day the value of all shares on the New York Stock Exchange dropped by $15 billion.

Bill Blundell of the *Journal* wrote from Beverly Hills: "One of the biggest scandals in the history of the insurance industry is beginning to break around Equity Funding Corporation of America, a financial-service concern with a go-go growth record in insurance sales."

In March 1973, Raymond L. Dirks, an unconventional stockbroker, received a tip from a disgruntled former employee of Equity Funding that sent him on a tense, investigative odyssey. He discovered that the kingpin of the scheme was Stanley Goldblum, the company's chairman and chief executive officer, but at least a thousand employees were aware of the fraud, and had been perpetuating it for nearly ten years.

The colossal fraud was born in Department 99 of the life insurance subsidiary of Equity Funding, a firm that had been started by Goldblum.

About 56,000 bogus insurance policies had been sold for cash and other major insurance carriers thought them completely legitimate. No fewer than 100 banks and insurance companies now found themselves with about two million shares of Equity stock that was virtually worthless. Some of Wall Street's most prestigious brokerage firms had been urging the public to purchase Equity Funding stock right up until the time the *Journal* story broke; they too had been duped.

The fact that the policies were bogus was well known among the company's executives. They managed to carry out the scheme through various forms of subterfuge, intimidation of employees, forgery, illegal scrutiny of their auditor's findings, and the faking of computer tapes. The executives took a perverse pleasure in the public's naivete. As one of them later testified, "People laughed and laughed about it."

But the joke was finally over. The day after the *Journal*'s story appeared, Stanley Goldblum quit, the stockholders charged the company with scheming to float the corporation's shares, and a ban was ordered on the insurer unit's operations.

The Securities and Exchange Commission followed this with a charge of fraud against Equity Funding. A consent order was entered, an investigator was appointed to oversee the firm, and audits of the various units of the company were undertaken. The *Journal* reported it thus:

A Wall Street Journal News Roundup
The Securities and Exchange Commission filed suit in federal district court in Los Angeles against Equity Funding Corporation; charging the company with fraud and other violations of federal security laws.

The filing was immediately followed by a court order consented to by Equity Funding. The order granted a permanent injunction prohibiting the company from fraudulent acts in the future, and provided for a plan of operation outlined by the SEC. Equity Funding, in consenting to the court order, didn't admit to any wrongdoings.

Three days after the *Journal*'s first story Equity Funding was ordered to file for bankruptcy under Chapter 10.

As the month of April progressed, the *Journal* printed other powerful stories.

April 9—Estimated that 66 percent of Equity Funding Life's reported insurance appears to be bogus.

April 11—Chemical Bank is sued over Equity debenture issue.

April 12—Salomon Brothers sued Boston Co.

April 18—Loews unit filed suit over shares it bought in concern.

April 20—*Before the Fall:* Many officers sold Equity Funding stock before scandal broke.

April 24—*Digging Deeper:* Firm's scandal grows, involves $120 million in nonexistent assets; scheme said to have begun in 1964;

bogus loans issued to a phantom policyholders; like fixing a horse race.

April 26—*Unsafe Combination:* Crooks and computers are an effective team, business would learn; firm's case points up fact; modern swindle is harder to uncover than old king; a heavy-betting bank teller.

April 27—Standard Oil Company of Ohio's employees pension fund sold 24,000 shares in firm March 19th.

April 30—Citibank said it was tricked into giving collateral back to firm; sources said official of firm convinced bank that quick return would save $700,000.

Throughout, *The Wall Street Journal* took the initiative in revealing the details of the fraud and the history behind what proved to be the most monumental swindle of modern times. Equity Funding Corporation of America had started as a financial-service institution in 1960 with assets of $10,000. In thirteen years the firm claimed to manage assets of $1 billion and advertised itself as outperforming every other major diversified financial company in the country.

The *Journal* exposed what had appeared to be a phenomenal success story as pure fiction. Equity Funding's assets were for the most part correct, but they had been obtained by illegal means: forging death certificates, counterfeiting bonds, and creating bogus insurance policies. Trading in the firm's stock, which had been as high as $80 a share, was suspended on the New York Stock Exchange, and the corporation filed for bankruptcy.

The newspaper was disturbed by the role of the New York Stock Exchange and by the fact that everyone seemed to have been fooled— investment advisors, bankers, lawyers, accountants, auditors, insurance examiners, members of the SEC, and of course the vulnerable shareholders. In the aftermath of the exposure the *Journal* wondered: "Why were so many analysts recommending Equity Funding only months and in some cases days before the collapse?"

Although Equity Funding stock had been worthless, major state regulatory agencies in California and Illinois authorized and approved its operation.

Established insurance companies accepted its policies at face value for reinsurance. Established auditors certified its accounts. Major banks extended its loans. Lawyers participated in the planning and execution. Reputable Wall Street firms underwrote and repeatedly recommended its stock—and venerable institutions, the Ford Foundation, Princeton University and many others, bought it. In short, the cream of this country's business and financial community was drawn in.

Not only did the *Journal* pin down the Equity Funding fraud, it raised grave questions about the role and performance of government regulatory agencies.

Several months later the *Journal*'s Bill Blundell and Priscilla S. Meyer wrote, "Predatory parent companies can and do siphon millions out of the insurers they hold, legally or illegally, and effectively thumb their noses at the regulators." The reporters identified several popular ploys:

—The Bum Asset Swap. One of the most common ways of removing money from an insurance subsidiary, this involves a transfer of cash or gilt-edged assets from the insurer to the parent, who replaces it with something of dubious worth (often its own debentures).
—The Shell Game. In this, a holding company milks insurance subsidiaries for cash and other assets. The parent simply concentrates what assets are left in subsidiary A, when it's facing an audit, moves them to subsidiary B when that company is due for examination, and so on. Since insurance subsidiaries in different states usually are audited at separate times, the weaknesses never show up unless one or more of the companies finally goes under.
—The Surplus Slurp. This is used to take cash out of insurance subsidiaries laden with money well in excess of their needs for reserves against insurance claims. The insurance subsidiary declares a hefty dividend to its shareholders—the parent.

Twenty-two men—twenty former Equity Funding employees and two accountants who audited the company's books—were indicted in November, 1973, by a federal grand jury in Los Angeles on 105 counts of fraud and conspiracy. A grand jury in Illinois, where Equity Funding's major life insurance subsidiary was chartered, handed up a similar indictment. Other criminal charges were started by grand juries in states where the firm did business; these were followed by a myriad of stockholders' and creditors' civil actions.

In 1974 William Blundell won a public-service award from the Scripps-Howard Foundation for his coverage of the Equity Funding collapse. In analyzing the firm's incredible deception, Blundell noted that it was an "idea company" that had capitalized on the emotions of the day.

In the soaring sixties, when it went public and became a hot stock, an idea was all you really needed. Carloads of hungry money poured into anything with certain buzz words in the corporate title: computer, systems, micro-this or that. Sometimes it didn't matter what the company actually did. The grandly titled Performance Systems Inc. peddled fried chicken, and not very good fried chicken at that.

Mobil's Maverick

On December 26, 1979, Paul Blustein, staff reporter for the *Journal,* wrote a story about William P. Tavoulareas, the president of Mobil Corporation. It told how Tavoulareas, a garrulous man with a thick Brooklyn accent and a head for figures, may have acted improperly in aiding his thirty-year-old son, Peter, to benefit from ownership in an independent concern, Atlas Maritime Company. Repeating a story from the *Washington Post,* Blustein indicated that Atlas managed ships owned by a Mobil-controlled maritime concern and several prominent Saudi Arabian citizens, including the son of Crown Prince Fahd.

Meanwhile, Rep. Dingell, who has launched his own probe into the affair, sent a letter to Securities and Exchange Commission Chairman Harold Williams questioning the veracity of testimony Mr. Tavoulareas gave under oath to SEC investigators in 1977: "It appears that Tavoulareas may substantially have misled the commission concerning these transactions and has involvement," the Congressman's letter said.

The communiqué said that the Mobil president was responsible for forcing George Comnas, the founder and controlling shareholder in Atlas, to relinquish his interest, thereby enriching the remaining partners, including Tavoulareas's son Peter.

Commenting in Blustein's article, Tavoulareas argued that his motives were based on his determination to preserve Mobil's good relations with the Saudis, and he especially wanted to protect his influential Saudi shipping partners against financial misfortune lest they become angry with Mobil.

While the *Washington Post* cited "personal disputes" between the younger Mr. Tavoulareas and Mr. Comnas, Tavoulareas told the *Journal* that Mobil and its Saudi partners were unhappy with Mr. Comnas's performance.

Blustein wrote that he had reached Comnas at his Massachusetts home, where the former Atlas executive labeled the contention that he had performed unsatisfactorily as "garbage."

Meanwhile Congressman John Dingell, one of the oil industry's most ardent critics, suggested that the Mobil president acted improperly in the affair by offering Mr. Comnas a $25,000-a-year consulting job with Mobil for three years in order to induce him to leave Atlas. Mobil, in a written response to a *Journal* question, said that Mr. Tavoulareas "didn't personally make the final decision on whether to get rid of Mr. Comnas, and he didn't personally give final approval to the details of the firing. Rather, he left those decisions up to others in Mobil; so it was in that sense that he 'wasn't involved.' "

The *Journal* story prompted Tavoulareas to write a lengthy letter to the editor. It concluded with these words:

I understand the difficulties in the publishing business, but I continue to believe that in this matter the *Journal* has deviated from its usual high standard of fairness. It has published material which is false and damaging to my reputation. At the very least the *Journal* should publish this letter and thereby attempt to undo a little of the damage it has caused.

The *Journal* printed the letter and right next to it another column about the oil executive, entitled "Mobil Maverick." In it Blustein commented that Tavoulareas was more than just a maverick. "He is also believed to be the oil industry's shrewdest negotiator and dealmaker, especially in the Middle East."

Tavoulareas told the *Journal* that he didn't have any regrets about having allowed his son to become involved in the shipping venture. "Here my son had an opportunity he may never get again. He knew Ari Onassis since he was a little kid, and that was what he wanted to do."

Characteristic of Tavoulareas's penchant for conducting business according to his own highly individualistic code, he said: "I come from a Greek background, where relatives help relatives." And Mobil's Saudi partners, he added, were delighted with the idea that young Tavoulareas would be participating. The Mobil president quoted a Saudi as saying, "I'm so pleased to have your son in here. Now I know I'll get attention from you."

But Tavoulareas was displeased with the *Journal*'s reportage. "I believe the article was inconsistent with the *Journal*'s reputation for fairness and accuracy [referring to the December 26 column]. The in-depth review of the entire relationship given by Mobil to your reporter before your article was published included the fact that there had been and continued to be full disclosure of these relationships to the management of Mobil and the Board."

Although Tavoulareas condemned the *Washington Post*'s original story, he was especially angered by the *Journal*'s failure to incorporate new information to clarify his position:

I was specially disappointed in the *Journal*'s article because at the time it was published, the *Journal,* unlike the *Post,* had in its hands documentary proof of the falsity of the charge (which most disturbed me) that corporate assets had been misused by me to enrich my son. When, following their original article, these documents were given to the *Post,* it printed a retraction or "correction" within 24 hours. Two weeks later the *Journal,* notwithstanding documentary refutation in its hand, chose to republish the original charges without making any reference at all to those documents. This was, I believe, unfair and warrants an apology and correction from the *Journal.*

Tavoulareas was seeking a retraction but the *Journal* found no flaw in its reporting and wrote as an introduction to Tavoulareas's letter:

While preparing the accompanying article, *The Wall Street Journal* was encouraged by Mobil Corp. to investigate charges against Mr. Tavoulareas that were contained in articles in the *Washington Post.* We did; a story ran in the *Journal* December 26th.

Mr. Tavoulareas believes the *Washington Post* retracted or corrected those articles; we believe the *Washington Post* amended and clarified some of the charges, but didn't retract what it published. Mr. Tavoulareas also contends the *Journal* ignored information Mobil provided that he believes proved the charges against him were false. The *Journal* did, in fact, provide this in its December 26 story. He also believes the *Journal* article was unfair; we don't.

On July 30, 1982, a federal jury found that the *Washington Post* had libeled Tavoulareas and assessed the newspaper $2.05 million in damages.

Critics who believe that *The Wall Street Journal* unfailingly takes the side of big business should realize from this exchange that the newspaper has only one objective: to report the truth without favor to any party.

Because it is primarily a business daily, the *Journal*'s eye is most often trained on the highest levels of management in the richest firms in the country. All corporate executives worry about bad publicity, but one of their worst fears—and perhaps the one that keeps many of them on their toes—is the fear of being weighed and found wanting by *The Wall Street Journal*.

Providing Electronic Information

We do not fight advancing technology—we attempt to envelop it, absorb it, and utilize it to allow us the opportunity to serve the business community, both nationally and internationally, with the best product representation of both techniques—print and electronics.

WILLIAM L. DUNN,
president/publisher of the
Information Services Group,
Dow Jones & Company

THE ALACRITY with which Dow Jones, along with Knight-Ridder Newspapers, authorized on March 3, 1981, the joint offer to purchase all of the stock of UA-Columbia Cablevision, Inc., in a transaction valued at $265.1 million, reflects the consensus that cable is a critical avenue for the future of newspaper organizations.

UA-Columbia, based in Westport, Connecticut, operates cable-TV systems serving 430,000 subscribers and also supplies cable programming through USA Network, equally owned by UA-Columbia and a unit of Gulf & Western Industries, Inc.

In an announcement of the UA-Columbia Cablevision offer, Warren Phillips, chairman of Dow Jones, and Alvah H. Chapman, Jr., president of Knight-Ridder Newspapers, were quoted as saying, "The company's management has built an outstanding organization and it has a very bright future—one in which it will continue to grow and will continue to be a leader in the fast-growing cable-television industry.''

The purchase by the two big newspaper publishers would have represented the second-largest cash offer for a cable operator—eclipsed only by Westinghouse's $646-million agreement to acquire Teleprompter, the nation's largest cable operation. The Knight-Ridder/Dow Jones acquisition would have made them the owners of one of the top ten cable-television systems as measured by subscribers.

In addition to investment opportunities the acquisition would have given the publishers entrée to the burgeoning electronic home-information market, which some analysts believe will one day provide serious competition to the printed newspaper.

On April 15, 1981, an unexpected snag occurred. United Artists Theatre announced a tender offer for nearly 50 percent of UA-Columbia's shares at a price $10 above the bid by the two publishers.

''I wouldn't draw any grim conclusions from this development,'' Phillips stated, ''because it's a normal tactic in this kind of situation and it wasn't entirely unexpected.''

Two weeks later UA-Columbia Cablevision filed two countersuits and a petition to the Federal Communications Commission aimed at blocking UA Theatre's rival $85-a-share tender offer. Thus began an attempt to stop UA Theatre from interfering with the $265.1-million merger with Dow Jones and Knight-Ridder Newspapers.

The publishers believed they had lined up enough votes to win approval of their proposed bid. On April 23 Phillips and Chapman raised their merger offer by $5 a share to $80. Then, on April 30, UA Theatre raised its offer for an increased interest in the cable television concern from $85 to $90 a share.

Then forty-eight-year-old Edward (Ted) Rogers joined forces with UA Theatre. Rogers's father had developed Rogers Batteryless radio in 1927, the first plug-in radio sold anywhere in the world. At one time the family interests included Toronto's most popular radio station, CFRB (standing for Canada's First Rogers Batteryless).

Rogers Cablesystem of Toronto, Canada's largest cable-TV company, has 1.3 million subscribers and covers 80 percent of the country, with additional franchises in California, New York, and Oregon. It also has an operation in Ireland. Rogers wanted to add UA-Columbia with its 430,000 subscribers and twenty-two cable systems to his empire. He would then be on the way to owning the world's largest cable-TV system.

In May Dow Jones thought they had a shot at the company. The following wire service printout tells the story:

05/21 Dow Jones—Knight don't plan (DJ) to alter UA-Columbia bid.

NY—DJ—A spokesman for Dow Jones & Co Inc and Knight-Ridder Newspapers Inc said their joint venture company completed yesterday the purchase of 166 802 shares of UA-Columbia Cablevision Inc common stock at $80 per share from certain trusts. This brings the joint holdings up to 380 813 shares. In addition the joint venture has an option from UA-Columbia for 600 000 shares at $80.

The spokesman added that in response to the proposal of Rogers Telecommunications Ltd and United Artists Theatre Circuit Inc to merge with UA-Columbia Dow Jones and Knight-Ridder do not intend to alter the proposal contained in the merger agreement among UA-Columbia Dow Jones and Knight-Ridder.

Dow Jones and Knight-Ridder believe their proposal is an eminently fair one for UA-Columbia's shareholders and believe they offer the strongest possible future opportunities and support for UA-Columbia as a company for its employees and for the communities it serves the spokesman said. 11 21 AM

The following day directors of UA-Columbia Cablevision met to decide whether to jilt the two big publishing suitors and accept the $90-a-share merger proposal from a joint venture of Rogers Telecommunications Ltd. and United Artists Theatre Circuits, Inc.

Several days later, on May 28, the *Journal* reported that Robert Rosencrans, president of the cablevision company, had "entered into negotiations" to merge as a joint venture with UA Theatre and Rogers Telecommunications at $90 a share. The move put an end to the publishers' acquisition efforts. Phillips and Chapman announced that they had no plans to sweeten their proposal, since the Dow Jones/Knight-Ridder bid had already been approved by the UA-Columbia Board.

One week later, on June 4, the publishing companies were on the verge of selling some 330,000 shares of the cable system's stock, along with their option to acquire another 600,000 new shares, to Rogers Telecommunications and UA Theatre.

Warren Phillips was to have a last hurrah. Technically one obstacle remained before the merger could be finalized. On April 22 UA-Columbia directors had approved and signed a definitive agreement to merge with the Dow Jones/Knight-Ridder venture for $80 a UA-Columbia share. Would Phillips hold firm, or would he release UA-Columbia from the agreement?

On June 11 Dow Jones and Knight-Ridder agreed to drop their bid and any pending lawsuits in return for which they would receive approximately $3 million.

A big one had gotten away, but Dow Jones lost no time in finding a replacement. On October 23, 1981, the company announced that it would pay some $80 million for a 24.5 percent interest in Continental Cablevision Inc., a concern that boasts 410,000 subscribers in ten states.

Why all this scurrying about to acquire cable-television systems? Because an infant technology called videotex makes it possible for cable television viewers to read the news on their home screens, transmit their opinions, and make push-button purchases of everything from fast food to theater tickets or a house.

In the summer of 1981 AT&T planned, then postponed, an attempt to sign up 180 of its Austin, Texas, telephone customers to participate in a videotex experiment that offered an electronic version of its Yellow Pages, sports news, weather forecasts, and a host of other services. A later stage would have allowed participants to select and order merchandise, enter personal information such as appointment schedules, and change entries when they wished.

AT&T has run into strong opposition from newspaper publishers whenever and wherever it attempts to introduce new technologies. Several newspaper firms including Dow Jones are experimenting with similar methods of conveying information; they feel threatened by the vast array of resources that the huge utility can bring to such a venture. The 1982 agreement between the Department of Justice and the Bell system ending an antitrust suit would allow AT&T to go into information dissemination. The Yellow Pages would remain a property of the Bell system, permitting a full-scale move into advertising by the phone company. Dow Jones fears the impact of AT&T's "Electronic Yellow Pages" on its own classified advertising revenue.

To date five of the nine largest cable acquisitions have been made by newspaper groups, and most major chains are aggressively stalking others. The reasons become obvious when you consider the possibilities of videotex.

Suppose you want to buy or rent a house. Sitting in your own home, you can press a few keys on a computer-terminal keyboard specifying your preference as to location, size, and price. Instantly, listings meeting your specifications start crossing the screen hooked up to the terminal; press another button, and the ads' full texts appear on the screen. Still another button will instruct a printer to convert the information into hard copy you can read on the bus going to work.

Today a substantial part of Dow Jones's news distribution is electronic. The man in charge of that area of operations is Bill L. Dunn, who in January, 1980, was named president/publisher of the information services group and president of the operating service group.

Dunn, who works at the South Brunswick, New Jersey, facility, joined Dow Jones as a production assistant in Chicago after earning his B.A. in economics at Iowa's Drake University. In 1963 he was transferred to Chicopee, Massachusetts, where he became production manager two years later. In 1969 he moved up to national production manager, and in 1975 he became a vice president.

Many things have changed in the past hundred years, but the central concern of Dow Jones has remained exactly the same—to distribute timely and accurate business and financial news. Information services is the division of the company charged with finding up-to-the-minute ways to do just that.

Basically there are two types of information-delivery services: one-way and two-way. One-way services supply users with one or more types of business and financial news such as *The Wall Street Journal, Barron's,* or the Dow Jones News Service. Two-way services allow users to stipulate the kind of information they want.

As one of the world's largest purveyors of electronic information, Dow Jones is more than prepared to deliver both types of service.

One-Way Information Services

AP-Dow Jones

AP-Dow Jones links two of the world's oldest and most reputable news-gathering organizations—the Associated Press and Dow Jones. Using modern high-speed computerized communications and drawing on the full resources of both organizations as well as its own staff of specialists stationed in fourteen key international financial centers, AP-Dow Jones provides its subscribers with in-depth coverage of all news that affects the financial markets. It is transmitted via teleprinter equipment over a worldwide network of leased circuits.

Nine separate services are available to banks, government agencies, brokerage houses, newspapers, and industrial and trading companies in forty countries. The first, the *AP-Dow Jones Economic Report*, started operations in April, 1967. It was followed by *Financial Wire, Eurofinancial Report, Canadian News Service, Bankers Report, Forex Report, Gold Report, Petroleum News Service*, and the *Euromarkets Report*.

The combined efforts of the two parent organizations have resulted in a number of scoops. For example, in early 1978 AP-Dow Jones reported exclusively that "Big Five" finance ministers would convene in a secret weekend session in Paris to discuss economic and monetary matters. That story plus follow-up news breaks put AP-DJ squarely ahead of its competitors.

The saga began when John Fiehn, AP-DJ's Brussels correspondent, received a tip that a secret meeting of top finance officials from the U.S., Japan, France, West Germany, and Great Britain was planned for the second weekend in February. Jack Norman in Washington made some checks and sent word to the managing editor in London that Treasury Secretary Michael Blumenthal would be meeting German Chancellor Helmut Schmidt in Bonn on Monday, February 13. This was startling because Blumenthal's trip to Germany hadn't been announced publicly. Late Friday afternoon AP-DJ moved a bulletin leading with the secret "Big Five" meeting and following immediately with the disclosure that Blumenthal would be talking with Schmidt the following Monday.

Over the weekend AP-DJ staffers in several countries began to

275

scramble around, fitting pieces together. A break came on Sunday afternoon, when the French grudgingly admitted that the "Big Five" meeting was taking place at Versailles. AP-Dow Jones opened the wire an hour early on Sunday evening with a story from Paris on the event.

This wasn't the only scoop of that hectic weekend. Word had come from AP-DJ's Luxembourg stringer via John Fiehn that finance ministers of the European currency bloc were meeting Friday evening in Copenhagen. A bulletin was rushed on the wire, along with the correct deduction that the meeting involved a devaluation of the Norwegian krone. The information on the krone was supplied from New York by news editor Jim Furlong, who had called currency dealers in that city. AP-DJ had a thirty-minute beat on the subsequent official announcement of an 8 percent devaluation of the krone within the currency bloc.

Bonn's John Geddes covered the meeting between Secretary Blumenthal and Chancellor Schmidt, which took place late Monday evening. A small band composed of AP-DJ's man Geddes and reporters from Reuters, the *New York Times,* and the *Washington Post* waited outside the chancellery in snow and subfreezing temperatures for the meeting to conclude.

While the four were marking time, they made up a large sign reading, "U.S. PRESS CONFERENCE HERE." Each word was on a separate card, one card for each of the correspondents. When Blumenthal and his party finally left the chancellery, the four hurried, cards in hand, to stand by the side of the road. It was now about 10:45 P.M. on one of the coldest nights of the winter.

Sure enough, the motorcade halted near the correspondents, who immediately began folding up the signs to have something to write on. Blumenthal got out of his car and allowed himself to be interviewed for about ten minutes, while the intrepid reporters struggled to take notes with numbed fingers.

Because of Geddes's extraordinary perseverance, AP-DJ was one of a handful of news organizations to have a story on the Blumenthal-Schmidt talks with quotations from one of the participants.

The Capital-Markets Report

As markets change, so does the information needed in the various marketplaces. With the recent flurry of activity in the fixed-income side of the securities industry, Dow Jones Information Services introduced in 1981 a specialty news service to meet the growing demand for information: the *Capital Markets Report*.

Traditionally, bonds were bought and held until maturity. They represented a "safer" investment than stocks since they guaranteed a specific rate of return. With the inflation spiral and subsequent decrease in the value of the dollar, however, the fixed-income market has changed dramatically. Secondary trading (the trading of bonds before they mature) has stepped up considerably as investors seek different maturity dates and higher yields.

The *Capital Markets Report* focuses on any interest-bearing instrument that makes up the fixed-income market. This includes U.S. government bonds, tax-exempt bonds, corporate bonds, financial futures, and money market funds. According to production manager James Feeny, the report delivers "any news that affects interest rates—the cost of money in any way." It's an important venture, he adds, because "virtually no one is currently providing the instant news needed by this market."

The *Capital Markets Report* has its own reporters and editors, who work at Dow Jones's New York headquarters. The staff of thirteen is headed by managing editor Phil Hawkins, who formerly wrote the "Bond Market" column for the *Journal*. They monitor and report any news that bears on the cost of money, from the performance of U.S. stocks in Europe to automotive strikes, which may ultimately affect the rate at which manufacturers seek to borrow money.

The *Capital Markets Report* is transmitted to desktop terminals through the computerized financial network called Telerate, which has over 2,000 subscribers and more than 3,000 systems on line. Since users are frequently away from their desks, the terminal service is also available by ticker as a backup. The *Capital Markets Report* does away with the bothersome phone calls and frantic searches previously required to compile timely information.

277

Obviously, this report is not intended for a mass audience. It is aimed primarily at major institutional investors in commercial banks, private and public pension funds, insurance companies, and mutual funds who deal extensively in fixed-income investments. But, James Feeny notes, "we do anticipate a spillover to smaller trust departments, banks, and savings and loan institutions—and even to some wealthy individuals who have $500,000 or more invested in the fixed-income market."

RADIO AND TELEVISION

The public's interest in financial and stock market news was mushrooming around the country. In 1968, Bill Kerby and his senior executives decided to move away from exclusive reliance on the printed word and slide ever so gently into voice and picture.

Thus, on May 1 of that year Dow Jones announced that it would begin supplying Dow Jones business newscasts for radio and television. They would be written by a special staff and drawn from news reports prepared by *Wall Street Journal* staffers, from *Barron's National Business and Financial Weekly,* and *The National Observer.* Initially nine business and stock market reports were issued daily and sold by Scantlin Electronics, Inc., as three-and-a-half-minute news "editions" to both radio and television stations.

It has been said in some quarters that *The Wall Street Journal* speaks with the voice of authority. It was only an expression until the launching of live "Wall Street Journal Report" broadcasts in the nation's leading radio markets.

In the fiercely competitive world of radio the "Report" is unique. Many radio stations carry home-grown business briefs (with the accent on stock market quotes), prepared and usually delivered over the phone by a local stockbroker. Other stations rely on general news programs supplied by national networks or syndicators for major business news items (such as the consumer price index or unemployment rate). No radio station, network, or syndicator, however, presents as timely and comprehensive a service as "The Wall Street Journal Report."

The "Report," heard Monday through Friday, seventeen times a day, originates live from a specially designed studio in the *Journal*'s New York newsroom. Broadcasts begin at 5:50 A.M. (EST) and continue throughout the day at ten minutes before the hour until the closing report at 9:50 P.M. (EST).

In addition two feature programs are prepared for Saturday and Sunday broadcasts: "The Wall Street Journal Weekend Report" and "The Wall Street Journal Weekend Review and Outlook." All broadcasts are transmitted via an Associated Press communications satellite to affiliates in the top fifty radio markets.

This ambitious schedule alone distinguishes the service from other radio ventures in busines reporting. But the "Report" also outdistances its competition in the kind of news it delivers: quality Dow Jones reporting coupled with exclusive on-the-scene reports from financial centers around the globe. The reports are presented in a nontechnical style, easily understood by the average radio listener.

"The Wall Street Journal Report" must maintain the journalistic standards set by its corporate fellows. To that end it draws on Dow Jones's global news-gathering resources. The broadcast writers and editors work under the direction of Sidney White. Minute by minute, hour after hour, they scan the broadtape and AP-Dow Jones news wire for possible stories, supplementing their information with material from that day's *Journal*.

Weekday broadcasts focus on late-breaking domestic and international news likely to have the greatest impact on the personal and professional fortunes of the listening audience. Items in a typical report may cover a wide range of business and financial issues, from movements in the prime rate to the effect of Brazilian frost on world coffee prices. As one might expect, weekday reports also deliver hourly updates on the stock market, the value of the dollar, and world gold prices—all matters of intense interest to many listeners.

The weekend features contain "evergreen" material (news that is less timely and therefore remains fresh for an extended period). "Weekend Report," for example, might summarize the findings of the latest *Wall Street Journal*/Gallup poll or analyze the impact of the corn surplus on retail meat prices.

In assembling each program the selection and mix of stories is critical. Another important consideration is how well the stories will make the jump from the printed to the spoken word.

The task is not as easy as it sounds. Broadcast writers and editors can't afford to take the time that their *Wall Street Journal* counter-parts have for preparing their stories. Nor can they assume the staccato style of the speed-conscious News Service staff. The broadcast team must meet seventeen deadlines each workday and still offer expert, entertaining reports that will keep listeners tuned to that particular station.

The use of actual comments from experts considerably strengthens the conversational yet authoritative nature of the "Report." For example, a staff broadcaster can say that prosperity may be around the corner for the housing industry. But the story has enhanced credibility when the deputy chief economist of the Commerce Department informs listeners that the slump appears to be bottoming out.

Similarly, actualities—as these commentaries are called—can lighten a straight business story by lending a human dimension to the issue. It's one thing to hear a report that consumers are profiting to the tune of $175 each from airline bumping practices on the Los Angeles-Washington run. But it's certainly more interesting to hear, from United Air Lines' director of corporate communications, how one passenger temporarily abandoned his wife and child for a later flight and payoff.

Actualities suit radio's one-on-one, highly personal style, but they must be used judiciously in the course of a two-minute report to ensure adequate time for other news stories.

Being selective—knowing what to include and what to leave out— is the greatest challenge of a limited-time medium like radio. To meet it the Dow Jones broadcast team is well schooled in both business journalism and radio techniques. Each member of the staff has written and edited for major radio stations or news services, and nearly all have served as radio correspondents in the U.S. and overseas.

As director of broadcast services Robert Rush views it, "With the voice-feed we have total control over the product. We can maintain a consistent level of quality in news content and delivery that people have come to expect from anything bearing *The Wall Street Journal* name."

"Rip and Read"

While the "live" service of the broadcast division reaches radio audiences in major markets, the "script-feed" "Wall Street Journal Business Report" continues to serve listeners in some 270 cities nationwide. (The services are noncompeting; stations in the top markets may not receive the script service.)

Eight times each weekday subscribing radio stations receive business, financial, economic, and stock market news summaries in script form, prepared by writers and editors in the broadcast division of Dow Jones. As with the live broadcasts, "Wall Street Journal Business Report" material is drawn from the *Journal,* the Dow Jones News Service, and AP-Dow Jones news wires. It is offered to radio stations in exchange for commercial time to promote the *Journal.*

Scripts, also referred to as "hard copy," are distributed on an exclusive Dow Jones circuit and received in subscriber stations on printers. The station's news director (or a news staffer) rips the script from the printer and prepares the copy for broadcast. Some stations use the scripts as is; others break the copy into shorter segments for broadcast throughout the day. Each script is handed to a station announcer who reads it on the air (hence the nickname, "rip and read").

While the "Report" is somewhat less dramatic than the live broadcasts, it covers the business and financial scenes with the same thoroughness and painstaking accuracy.

As expanding technological capabilities permit the "Report" to reach more markets, the script service is expected to be phased out in favor of live broadcasts. Meanwhile "The Wall Street Journal Business Report" continues to be a valuable service to areas in which satellite transmission is not yet available. And as the interest in business news continues to grow, the "Report" will follow, moving into smaller markets whose listeners are just as eager for concise, authoritative business reporting as their big-city cousins.

Consumer Service

The success of "The Wall Street Journal Business Report" led Dow Jones's broadcast division to introduce "Consumer Service."

A five-person staff now provides five consumer-oriented news features per week to fifty-nine radio stations nationwide. They cover topics from the pages of the *Journal* dealing with products, mortgages, money, and any of the vast number of subjects of concern to the average consumer.

THE DOW JONES REPORT

"There were no fireworks in the market . . . just the dull thud of collapsing stocks."

This lively lead-in to a stock market final report before the July 4, 1978, holiday was heard by several thousand New York-area callers who dialed the "Dow Jones Report."

Initiated in August, 1976, the "Report" provides callers with a one-minute summary of market trends and statistics and stock and commodity exchange activities delivered in a fast-paced, lively style. The phone report averages over 50,000 calls a day; its peak was more than 78,000 calls in one day. During two months in '78, when the stock market was especially active, more than one million calls were received each month. In 1977 it logged more than seven million phone calls.

The first "Dow Jones Report" is available to customers at 9:15 each weekday morning; the report is updated every half-hour until the close of the stock exchanges at 4:00 P.M. In addition there is a final daily report and a weekend report.

"Our news is kept current," said Alan Zimmerman, a Dow Jones broadcaster. "With thirty-minute deadlines we are forced to think in immediate terms. The real challenge, however, is to provide the caller with this information in fifty-seven seconds."

Dow Jones sells the "Report" to the New York Telephone Company, which in turn makes money from the message units and toll charges incurred by callers. Buffalo, New York, was the second city to utilize the "Dow Jones Report"; others are scheduled.

TELEVISION

In 1979 the broadcast division launched a business news report for use on television. The three-minute newscast, called "The Wall Street

Journal Television Business Report," was first aired on New York's WPIX-TV and soon after was carried by twelve stations nationwide. Today more than twenty-five television stations broadcast the program.

The television script was designed for an evening time slot and contains a mixture of news from that day's edition of the *Journal* and selected items from the following day's edition. The script is sent to subscribing stations—more than 150 of them—over Dow Jones's national communications network; it is read by the stations' own announcers.

Future plans call for full production of the newscasts using Dow Jones announcers. According to information services vice president William Clabby, "The script service is just a beginning." He anticipates a videotape television service to be offered soon, delivered via satellite by his announcer, and available to stations in the top 100 U.S. markets.

While through-the-air broadcasting has held center stage with the American viewing public since the birth of television, a large part of the future may belong to cable. As subscriber and pay-TV increase their household penetration, Dow Jones is ready with plans.

Subscribers living in selected areas of the country are already familiar with continuous, one-way general news offerings. In the near future Dow Jones will enter the market with business news twenty-four hours a day, seven days a week. This service, in which the TV screen displays printed news, will be devoted exclusively to business and financial information drawn from the *Journal* and the Dow Jones News Service.

Two-Way Information Services

NEWS/RETRIEVAL

William Clabby describes *News/Retrieval* as "nothing more than a system for storing the information Dow Jones generates for its publications for extraction by people who want news on command." That simple definition, however, doesn't begin to describe the value *News/Retrieval* has for some 18,000 subscribers nationwide, making Dow Jones the world's largest news-on-demand supplier.

News/Retrieval, under the joint direction of Clabby and another information services vice president, Carl Valenti, is the first business-information service specifically designed for the busy executive who needs precisely selected information delivered with the speed of a wire service. The data base initially contained up-to-the-minute news from Dow Jones's domestic and international news wires, articles from *The Wall Street Journal,* in-depth financial analyses of companies and industries from *Barron's,* and selected business items from the *New York Times.*

News/Retrieval is, quite literally, a ton of business and financial information that few libraries or offices would have the time, space, or inclination to store, let alone find. Subscriber access is amazingly easy, thanks to careful planning by Dow Jones management.

By the late 1960s people were talking about the feasibility of electronic newspapers. Although Dow Jones was deeply rooted in the newspaper business, its News Service had considerable experience delivering news electronically. A union of the two sources was a natural step.

Clabby explains that simplicity was a critical objective of this union. "There are a lot of data bases out there serving good purposes," he says, "but it often takes a library science major to extract the information." In creating a service subscribers will buy, he notes, "The secret of the sale is ease of retrieval."

For *News/Retrieval* that secret is its reliance on the language most familiar to primary users in the brokerage community: stock symbols. The data base carries information on about 6,000 publicly held companies. Subscribers retrieve the stored information by pressing keys on a retrieval terminal, and the requested item appears on a cathode-ray tube (CRT) screen.

For subscribers across the country Dow Jones *News/Retrieval* serves as a giant filing system without the enormous amount of time needed to file and retrieve information—not to mention the immense space needed to store it. Like any system, however, its usefulness is only as good as the quality of its information and its accessibility.

For that reason, Clabby reports, *News/Retrieval* plans to broaden its data base from ninety-day to one-year storage by 1982. And as the service widens in appeal beyond its current core audience, Clabby suggests that *News/Retrieval* may eventually switch from the language of stock symbols to one we all know well: English.

Unwilling to miss any opportunity, Dow Jones began to link up with manufacturers of home computers. Working with Apple units and Radio Shack systems, Dow Jones information packages can now be purchased in 7,000 stores selling personal computers. Commodore, Atari, Texas Instruments, and IBM are also using Dow Jones services, creating an almost limitless set of outlets for information prepared by the world's leading warehouse of daily business and financial data.

INTERACTIVE CABLE TELEVISION

Dow Jones first began offering news and financial information using in-home video screens and teleprinters in 1979. The recipients were six families in Las Colinas, a residential and commercial development in Irving, Texas, between Dallas and Fort Worth.

Beginning the following summer, some cable-TV subscribers were able to house-hunt at home. They also have many more innovative information services at their command, thanks to compact computer terminals and a two-way cable link to several data bases.

Participants in the Park Cities (two high-income suburbs near Dallas) experiment had instant access to information ranging from stock prices, corporate financial reports, and business and financial news from Dow Jones to classified advertising, entertainment schedules and restaurant guides, sports scores, and local news from the *Dallas Morning News*. The two-way cable link, unlike more common one-way systems, allows users to select precisely the information they want and to retrieve it when they want it.

On May 28, 1981, Dow Jones announced the establishment of Dow Jones Cable Information Services to supply its data base to cable-television systems. The growing, diversified information conglomerate had reached agreement with six cable-TV systems on providing the service, which allows two-way interactive cable subscribers to call up information from the *Journal, Barron's,* and the Dow Jones

News Service. Dow Jones was now offering information from local newspapers, transactional services with local banks and stores, and other data.

By mid-summer, in cooperation with Tocom, Inc., 2,000 home interface terminals were being produced, with an initial order for $810,000. Dow Jones described it as the first widespread use of cable television for delivering home information-retrieval services. The service would be available in Bergen County, New Jersey; Clearwater, Florida; South Pasadena, California; Lakewood, Colorado; Fort Worth, Texas; and St. Louis, Missouri.

It is too soon to predict how successful this will be, but business has been less than brisk in the Park Cities, Texas, location where 6,000 potential subscribers were offered unlimited access to Dow Jones *News/Retrieval* for $40 a month. By June, 1981, only thirty people had signed up for the service, a far cry from the hundreds that had been expected.

It may be that Dow Jones Cable Information Services are slow to get started, or, like the ill-fated *National Observer,* they may simply be a good idea whose time has not yet come.

Speaking on the Presidency

We have a long-standing tradition of avoiding formal endorsements of political candidates.

ROBERT BARTLEY, editor

IN 1972 BOB BARTLEY, then associate editor of the *Journal,* said of his paper's refusal to formally endorse candidates:

Every four years we write an editorial trying to explain why. The short answer is that we don't think our business is trying to tell people how to vote. We think our business is trying to add something to the public discussion of issues. Someone following what we say on the issues ought to have a good idea of precisely where we stand, whether that is pro, con, neutral or confused. We think that ultimately that serves a far more useful purpose than does the exercise of pigeonholing ourselves in one political camp or another.

The editors may not come out directly in favor of one candidate or officeholder, but there is ample evidence that they are seldom neutral. In years past they were quick to take note of blunders, bad judgment, and incompetence on the part of such leaders as Roosevelt—both Theodore and Franklin—Harry Truman, Adlai Stevenson, John F. Kennedy, and Lyndon Johnson. High praise, with an occasional round of criticism, was meted out to Dwight Eisenhower and, during his first term in office, Richard Nixon.

Since the early 1970s White House reporting has become decidedly more important to the nation. As a result *Journal* editorials and columns have given increased space to the news emanating from the Oval Office. The comments on our chief executives and their policies have produced some lively copy.

Scooping Nixon's Wage-Price Freeze Announcement

On Sunday evening, August 15, 1971, President Richard M. Nixon sat down before television cameras in the White House to discuss economic policy. The speech had been announced only hours earlier, yet when it was over, at approximately 9:25 P.M., the administration's economic policy was dramatically reversed, the international monetary system historically altered.

Nixon's speech triggered the most exhaustive news coverage the *Journal* had given to a single news event in the last twenty-five years. Monday's two-star edition of the *Journal* had gone to press two hours earlier—too soon to carry details of the speech or reactions to it. Yet business and labor, wages and prices, imports and exports were all significantly affected.

By the time the three-star edition was put to bed, shortly after the President had concluded his remarks, the paper carried a complete page-one story by Washington correspondent Dick Janssen and a broad reaction story. The stories made 400,000 copies of the remaining 675,000 press run. It was the first time that a page-one leader had been completely switched between editions.

Until 2:00 P.M. Sunday no one at the *Journal* had any solid information on how big the Nixon story would be.

The paper's European news editor, Ray Vicker, had been having difficulty reaching his contacts in London during the latter part of the preceding week. In Washington Dick Janssen had had a similar problem. People "in the know" had suddenly become reluctant to talk.

"We were both getting vibrations that something was going to happen," recalls Janssen, "but there was nothing definite."

The first concrete evidence that a major news event was about to occur came when Janssen made a telephone call early Sunday morning to a former *Journal* staffer working in the Treasury Department. The staffer informed him that some sort of economic pronouncement would be made around 8:00 P.M., either by the White House or the Treasury.

Monday's *Journal* as originally laid out included a leader by Al Malabre on consumer spending and an "Outlook" column by Dick Janssen. Both stories were written on the assumption that there would be no major economic developments before the paper got out.

After the telephone tip, however, Janssen began to have second thoughts. He discussed the situation with Washington bureau chief Alan Otten, and they agreed that something had to be done. Janssen went to work at his typewriter. It was shortly after 2:00 P.M.

By 4:30 Janssen had written a completely new "Outlook" article based on what he described as "advance inklings." Piecing together his observations of recent administration activity, adding several congressional quotes and a stack of economic statistics, he produced a penetrating analysis of why the President was changing his economic "game plan." The column covered unemployment, inflation, the international monetary situation, the domestic political picture, and the reasons why changes in economic policy were necessary. But Janssen, like almost everyone else, still did not know what the changes would be.

In the meantime Al Otten had called managing editor Fred Taylor in New York and told him that Nixon's forthcoming statement was expected to be significant. The decision was made to stay with Al Malabre's leader on consumer spending, but Max Solomon at the New York rewrite desk was prepared to handle the editing of any inserts if that became necessary.

At 4:30 the White House announced that President Nixon would address the nation on network television at 9:00 P.M. No clue was given to the contents of his speech. The timing of the address meant that the *Journal*'s two-star edition would already be in the works. Dick Janssen's revised "Outlook" column would run, but there was no way to print any later developments.

Soon after that the White House scheduled briefings for TV personnel at 7:30 P.M. and for the general press an hour later. The sessions would provide background information and an opportunity for reporters to question "high administration officials." But the timing for the *Journal* was still bad.

When briefings are given prior to a presidential address, reporters are usually restricted to the White House grounds until air time. The reason is obvious: Nobody scoops the the President on his own story.

An 8:30 P.M. briefing meant that *Journal* reporters would not be able to file stories until around 9 P.M., when the next day's three-star edition would have already gone to press. The 7:30 briefing, although it was for TV personnel, at least offered a possibility of copy making the Monday edition.

Ron Ziegler, the White House press secretary, had set ground rules for filing stories on the briefing. Janssen wryly described them as more complicated than the economic program itself. Despite the rules and the schedule, however, there might be an opportunity to prepare copy for Monday's three-star edition. Accordingly, Janssen decided to attend an earlier briefing for TV personnel.

Since there was still no information about the broad significance of the speech, a decision was made to report it on page three. Max Solomon would rewrite the key points for a page-one leader.

In New York, news editor Charlie Stabler had a hunch the story might develop and began lining up bankers across the country for their reactions. News editor Pete Keller began telephoning bureau chiefs, advising them to be ready to call top business executives in their areas. Dick Janssen would attend the 7:30 briefing, Al Otten would attend the 8:30 session, and staffer Jim Large was delegated to watch the speech on TV in the *Journal*'s Washington office.

Shortly after the first briefing had begun, it became apparent this was to be no ordinary speech. As the points covering domestic policy were disclosed, "there was some whistling and quite a few people saying 'whew,' " Janssen recalls. The international implications were more technical, but there was no mistaking this was a major story.

"All the things we had been writing about for so long were all there in one package," says Janssen. "After eight years on the job, this was it. I'm sure glad I wasn't on vacation."

Just before 8:30 P.M. the first briefing ended. Janssen raced to the

Journal's White House phone link and called Bob McGilvray, the head desk man at the Washington bureau. After taking the main points McGilvray flashed the word to New York. News editor Pete Keller immediately called Fred Taylor at home and told him what the President was about to say. There was no question that the story had to go on page one, replacing Al Malabre's leader on consumer spending.

By this time Janssen was back in the Washington office, writing like mad. Jim Large was getting quotes directly from Nixon's televised speech, Al Otten was working on the material from the general press briefing, and Bob McGilvray was putting it all together. The first copy started arriving in New York minutes after the President had gone on the air.

Meanwhile news editors Charlie Stabler and Pete Keller started calling bankers and business executives for their reactions. The entire package was ready in time for Monday's three-star edition.

At nine the next morning, twelve hours after President Nixon had made his dramatic reversal in economic policy, Fred Taylor arrived in the *Journal*'s New York office to start working on Tuesday's paper. Other assignments were quickly handed out.

At ten o'clock Fred Taylor, page-one editor Mike Gartner, Charlie Stabler, and Jack Cooper held an editorial strategy meeting. All aspects of the President's speech were discussed, and plans were made for continuing coverage. This would be more than a one-day story.

By noon Ray Vicker's copy began coming in from London. Because of the time difference a great deal had already happened. London stock prices were dropping sharply. In France, West Germany, South Africa, and elsewhere foreign exchange trading was halted altogether. Businessmen and labor leaders abroad, like those at home, also had comments on the situation.

Enormous amounts of copy were coming into the newsroom in New York, and the task of dealing with it was complicated by the fact that almost one-third of the staff was on vacation. Even so, everything was ready when Tuesday's *Journal* went to press. It was a historic edition. There were twelve major stories in addition to commentary in the regular columns, Dan Dorfman's "Heard on the Street," the

Labor Letter, and the editorial page. The Nixon speech and its rami-
fications had been carefully and comprehensively covered with remarkable speed.

Spiro Agnew's Dilemma

Early in May, 1973, Jerry Landauer of the *Journal* started hearing
rumors about payoffs to Vice President Spiro Agnew. There were
reports that three Maryland engineers and contract consultants, long-
time friends of Agnew's, were trying to save their own necks by
blowing the whistle on the Vice President. According to one source
Agnew had accepted $15,000 from a retired Maryland industrialist
and a "hefty celebrity discount" on a luxury hotel suite.

Unfortunately, Landauer, a tenacious investigative reporter, did not
have enough hard evidence to write the story. It was not until the
following August that he finally hit pay dirt.

One Sunday Landauer talked to George Beall, the U.S. Attorney
for Maryland, by phone, and to the prosecutor's surprise and dismay
recited the first paragraph of a letter Beall had written to Agnew,
nearly word for word. The reporter, according to Beall, claimed he
had a source inside Agnew's office and that *The Wall Street Journal*
was about to print the story. Instead of running the story in its Monday editions, however, the paper held off a day to get additional
information and comment from Agnew. The *Journal* didn't yet know
whether the investigation covered the period when Agnew was county
executive, governor, or vice president, or why the alleged payoffs
had been made.

Landauer's article on August 7, 1973, began:

Vice President Spiro T. Agnew was formally notified by the Justice Department last week that he is a target of a far-ranging criminal investigation—
by the U.S. Attorney's office in Baltimore. The allegations against him include bribery, extortion and tax fraud. . . . The investigation is being carried on in strictest secrecy. On receiving the Justice Department notice, the
Vice President sought a White House audience presumably to inform President Nixon.

In his memoirs the President says that *The Wall Street Journal* had
the scoop on August 7, 1973, but the Vice President himself made

the newsbreak. The *Journal* had informed him of their story earlier in the day and asked him for a statement. The Vice President refused; instead he called a news conference and scooped *The Wall Street Journal*. Two months later, on October 10, Mr. Agnew resigned after pleading no contest to a count of tax evasion.

Jerry Landauer had been working on that August 7, 1973, story since 1968, when Spiro Agnew was governor of Maryland. It won him the 1974 Drew Pearson Prize for investigative reporting and the Worth Bingham Memorial Prize. "The Agnew story epitomized the careful, painstaking work of Mr. Landauer," said Norman C. Miller, who had become chief of the *Journal*'s Washington bureau. "He had investigated allegations concerning then-Vice President Agnew for over four years before satisfying himself of their accuracy."

Born near Stuttgart, Germany, in 1932 Landauer and his family settled in New York in 1938. A Phi Beta Kappa graduate of Columbia College, the reporter worked for the *Washington Post* and as a Senate reporter for United Press International before joining the *Journal*'s Washington bureau in 1962.

Landauer died of a heart attack in 1981, at the age of 49. His colleagues remember him as a meticulous reporter. "You've got to have documents," he used to say in describing how he assembled material for his stories. He trained any number of young reporters to pursue the complex, probing stories he loved to write; he advised them to hand-deliver letters to officials, get receipts, and wait for written responses so there couldn't be any confusion about the facts.

Said Laurence G. O'Donnell, managing editor of the newspaper:

Jerry Landauer was a reporter in a class by himself. He understood better than most that leaders who violate the public trust profoundly threaten a free society. So he dedicated his life to ferreting out significant wrongdoing by leaders in government, business and public institutions.

Watergate

The *Journal* was slow in covering the break-in at the Democrats' election headquarters in the Watergate. This was not deliberate; the newspaper simply didn't think it was important enough. They soon made up for lost time, however, and joined the rest of the nation's press in inquiring about President Nixon's role in the cover-up.

Eventually Nixon found himself on the brink of impeachment proceedings. There was a possibility that he could avoid them if he obeyed a court order to surrender tapes of conversations held in the Oval Office pertinent to the Watergate break-in. Nixon refused but suggested a compromise—summaries of the tapes validated by a highly respected member of the U.S. Senate.

The following story, reprinted from the Dow Jones & Company newsletter, illustrates the tribulations of several *Journal* reporters in covering the hearing at which Judge John Sirica would decide whether or not to accept the President's compromise.

In the world of journalism, minutes lost often determine the effectiveness of a reporter in getting the story to the newspaper.

For the Dow Jones ticker, President Nixon's decision to surrender the Watergate tapes was a resounding victory over competing wire services of the Associated Press and United Press International.

The triumph came despite the fact that best-laid plans went awry. It was a tribute to the teamwork of two *Journal* Washington bureau veterans— Monroe (Bud) Karmin and Ron Shafter—who for many years have starred for the bureau's football team in their battles on the athletic field.

On the gridiron, Bud is the fleet-footed scatback; Ron, the dependable lead blocker. This pigskin experience paid off in the corridor outside Judge John J. Sirica's courtroom when the President decided to obey the court and deliver the controversial Watergate tapes.

Though Bud and Ron were prepared, the unexpected intruded and instinct alone won the game. But, first, the scene: Judge Sirica's courtroom, every seat filled with attorneys, journalists, and spectators.

No telephones in the courtroom, of course; they are down the corridor, 50 yards away. There are just four pay phones to serve representatives of every major news organization. So, Bud and Ron develop a strategy to be first with the news.

Ron stakes out a phone.

Bud will be inside the courtroom.

As soon as Judge Sirica issues his ruling, Bud will burst from the courtroom and signal the decision to Ron who will dictate to the ticker in New York the pre-arranged headline and lead paragraph. Then, Bud will arrive to add on.

Judge Sirica has three options.

(1) He could decide to accept President Nixon's compromise proposal, summaries of the tapes validated by Senator John Stennis of Mississippi, thus defusing the Congressional move for impeachment. If the Judge chooses this course, Bud will rush from the courtroom and signal Ron by raising his left arm.

(2) He could decide to reject the compromise and hold the President of the United States in contempt of court, an unprecedented action that would fuel the move for impeachment. If the judge chooses this course, Bud will rush from the courtroom and signal Ron by raising his right arm.

(3) He could find some legal technicality to avoid a decision on the major issue involved. If the Judge chooses this course, Bud will rush from the courtroom and signal Ron by placing both hands atop his head.

A surefire game plan, right? Wrong, as subsequent events proved.

All in readiness, Ron stations himself at the telephone. Bud selects the last seat by the door in the rear of the courtroom. Rapidly, all the seats, including the jury box, are filled. The burly marshals begin throwing people out and, horror of horrors, locking the door.

Shortly after 2 P.M. a solemn Judge Sirica enters the courtroom and assumes his seat at the bench. At one counsel table are seated staff members for Special Watergate Prosecutor Archibald Cox, fired over the weekend by President Nixon. The President's action brought the resignations of Attorney General Elliot Richardson and his deputy, William Ruckelshaus. With the Executive and Judicial Branches of government at loggerheads, the nation is in a constitutional crisis.

At the other counsel table are the White House men. Charles Wright, the President's constitutional lawyer, is there along with Leonard Garment, a faithful and trusted Presidential counsellor. Both are deadpan, giving no indication of their plans.

The court is called to order, and Judge Sirica begins reading the pertinent portions of the legal opinions affecting the case. The reading takes approximately 15 minutes. There is not a sound in the room except for the Judge's droning voice. At 2:18 P.M. the Judge asks the crucial question: Does the President of the United States have a "response" to make to the court orders?

All eyes fix on Counsellor Wright as he arises and approaches the bench. Now we sit with Bud as he awaits the dramatic announcement. Over the weekend the White House had advised the court of its compromise proposal. Remember, if Mr. Wright officially offers the compromise and Judge Sirica accepts it, raise the left arm. If the judge rejects the compromise and holds the President in contempt, raise the right arm. If the decision avoids the issue, place both hands on top of the head.

295

"The President of the United States is not prepared to file a response," Mr. Wright begins, "because of the time factor involved, etc." (Damn, thinks Bud, he's going to ask for a continuance and we'll have to go through all this again.)

"But I am authorized to say that the President of the United States will comply in all respects," Mr. Wright continues, "with the order of the court . . ." (My God, he's going to surrender the tapes. He's not supposed to do that. Can it be true? There must be a hooker.)

"The President has reached this decision because as a result of this proposed compromise, the constitutional crisis that has gripped the nation, instead of abating, has reached grave proportions," Mr. Wright explained. Then he declared finally, "This President does not defy the law." (He's doing it. He's really doing it. He's surrendering the tapes. I gotta go with that.)

At that moment, Fred Graham of CBS, seated at the front of the courtroom, rose to his feet and began to leave quietly. But is the door open? The marshalls locked it earlier. Bud slipped from his seat and tried it. The door was unlocked.

Bud put his head down and bulled through the first wedge of spectators outside the courtroom door. He zigzagged through the secondary and broke into the clear.

(Right arm? Left arm? Hands on head? Damn, the game plan didn't call for the President to deliver the tapes! What signal? None. Run. Run. Run. But run with your arms at your sides. Don't raise either one, or Ron will go with wrong lead.)

And so, as he had done so often for good old Dow Jones on the gridiron, Bud ran with the ball—albeit with his arms at his sides.

At the other end of the corridor was Ron Shafter. For twenty minutes, Ron had been waiting, chatting occasionally with a CBS agent who also was staking out a phone. Then the courtroom door burst open, the crowd of spectators parted, and out slithered Bud Karmin.

(There go the doors. Listen to those guys trying to break through. Here they come, a whole gang of them. Now I know what a kickoff return man feels like with the Redskins special team bearing down on him. There's Bud in the lead. Right arm? Left arm? Hands on head? There's no signal? What's he doing? He just keeps coming and coming.)

Ron ran—to the phone. But the CBS agent had commandeered it, so Ron alertly grabbed the phone CBS had staked out and dialed the ticker in New York.

Bud, who started with several steps on CBS's Graham, widened the gap over the 50 yards.

Ron held out the phone, and Bud, huffing and puffing, dictated a head-line: PRESIDENT NIXON AGREES TO PRODUCE WATERGATE TAPES.

And then the lead graphs:

Washington-DJ-President Nixon agreed to produce the Watergate tapes for District Court Judge John Sirica.

The President does not defy the law, White House Counsel Charles Wright told the court.

Wright said the President had hoped his prior compromise offer would end what he calls the constitutional crisis.

However, the counsel said it was evident from the events of the past weekend that this hope was not fulfilled.

Therefore, Wright said, the President "will comply in all respects" with the previous order of the court that has directed him to produce for Judge Sirica the actual tapes for the Judge to hear in private.

The dramatic announcement by Wright reversed a position that the White House had filed with the court over the weekend.

While Bud was dictating, the herd of other correspondents charged up to the phones. Ron blocked them aside, one by one, as he does so often on the football field.

The Ticker ended the story at "2:28 P.M. EDT"—minutes ahead of the competition. Ron and Bud shook hands and took off after Mr. Wright and Mr. Garment as they emerged from the adjourned courtroom.

More information was needed for *The Wall Street Journal* story.

"A Pleasant but Plodding Wheelhorse"

On December 6, 1973, Gerald Ford was sworn in as the fortieth Vice President of the United States. The *Journal* wrote: "The Michigan congressman isn't a creative man. . . . Rather he is a pleasant but plodding wheelhorse who often speaks and apparently thinks in clichés."

Slightly more than a year later, in January, 1975, the newspaper had a complimentary column on now-President Gerald Ford. It said that he had grasped the office of the presidency but qualified its stand by adding: "Of course, all this could change by cherry blossom time since the moods of Washington are always mercurial."

297

Three months later the *Journal* carried a long front-page piece that said, "Ford is restoring a sense of purpose to the administration." The newspaper noted that the administration, once demoralized and nearly paralyzed by the scandal that drove President Nixon from office, had been revitalized by President Ford.

For the most part the *Journal* was ambivalent in its feeling for Ford. Only months before the 1976 election, when the President was being challenged by Jimmy Carter, Jerry Landauer wrote a story saying that there was some suspicion that a number of political contributions had been diverted to Gerald Ford's personal use or to other uses that the contributors had not intended.

The allegations were flatly denied by none other than Leon Jaworski, the former special prosecutor during Watergate. Jaworski told newsmen that he had looked into the same charges against Ford and had "found nothing that called for further investigation."

According to Ron Nessen, Ford's press secretary, "A far more serious challenge to the President's reputation for honesty was raised when Watergate special prosecutor Charles Ruff launched a secret investigation in July, 1976, into charges that Ford misused contributions to his congressional campaigns in Michigan."

An article by Landauer in the September 21 *Journal* publicized the investigation. It couldn't have come at a worse time. It was two days before the first campaign debate with Jimmy Carter and exactly six weeks before election day.

Finally, on the thirteenth of October, just nineteen days before the election, Ford was exonerated of any wrongdoing in connection with his congressional campaign contributions. But the President still had to worry about the impression he made on voters during his debates with Jimmy Carter.

After the second debate the *Journal* reported that a 1973 Internal Revenue Service audit of Ford's tax returns from 1967 to 1972 showed that he had not violated any laws but that he and his wife must have been able to survive with only $5 to $13 a week in spending money. The audit also revealed that four times in 1972 the Fords purchased clothes with checks drawn from a political-funds account maintained by Ford, and that the IRS had "docked" the Fords $435 in tax on the income. It also revealed that Ford had paid $1,167 for a Vail, Colorado, ski trip out of the same political account, to be later reimbursed with a personal check. Finally the report found Ford had drawn the latter check on an already overdrawn account, showing a debit of approximately $3,000.

The *Journal* reported the facts but the American people chose their President. It was not Gerald Ford.

Carter's Policy—"An Abject Failure"

Speaking from its usual conservative Republican viewpoint, the *Journal* found Jimmy Carter the most attractive of the Democratic candidates. In July, 1975, Norman C. Miller wrote an article illustrating the paper's favorable attitude toward Carter. Miller presented Carter's platform, mentioned his "dark horse" status, and said, "His engaging personality and tireless campaigning are impressing many Democratic politicians around the country." It did not hurt, of course, that Carter was a fiscal conservative and a foe of big government.

The *Journal*'s enthusiasm waned after Carter was elected. The new President was criticized for his foreign policy, for not doing more to preserve the governments of Panama, Ethiopia, and Iran, and for failing to see the global significance of setbacks in these countries.

As the 1980 election neared, Bob Bartley's editorials took aim at the other candidates but managed to hit the incumbent President the hardest. For example, "Mr. Carter has been a weak leader because, far from being out in front of the people, he has had to be led kicking and screaming to go in the direction the nation needs to go and wants to go."

The *Journal* took a particularly vehement stand against Carter's handling of the Iranian hostage crisis, calling his policy "an abject failure."

On March 27, 1980, Bartley denounced Carter's windfall-profits tax as the "Death of Reason" and ran the editorial with a black border. "Barring a redemptive miracle," it said, "the United States Senate today will sacrifice the nation's future security to its own unslakable thirst for revenues. It will give final approval to the massive, falsely labeled, 'windfall-profits tax.' "

In his conclusion Bartley wrote:

President Carter conceived the brilliant idea of removing price controls on domestic crude oil but taxing away most of the added revenues that he presumed would flow from letting prices rise above the ceilings. The DOE [Department of Energy] bureaucracy found ways, as we noted in this column yesterday, to preserve and expand its power even after decontrol. . . . The oil revenues tax Congress will pass today—again barring some last-minute conversion—will combine with raging inflation to run the American crude oil production industry into the ground. It will solidify OPEC's grip on oil prices, leave us politically and militarily exposed from further dependence on imported oil, drain huge funds out of the savings/profit pool needed to stimulate investment and productivity, and increase the incentives for inflationary money creation. To find a similarly destructive single piece of legislation, you have to hark back to the Smoot-Hawley Tariff, which helped throw the world into the Great Depression.

Carter was so furious at the editorial, a White House aide reported, that he stopped reading the *Journal*.

On election day, November 4, 1980, Bartley wrote "Carter II?" *The Wall Street Journal* had abandoned its long-standing policy of not supporting any political candidate.

Clearly the next president will be severely tested no matter which candidate wins, and there is no guarantee that either could cope successfully. But the tests will be difficult enough without all of the baggage Mr. Carter acquired during his first stumbling term. If he is inaugurated again in January, he will have to deal not only with the nation's problems but with a long list of enervating distractions that would sap his ability to lead and govern.

The following day, in celebration of Ronald Reagan's landslide victory, Bartley concluded his editorial:

The stakes here are enormous; if the Reagan administration fails, the nation will not have this opportunity soon again, and will likely lurch in directions quite the opposite of what Mr. Reagan intends. But the opportunity is equally great. If Mr. Reagan can manage the government and make his policies work, we will look back on Tuesday's election as the start of a new era for the nation and the world.

300

Reagan's Conservative Attraction

At the end of 1980, Bob Bartley's "Review & Outlook" column promised its readers that with "a bit firmer hand at the tiller [Reagan], the American nation will right itself."

Then, on January 8, just eleven days before his inauguration, President-elect Reagan wrote a lengthy *Journal* essay. He noted that the United States stood alone among industrialized powers "in the adversary nature of the relationship between its government and the business-industrial sector."

Mr. Reagan urged a unity, a collective spirit to overcome this attitude:

The nation belongs to all of us. To solve our problems we need the help and talent of a wide range of well-motivated Americans. The business and industrial sector has a vital stake in this process and we shall look to it to provide men and women for both short-term government careers and voluntary assignments, to help us put our nation on the proper track.

Bartley's inauguration day message to *Journal* readers was optimistic:

Today we will start to learn, embarking with Mr. Reagan on a new experiment and a new adventure. He has the ideas and the mandate, and if he can actually bring them to pass and make them work, it will seem one great stroke of dramatic plotting. For if this happens, our 40th Presidency will have been a historical watershed.

The next morning—January 21, 1981—Bartley called on Mr. Reagan to renounce the deal made by former President Carter with Iran:

. . . bargaining with human lives against money and contracts, has an unfair advantage. We should not hesitate to make it clear that an agreement negotiated under such conditions is worthless and equally clear that anyone who attempts the same thing in the future will not be treated so gently.

The editorial reiterated Bartley's previous suggestions (which had not been followed) of immediately reducing the difference between investment income, taxed at rates of up to 70 percent, and labor income, taxed at a maximum of 50 percent. It also expressed regret that the President had not been bolder in accepting the reductions for investment income, cutting projects instead of capping them, and reducing spending for social programs.

However, Bartley still found much to praise in the President's policies. Said one editorial:

Mr. Reagan concluded his Wednesday night address by challenging his critics to provide an alternative. Other than even more of the same, we see none. And given the clear failure of past thinking, it's refreshing to have an idea that offers hope for recovery.

A philosophical bond exists between the current resident of 1600 Pennsylvania Avenue and many of the people who work at 22 Cortlandt Street (the *Journal*'s headquarters since 1972); still, Bartley and his editorial writers try to be objective. They criticize Reagan from time to time, although not nearly as often as they have done with other presidents.

On June 3, 1981, "Review & Outlook" column titled "A Reagan Blunder" accused the President of faltering on the question of what to do about the World Bank. "Mr. Reagan blundered when he allowed his administration to be maneuvered into backing a big increase in World Bank funding," it said.

A June 22 column, "The Imperial Presidency?" repeated an earlier plea to the Reagan administration to renounce President Carter's deal with Iran for the release of the hostages. If Reagan reaffirmed the executive order requiring U.S. banks to surrender the $3 to $4 billion in Iranian assets they held to the New York Federal Reserve Bank, private citizens and corporations would be deprived of the opportunity to make independent claims against Iran.

Urging the U.S. Supreme Court to override this attempt to allow foreign policy to take precedence over constitutional rights, the editorial concluded: "If the Supreme Court allows the Executive Orders to stand, Americans who in good faith supplied goods and services to Iran will be denied a right to collect in court the money they are owed."

On July 2 the Supreme Court ruled unanimously that President Carter had had the authority to make the agreement with Iran that freed the fifty-two Americans who had been held hostage in Iran. As a result of the ruling U.S. companies and individuals, who have filed about 2,500 claims totaling an estimated $3 billion, will have to take their cases to the international tribunal established under the terms of the agreement.

The *Journal*'s editorial of July 10, 1981, remained steadfast in its opposition to the Court's decision.

As we have said before, such abuses of U.S. law and procedures, not to mention pocketbooks, seem to us overly generous toward the Tehran barbarians. The U.S. has no moral obligation to live up to such an onerous deal made at the point of a gun. It's too bad that the Reagan administration didn't take our original advice and renounce it.

On the following Saturday 100 banks around the country transferred almost $2 billion of Iranian assets to the Federal Reserve Bank of New York. By July 19 $1 billion of this amount would go directly to Iran, the remaining $1 billion to a special escrow account at a foreign central bank.

David Stockman, President Reagan's director of the Office of Management and Budget, apparently had limitless power over the nation's economic policies and the federal budget.

Stockman's supply-side economics and neoconservatism were, and still are, strongly influenced by *Wall Street Journal* editorials. In the late 1970s Stockman spent a great deal of time with Republican Congressman Jack Kemp of New York. Kemp, in turn, introduced Stockman to Dr. Arthur Laffer, the supply-side innovator, and Laffer's speech writer, Jude Wanniski, a one-time Dow Jones writer.

As Wanniski was completing the manuscript for his book on supply-side economics, *The Way the World Works,* he permitted Stockman to take an advance look at his work. Says Wanniski, "We were plotting and scheming how to take over economic policy." Even then it was obvious that the person chosen to head the Office of Management and Budget would have direct access to President-elect Reagan and would serve as a virtual deputy president. Stockman was not himself seeking the position, but he expected to have some say in the selection.

After the 1980 election a task force was rushed to Ronald Reagan's Pacific Palisades home to prepare the agenda for the first 100 days of his administration. Stockman, working with Kemp and others, wrote a twenty-three-page report, "Avoiding a G.O.P. Economic Dunkirk," which included a plea to the President to declare a national "economic emergency."

The President was impressed with Stockman's work and was ideologically supportive of the economic report. In December, 1980, Wanniski slipped a copy of it to Leonard Silk, economics reporter for the *New York Times*. The result was the first news column that not only hinted at Reagan's economic mission but also brought Stockman's name to public attention. As Wanniski puts it, "It elevated Stockman to a pivotal force."

Jude Wanniski attended a dinner honoring David Stockman in New York City a few days before President-elect Reagan took office. The occasion was designed to woo the Wall Street establishment. Among those present was another neoconservative, Robert L. Bartley, editor of *The Wall Street Journal*.

Bartley's influence with the new administration was destined to be significant. In the early 1970s he had put forth a set of drastic remedies for the inflation and unemployment that were spreading across the nation. He favored shifting individuals and firms into lower tax brackets, adjusting tax rates to inflation, dismantling federal regulations, returning to a convertible currency, and finding a way to restrict the money supply.

Today much of this economic philosophy is packaged as "supply-side economics," and Bartley's influence is becoming increasingly strong in Washington. One of his colleagues, Paul Craig Roberts, left his position as associate editor of the *Journal*'s editorial page to become Assistant Secretary of the Treasury in Reagan's cabinet. (In the winter of 1982, Roberts resigned his Treasury post to accept the William E. Simon Chair for Political Economy at the Georgetown University Center for Strategic and International Studies.) The *Washington Post* reported that ". . . others in the *Journal*'s inner circle of guest writers are playing important roles in the early stages of the Reagan administration's economic planning."

Bartley admits that he owes most of his economic ideology to his former employee, Jude Wanniski. The editor hired Wanniski, former Washington columnist for *The National Observer*, shortly after he took over the editorial page in 1972. Wanniski, the son of a Pennsylvania coal miner, grew up in Brooklyn, New York, and was educated at Brooklyn College and the University of California. Says Bartley, "Jude had a tremendous influence over the tone and direction of the page. He taught me the power of the outrageous."

In addition Wanniski began to educate Bartley about the radical economic theories of his friend Arthur B. Laffer, whom Wanniski had known in Washington when Laffer was chief economist at the Office of Management and Budget. Laffer, a classical economist, had long rejected the monetarism approach of Milton Friedman and found little to praise in the theories of John Maynard Keynes, which encouraged government spending to keep the economy healthy.

Laffer had little support among his fellow economists, but he had the complete support of Jude Wanniski. From his Dow Jones office Jude would telephone Laffer at the University of Chicago every morning at 10 A.M. to review the day's events with his mentor, then pass them along to Bob Bartley.

Wall Street Journal editorials began to echo Laffer's projections. In December, 1974, for instance, Wanniski wrote a lengthy editorial extolling the concepts of Robert Mundell, a Canadian economist and collaborator of Arthur Laffer. Mundell was urging a policy of extremely tight money combined with tax reductions. "Nobody understood what he was talking about," recalls Bartley. "I thought it was a little wacky myself." (Several years later President Carter incorporated the tight money policy, and President Reagan announced the tax cut to go along with it.)

Bartley gradually began to give space to an assortment of experts who supported his and Wanniski's views on the economy. There was Arthur Laffer, of course, his fellow supply-sider Dr. Norman B. Ture, until July 1, 1982, Under Secretary for Tax and Economic Affairs, and businessman Lewis Lehrman, an outspoken advocate of the gold standard. (Lehrman had helped Jack Kemp and David Stockman prepare the twenty-three-page preinaugural report to President Reagan.) George Gilder, author of the bestseller *Wealth and Poverty,* and Irving Kristol, editor of *The Public Interest,* were enlisted to explain the new conservative economics to readers.

Meanwhile Wanniski, who had started it all, began to lose favor

305

with some of the senior management at Dow Jones. Company policy on conflict of interest discourages reporters' involvement, directly or indirectly, in government activities. In 1975 Wanniski lobbied President Gerald Ford's advisor Donald Rumsfeld to persuade the administration to abandon its 5 percent surtax plan. The following year, while in Atlanta, the reporter tried to convince President-elect Jimmy Carter's staff of the benefits of supply-side economics. In 1978 Wanniski violated the rules of the firm for the last time by handing out political leaflets for New Jersey senatorial candidate Jeffrey Bell. Soon after that Wanniski resigned to become a private consultant and, eventually, a member of President Reagan's inner circle of advisors.

On August 13, 1981, Reagan signed into law two of the most far-reaching domestic economic measures since the New Deal, thus inheriting responsibility for the fate of the economy.

One bill provided the largest tax cut in this century and the other authorized the sharpest cutbacks in domestic spending in five decades. Together they represent, said the President, "A turnaround of almost a half a century of a course this country has been on. . . . They mark an end to the excessive growth in government bureaucracy and government spending and government taxing."

Bob Bartley was and is aware that the basic question is whether this experiment in economics will work. If, as he and others have promised, it produces vibrant growth and lower inflation, conservative Republican policies will probably sweep the nation. If it fails, producing still larger budget deficits and deepening recession, it will be a major defeat for both Reagan and his leading supporters at *The Wall Street Journal*.

A lead story, "The Education of David Stockman," appeared in the December, 1981, *Atlantic Monthly*. It offered, with ample quotations from budget director Stockman, a stunning confession that the Reagan administration's vaunted economic policy cannot work. Moreover, Stockman admitted, the White House knows it.

In the November 16 "Review & Outlook" editorial, the *Journal* angrily defended Stockman:

The chop-licking over David Stockman's outburst of candor in *The Atlantic Monthly* has been disgraceful. . . . Congress's collective toe has been smarting for some time getting stepped on in Mr. Stockman's drive to cut spending. . . . About David Stockman, let it be said that he got far more expenditure restraint than most budget directors or budget committee chairmen have before turning, as all of them invariably have, to leading the drive for higher taxes. . . .

In private Bob Bartley defends his own stand on Reagonomics in more temperate terms: "I think these are very important ideas. . . . But I couldn't give you any guarantee that they'll work. Maybe they won't. I just can't see anything else on the horizon."

The young editor may be mellowing as he approaches middle age.

19

Phillips at the Helm

Bullish Wall Street Journal Is Largest Daily in U.S.
Headline, New York Times,
January 3, 1980

WARREN PHILLIPS, chairman and chief executive officer of Dow Jones, is the son of a New York garment worker. He was born on June 28, 1926, and graduated from high school a few weeks before his fifteenth birthday. Phillips served in the Army during World War II and then earned a degree in economics at New York's Queens College.

Rejected by Columbia University's Graduate School of Journalism, Phillips joined *The Wall Street Journal* as a proofreader. He was soon promoted to copyreader and later switched desks to write the "What's News" column. In 1949, after failing to land an overseas assignment, Phillips quit the *Journal* for a job with the Armed Forces paper, *Stars and Stripes,* in Germany. He continued to contribute to the *Journal* on a free-lance basis, and after a few months managed to get himself rehired as its German correspondent.

In 1950, Phillips was named chief of the London bureau, covering such stories as Europe's recovery under the Marshall Plan and Winston Churchill's return to power. He returned to New York a year later and was successively foreign editor, news editor, managing editor of the Midwest edition, and (in 1957) managing editor of the *Journal*. Phillips was recognized as a man with dual abilities: He was both a first-rate journalist and a skilled executive. "Every managing editor has his own talents," claims a former Dow Jones executive. "Warren stood out mostly for his organizational and administrative ability. Others may have been more brilliant newsmen but were lousy administrators."

Phillips's achievements were recognized both in and out of Dow Jones. In January, 1959, the U.S. Junior Chamber of Commerce named him one of America's ten outstanding young men of 1958. The list also included twenty-four-year-old singer Pat Boone and thirty-five-year-old Dr. Henry Kissinger.

After eight and a half years as the *Journal*'s managing editor, Warren Phillips became executive editor and, in 1970, vice president and general manager. His climb to the top was hastened when Vermont C. Royster, the *Journal*'s editor and the firm's senior vice president, retired at the age of fifty-seven. Phillips was named editorial director of Dow Jones & Company on January 11, 1971. A little over a year later, on March 15, 1972, he became executive vice president of the company, succeeding the late Buren H. McCormack. Eight months after that William Kerby became chairman of the board and Phillips was named president, a director, and a member of the executive committee of Dow Jones & Company.

Phillips succeeded Kerby as chief executive officer on March 19, 1975, but retained his title as president. When Bill Kerby retired at the end of that year after forty-five years with Dow Jones, the fifty-year-old Phillips assumed the additional title of chairman of the board.

A slim, dapper man with a precise manner, Warren Phillips is credited with being the primary architect of the company's diversification efforts. He is lauded by analysts and financial observers as an accessible and candid spokesman who has substantially improved his company's image.

But Phillips is not without his critics. One, Ben Bagdikian, who teaches at the University of California, Berkeley, Graduate School of Journalism, says, "With growth has come managerial efficiency instead of individuality." In Bagdikian's opinion, management at Dow Jones has tightened its control over stories, making the newspaper less of a "reporter's paper" with personal touches and imaginative writing, and more of an "editor's paper," preoccupied with efficiency. "With the growing competition in business reporting," says Bagdikian, "the *Journal* is becoming more conventional in the manner of bureaucracies and others who want to play it safe."

Phillips flatly rejects this evaluation. He insists that he is aware of the shortcomings of bureaucratic control and is quick to remind his critics that he regularly meets with staffers and makes it a point to visit every *Journal* bureau at regular intervals.

Many professionals argue that the *Journal* fails to mirror the full range of business activities, pressing hard in some areas and tiptoeing around certain others. One in particular: the tendency of banking and industry to form agglomerations. Ben Bagdikian wrote:

Yet like all other major media in the U.S. the *Journal* avoids systematic examination of the larger question, the impact of giantism on the economy. Its reporting rarely permits a glimpse of the concept that dominant corporations, as much, if not more, than government, inhibit a truly "free marketplace."

Los Angeles Times writer A. Kent MacDougall, a *Journal* reporter from 1960 to 1970, says:

I would make the point that the *Journal*'s sins are of omission rather than commission. It does not tell with any consistency how businessmen really do business. It does more than any other paper but it doesn't get to the heart of what business is. . . . The *Journal* points to rotten apples in the barrel, but when it comes to oligopolistic capitalism as it has evolved in the United States, it does not stand outside the system and look at it with detached perspective. It doesn't have to be a critic's perspective, just an outsider's perspective, the way journalism is supposed to be.

Most of the criticism from former and present staff members at Dow Jones centers around the paper's failure to cover what they believe to be the most vital issue of our times—the concentration of control by multinational banks and corporations, which manage to circumvent the free marketplace system.

Shortly after becoming chairman, Warren Phillips began his fight to liberate reporters from government attempts to limit the freedom of the press. He sees a direct threat to future investigative reporting as a result of increased pressures from judges to make reporters divulge their confidential source. The issue, as Phillips sees it, is "whether, by limiting what is published, we are going to let the government deprive the public of much of what it should know."

One of the most powerful branches of the U.S. government—the Securities and Exchange Commission—has usually been a friend of the *Journal*. But when the thin line defining a reporter's license to serve society is drawn, the relationship becomes strained.

On May 19, 1975, the commission received an appeal from Dow Jones & Company and Ken Bacon, one of its reporters, stemming from the denial of a request for access to investigatory records compiled in the course of the commission's investigation of Phillips Petroleum Company. That investigation resulted in the filing of an injunctive action against Phillips Petroleum and four individuals in which orders of permanent injunction by consent were obtained against all defendants.

In essence the federal agency's complaint alleged that Phillips Petroleum had violated the Securities Exchange Act by filing with the commission certain reports and by soliciting proxies from shareholders of Phillips by means of proxy material that failed to disclose that the defendants and others had created a secret fund of corporate monies to be used for illegal political contributions and other unlawful purposes.

In the Dow Jones appeal the commission's attention was directed to the fact that the enforcement action filed against Phillips Petroleum and others in March, 1975, had been completed and that this distinguished the case from others in which the agency had withheld investigatory records. However, the critical fact was not that orders of permanent injunction had been entered against the defendants in one particular enforcement action, but that the commission's inquiry was continuing. While the commission agreed with Dow Jones's contention that complete disclosure of the nature and extent of the illegal use of corporate monies is in the public interest, it was to protect the company from such disclosure that access to the commission's investigatory records was denied at that time.

Arguments based on the Freedom of Information Act did not help

Dow Jones's lawyers. The primary reason given for denying reporter Bacon access to the investigatory records of Phillips Petroleum was that disclosure of the commission's file, or any portions thereof, would hamper their enforcement proceedings. The records were therefore exempt from compelled disclosure. The commission also argued that disclosure of the records might tend to deprive the subjects of the investigation, who might be named in further proceedings by the agency, "of a right to a fair trial or an impartial adjudication," and could "constitute an invasion of personal privacy" of persons who were investigated but not named in the commission's enforcement action.

George A. Fitzsimmons, appeals secretary for the SEC, wrote: "Accordingly, IT IS ORDERED that the request of Dow Jones & Co., Inc., and Ken Bacon for access to the investigatory records relating to Phillips Petroleum Company be, and it hereby is, denied."

In the next SEC docket Fitzsimmons responded to another Dow Jones appeal. On May 22, 1975, Byron Calame, then bureau manager for the *Journal* in Pittsburgh, appealed to the agency under the Freedom of Information Act to reverse the denial of his request for access to preliminary proxy material filed by Gulf Oil prior to their 1974 and 1975 annual shareholder meetings, along with any related correspondence.

The SEC acceded to Calame's request, but there was one catch: The information would not be made available until ten days after Gulf was notified of the commission's intention to do so and a copy of their appeal decision furnished to the company.

It was a victory of sorts, but ten-day-old news was not much use to Byron Calame.

The Securities and Exchange Commission maintains that most of its leads to possible violations come from complaints by the investing public. This category is followed by leads resulting from the agency's routine and special examination program for broker-dealers, investment advisors, and investment companies. "Next, there are three categories of leads which appear to be of roughly equal importance," says Ira H. Pearce, special counsel for the SEC. "These are information obtained from the news media, the commission's market surveillance program, and information supplied by informants."

Wall Street Journal and *Barron's* reporters dismiss the SEC's contention that the news media are only minor contributors to the caseload of fraud, bribery, and other violations the agency handles. Warren Phillips recalls with pride Dow Jones's role in alerting the SEC to the Equity Funding, GeoTek, and Home-Stake swindles.

SEC counsel Pearce attempts to set the record straight:

While it is very difficult to state with any great degree of accuracy the percentage of leads to violative activity coming from the news media, it is probably reasonable to estimate that approximately 10 percent of the commission's recent cases originated solely or in part on the basis of information obtained from the news media. However, it is not possible to make any informed estimate as to the percentage of such leads that come from any particular newspaper because our records are not maintained in such a way as to make that information readily available. The commission's home office routinely monitors the major financial publications throughout the country, and each of the commission's fifteen regional and branch offices monitor the local financial publications in their respective geographic areas. As a result, the home office and each of the regional offices has initiated one or more investigations as a result of leads which came to their attention in whole or in part from information obtained in the news media.

One of Warren Phillips's earliest moves as chairman was the appointment of Ray Shaw as president and director of Dow Jones & Company. Shaw also assumed the duties of chief operating officer.

An intense, no-nonsense man, Ray Shaw was an Associated Press reporter and editor until Warren Phillips brought him to the *Journal* as a rewrite man in 1960. Oklahoma City born and Oklahoma University educated, Shaw moved up the corporate ladder rapidly, first as page-one editor, next as a reporter covering stories on advertising and marketing, then as department head of the "Business Bulletin" column. In 1963 he was transferred to the Dallas bureau as managing editor of the newspaper's Southwest edition.

When Dow Jones and the Associated Press established their financial news service for overseas subscribers in 1966, Shaw became the wire's managing editor. In 1971 he became assistant general manager of Dow Jones, went on to fill a number of slots in the management hierarchy, and was named executive vice president in November, 1977. Under a reorganization plan in 1979, Warren Phillips relin-

313

quished the title of president, and Ray Shaw was elevated to the post.

As president, Shaw has full responsibility for the operation of the company. This includes acquisitions, new products and services, marketing, and a host of other activities. Among Ray Shaw's challenges are keeping up with the technological advances that will make Dow Jones's operations more efficient and cost-effective, monitoring potential threats from rival companies, continuing to increase the *Journal*'s marketing position and regional flexibility, and keeping abreast of readership demands at a time when the market for his firm's services is growing at twice the rate of the general population.

On New Year's Eve, 1979, Ray Shaw circulated to all Dow Jones employees the company's updated "Conflicts of Interest Policy." Few organizations, including other newspapers, place such restrictions on their employees, demand such caution when dealing with the outside world, or emphasize so strongly the dangers inherent in even a hint of wrongdoing.

The policy statement incorporates guidelines for complying with the Foreign Corrupt Practices Act, for serving on government advisory and corporate boards, and participating in civic, charitable, and political organizations. Its sole aim: "building and maintaining our Company's reputation for trust."

Any code of ethics is only as good as its enforcement. The management of the company is diligent about carrying out its responsibilities on this score. Conflicts of interest are also taken into account when it comes to appointing directors. Dow Jones has to be on the alert that the members of its governing board do not pose a threat to its objectivity.

For example, Coca-Cola's powerful past chairman and chief executive officer, J. Paul Austin, was a director of Dow Jones & Company until 1981. Executives at Dow Jones felt that this was a safe appointment since there seemed little likelihood of a link between publishing and soft drinks.

When John Huey and John Koten, reporters for the *Journal* in Atlanta, wrote a series on the corporate battles going on inside Coca-Cola, they clearly identified Austin's ties with Dow Jones in each article in the series. They also uncovered some dramatic pieces of information that angered most officials at the giant corporation.

Most newspapers depend on corporate advertising for a large share of their revenues. Ray Shaw is keenly aware that this leaves them open to the suspicion that they may be guilty of conflicts of interest. At a Magazine Publishers Association symposium in New York not long ago consumer advocate Ralph Nader was asked: Is not the press at least implicitly dependent on advertising and therefore on big corporations?

Shaw was delighted that Nader's reply included this remark:

. . . the press that has prospered the most in terms of quality of its reporting is the press that has sought to give the public the facts no matter where they may fall. And the leading example of this is *The Wall Street Journal* which could have become just a business pap sheet in the early '40s and late '30s and instead has become the leading reporter on business irresponsibilities, as well as straight financial reporting, in the country.

In 1978 *The Wall Street Journal* assigned a correspondent to get a job at Texas Instruments, Inc., to find out how the company thwarted union organizers and kept its wages low. On learning what had happened, the firm's officials were so furious that they sent a senior vice president to New York to try and kill the story. The editors not only refused, they decided to run the story earlier than they had originally planned.

Pressure from public relations representatives is a constant problem at *The Wall Street Journal*. PR people generally have one of two objectives: getting favorable coverage for their clients or suppressing information that would make the clients look bad.

The general feeling in the *Journal*'s newsroom is anti-PR, and particularly some of the PR agencies. Writing in *The Corporate Communications Report,* editor Richard Blodgett said:

There are also some specific rules at the *Journal* that tend to inhibit a PR man's role. Reporters are forbidden to use information in agency-prepared press releases without first checking the facts back with the company itself. And when it comes to dealing with internal PR men, *Journal* reporters are allowed to accept their answers on factual material but are expected in most cases to get any further explanation from an operative executive.

315

Journal reporters detest public relations people who (1) waste their time on minor stories; (2) won't permit journalists to meet with operating officials; (3) send out press releases late in the afternoon; (4) distribute numerous copies of the same release; and (5) send photographs, knowing full well the *Journal* doesn't use pictures.

On the other hand *Journal* writers tend to be hospitable toward PR representatives who keep them abreast of events in the industry, inform them of future annual meetings, executive retirements, and the like, and keep their distance when they have no information to offer.

A former *Journal* reporter, Richard Blodgett suggests that a company can score points by making its economist and other key officials available on a no-quotation basis to give a journalist accurate insights into industry developments.

Blodgett's "Ten Commandments for Dealing with Dow Jones" are:

1. Know which reporter is assigned to follow your company, and never seek to bypass him and deal with somebody else.
2. Be alert to any possibility for a Dow Jones interview. These are the interviews that appear on the ticker and, in many cases, in the next morning's *Wall Street Journal*. Reporters are required to produce a certain number of them, and often they are grateful if you offer to make your chief executive available for one.
3. Be cooperative but not pushy. *Journal* reporters are trained to look down on pushy or uninformed PR men.
4. Allow the reporter to deal directly with your company's operating executives when he wants. If he can never get by the PR manager, he will end up thinking that you are making it unnecessarily difficult to cover your company or that you have something to hide.
5. Be alert to solid industry stories in which your company might be mentioned positively. You should have no qualms about submitting a brief memo to the reporter outlining your story idea.
6. Be aware of why Monday is the best day to release news and Thursday and Friday the worst days.
7. Get your releases out as early in the day as possible. If you expect a late-breaking story, try to let the reporter know in advance that something will be coming.
8. Don't threaten reprisals when you feel you've been wronged. Reporters

don't care if you yank your ads. If a clearly inaccurate statement has been made in the paper, the *Journal* will print a correction on request.

9. Have patience with young reporters. The *Journal* has long preferred to train neophytes rather than take on experienced hands. The advantage is that younger reporters tend to be less expensive and more aggressive. The disadvantage is that they occasionally don't know what they're doing.

10. Be aware that you may be able to hoodwink a young reporter but that it is self-defeating in the long run. While young reporters can be gullible, their work is reviewed by hard-nosed editors who have been around a long time. These editors don't forget easily if they think you are trying to put one over on them.

As an eleventh commandment Blodgett suggests ". . . the best way to get Dow Jones to print a news announcement quickly is to say you're releasing it to Reuters in ten or fifteen minutes."

Two key people at Dow Jones & Company are Paula Jameson and Peter Kann. One is and the other was assistant to the chairman of the board. Kann, Warren Phillips's heir apparent, was given the title in March, 1979. The following September, at the age of thirty-six, he was named associate publisher of the *Journal*. In announcing the appointment Phillips said: "Ray Shaw, President of Dow Jones, and I are delegating to him the authority to act on our behalf in working with the *Journal*'s news and sales department heads and staffs in the continuing efforts to strengthen the paper." Later that year Peter Robert Kann also became vice president of Dow Jones & Company.

Paula Jameson was named assistant to the chairman of the board at the beginning of 1981. She had practiced law in the District of Columbia and Fairfax County, Virginia, before joining Dow Jones's legal staff in 1977, becoming house counsel two years later. Her present job is somewhat all-encompassing, but essentially she's concerned with finding ways to make her boss's life less hectic.

Dow Jones's Reorganization

The year 1980 began with a newly restructured Dow Jones management, marking a transition from a mostly "vertical" structure, with authority divided primarily along functional lines—news, production, administration, for instance—to a "horizontal" structure organized for the most part around product lines.

The company is now divided into seven principal operating groups headed by senior executives who have the title of president and/or publisher or associate publisher of their respective operating groups. These executives also carry the corporate titles they had prior to the reorganization. They report to Ray Shaw, president and chief operating officer, and Warren Phillips, chairman and chief executive officer, and are assisted by staff executives in areas such as finance, legal, planning, and public affairs. Beneath the operating-group heads are other key executives, some of whom carry the title of vice president of their operating group (as distinguished from vice president of the corporation).

The seven operating groups are: *The Wall Street Journal,* Community Newspapers (Ottaway Newspapers, Inc.), Books (Richard D. Irwin, Inc.), International, Magazines, Information Services, and Operating Services.

In explaining the reasons for the reorganization Warren Phillips said:

One purpose is to give responsibility for the planning, decision-making and interdepartment coordination of each publication or service to the operating executives directly involved. By giving them this responsibility for their total enterprise, we hope to make their jobs broader and more challenging, and to enlarge their future managerial skills.

A second purpose is to clear up some of the organizational ambiguities—some duplications of responsibility and confused reporting lines, for example—that have grown up as we have expanded.

Until 1970 *The Wall Street Journal* accounted for about 94 percent of Dow Jones's net income. Responsibility for integrating operations across functional and departmental lines lay with a few top executives. Now, with the growth of community newspapers, books, news services, and other lines of business, the *Journal* accounts for about 60 percent of the company's profits. Thus, says Phillips, "It makes less sense for the same few key people to handle the interdepartment coordination and key decision-making for each of these many activities."

Other Key People

DONALD MACDONALD

Reporting directly to Warren Phillips is Donald A. Macdonald, vice chairman and director of Dow Jones & Company. A native of Union City, New Jersey, Macdonald earned both his B.S. and his M.B.A. at New York University. He worked briefly for the Royal Exchange Assurance Company and the Pacific Fire Insurance Company, served in the Army, and was discharged with the rank of captain in 1946. After the war he took a job at Olson Electric, Inc. In 1953 Macdonald placed an ad in *The Wall Street Journal,* and a few days later he was invited to become one of the newspaper's sales representatives. Within two years he was manager of the New England and Canadian territory, working out of Boston. He served successively as Eastern edition advertising manager, executive advertising manager, and Dow Jones advertising director. In 1967 he was named a member of the company's management committee.

Macdonald, Dow Jones's self-styled advertising "guru," was until recently concerned about *Book Digest.*

Founded in 1973, *Book Digest* became one of the fastest growing magazines in the nation. By March of 1978 its circulation was more than one million. Dow Jones acquired *Book Digest* in 1978 for slightly more than $10 million cash. The magazine was formerly owned by several interests, including the company's founders, John J. Veronis, president; Martin L. Gross, editor; and Peter Veronis, publisher.

Was it a wise investment? *Book Digest* had an after-tax operating loss of $2.4 million in 1979, compared with a loss of about $1 million in the last five months of 1978. The monthly magazine has been a consistent money loser. Dow Jones reported a decrease of 12 percent in its third quarter 1981 net income, reflecting a sharp writedown in the book value of *Book Digest* following a $1.7-million projected loss for the year. For the entire year 1981, Dow Jones took a $9.4 million write-off on the magazine.

Determined to head off disaster, Macdonald reduced selectively the magazine's circulation from one million to 400,000, changing it from a magazine of broad popular appeal to one with a targeted audience of better-educated, higher-income readers.

319

"It's a positive move because it will give us control over the magazine's demographics, which we haven't been particularly pleased with," said Macdonald. To enhance this control, and "to eliminate problems arising from divided authority," Dow Jones repurchased the 20-percent interest that had been acquired by *Reader's Digest* in January, 1980.

Another of Macdonald's steps was to reduce *Book Digest*'s advertising rate from $10,000 for a black-and-white page to $4,000. Peter Veronis, one of the magazine's founders, left, and editor Martin Gross turned over the reins after publication of the May, 1981, issue.

Book Digest operated as a division rather than a subsidiary of Dow Jones & Company. Raymond Sokolov succeeded Gross as editor-in-chief of the magazine. A Harvard graduate and a Fulbright scholar at Oxford, Sokolov was formerly book review editor for *Newsweek,* food and restaurant editor of the *New York Times,* restaurant editor for *New York* magazine, and a columnist for *Natural History* and *Inside Sports.*

Following a failed attempt to find a buyer for *Book Digest,* publication of the magazine ceased after release of its June 1982 issue.

Macdonald also maintains loose control over *Barron's* and with vice president Ed Cony makes policy and oversees the international group, which includes *The Asian Wall Street Journal, The Asian Wall Street Journal Weekly,* the international air edition of the *Journal,* Dow Jones International Marketing Services, and other ventures and investments overseas.

Macdonald, on September 10, 1979, launched the "international air edition." It is distributed throughout Europe, providing timely business reading to a select audience not otherwise reachable on a daily basis by any other Dow Jones publication. The international air edition is actually the Eastern edition stripped of Eastern edition advertising. It contains fourteen or fifteen pages of news and a maximum of four pages of advertising aimed at *Journal* readers in Europe.

Prior to the introduction of the international air edition, the Eastern edition had a circulation of 5,400 in Europe. The new edition was designed to cut air freight costs by reducing the weight of newspapers sent to Europe. By 1981 the air edition, which is also available in the Middle East, had a circulation of over 6,500. (The international air edition will be absorbed by a new edition, *The European Wall Street Journal,* scheduled for publication in 1983.)

EDWARD CONY

Edward Cony joined the *Journal* in 1953 as a reporter in the San Francisco bureau. A graduate of Reed College in Oregon, he has an M.A. in journalism from Stanford University. After San Francisco, he worked in Los Angeles, Jacksonville, and New York. He won a Pulitzer Prize for his 1960 story on Prudential Life Insurance president Carrol Shanks's questionable dealings with Georgia Pacific Corporation.

In 1964 Cony was named assistant managing editor of the *Journal*'s Pacific Coast edition (now the Western edition), and the following year became managing editor of *The Wall Street Journal* succeeding Warren Phillips. He was named executive editor of Dow Jones publications and news services in 1970, vice president of Dow Jones in 1972, and vice president/news in 1977.

Cony played a leading part in starting *The Asian Wall Street Journal* in late 1976 and *The Asian Wall Street Journal Weekly* in 1979 and in negotiating acquisition of minority interests in newspapers in Singapore and Malaysia. He continues to take an interest in the *Journal*'s news coverage as a member of the management committee, but he is primarily occupied with the international publications and certain domestic news operations of *Barron's* and the Dow Jones News Service.

GEORGE FLYNN

When Donald Macdonald, former senior vice president, was elected vice chairman as part of the management reorganization, George Flynn was named senior vice president.

Flynn, now in his late fifties, began learning the printing trade as a boy in Elizabethtown, Illinois. He later studied publications management at the University of Illinois School of Journalism.

Flynn joined Dow Jones in Chicago as assistant production manager in 1956, and later that year held the same position in Washington, D.C. In 1957 he was transferred to Dallas as production manager of the Southwest edition. In 1958 he was named production manager of the *Journal*'s Midwest edition in Chicago, became assistant to the national production manager, then moved to Riverside, California, as production manager of the Pacific Coast edition, where he was responsible for starting up the *Journal*'s pioneering microwave facsimile operations between San Francisco and Riverside.

In 1963 Flynn moved to the New York office as national production manager, and in 1966 was named business manager of Dow Jones. He filled several different vice presidential positions, and when Dow Jones was reorganized into seven operating groups, Flynn became president of the affiliated companies group, responsible for the Ottaway newspapers, Dow Jones's newsprint mills, and Richard D. Irwin, Inc., a book publishing firm that had merged with Dow Jones & Company in July, 1975. Irwin, which specializes in books on business and economics, has its headquarters in Homewood, Illinois. By 1980 its yearly earnings were more than $5 million.

In July, 1980, the Dow Jones Books division (established in 1964) was consolidated into Dow Jones-Irwin to strengthen the company's book publishing and marketing interests and streamline operations by eliminating duplication of services.

BETTY DUVAL

With all its sophisticated technologies, worldwide outlets, and impressive profits, Dow Jones remains a relatively small company. Fewer than 5,000 employees work in 229 locations around the globe. This constitutes one of the firm's greatest challenges. It is essential to be aware of individual needs, productivity, job satisfaction, and potential for advancement. The person who keeps track of these things is Betty A. Duval, who joined Dow Jones in December, 1980, as vice president/staff development.

Duval came to Dow Jones after twenty-three years at General Foods, where she was involved in development, organizational planning and human resources. To get a handle on her new job, she rode delivery trucks at four in the morning and sat behind the copy desk just before deadline. "Because of the nature of our products, we get a lot of quantitative data on circulation, linage, and the like that tell us how we're doing," says Duval. "We need the same type of feed-back between managers and individuals, and it has to be two-way feedback."

Consideration for personnel has seldom been a priority at Dow Jones. In 1979 one longtime bureau chief was called to New York for what appeared to be a routine meeting. Instead he was told by the managing editor: "I don't think things are working out. You're going to have to leave."

Another episode, still talked about at 22 Cortlandt Street, revolved around preventing Dow Jones staffers from practicing what they believed to be their constitutional rights. At the time of the first Vietnam moratorium in the fall of 1969, several *Journal* reporters asked that the DJ ticker be suspended for one minute, as their way of protesting American involvement in Vietnam. Management refused. The reporters then requested time off to march in a moratorium parade.

They were spotted carrying signs in the *Journal*'s logotype saying: "We are Wall Street Journalists." Warren Phillips and Ed Cony were furious. They didn't fire anyone, but they expressed strong misgivings about the use of the logo and about their employees marching in political demonstrations. At the second moratorium in Washington several reporters from the *Journal* marched, this time without signs.

There are other areas of friction between management and staff. A veteran subeditor observes that the senior people at 22 Cortlandt Street have "read the management manual for industry and are applying them to the newsroom."

Clearly Warren Phillips is aware of the problems. Betty Duval's presence is a step toward correcting them.

The Competition

Dow Jones would rather not think about competition, but its executives are smart enough to know that it can't be ignored. That's why they're keeping their eyes on *The Economist,* the 139-year-old British weekly that now boasts an American edition.

In just ten years the North American *Economist* has quadrupled its circulation, which is now about 50,000 in the United States. The regular edition sells about 150,000 in Great Britain, the British Commonwealth, and elsewhere around the world.

Although the *Economist*'s format differs greatly from that of *Barron's,* Dow Jones's financial weekly, both publications offer comprehensive reports of the week's events, with dispatches from all over the globe emphasizing business and economic news. They also feature technical reports and charts on such subjects as the interaction of inflation and exchange rates in the European monetary system.

As Americans increase their interest in foreign financial matters, *The Economist* stands a good chance of boosting its U.S. circulation. The magazine currently has nine full-time foreign reporters, four of them in the United States, and a string of part-timers in major cities around the world.

Although *Barron's* has its own staff, it can also turn to *Wall Street Journal* reporters when necessary. So, too, *The Economist* has *The Financial Times* of London, a half-owner in the magazine, to fall back on.

The Economist is available on Mondays. Film is flown in from London each Thursday. It is reproduced by offsetting in the R. R. Donnelley plant in Stamford, Connecticut.

At present *The Economist*'s U.S. sales are a mere one-fifth of *Barron's,* but, says David Gordon, managing director of the British weekly, "We think that we have in North America a very great potential for increasing circulation. We expect to reach more and more of the same kind of top people in the United States as we reach here and elsewhere."

In addition, the daily *Financial Times* continues to press hard on *The Wall Street Journal,* with its 255 specialist journalists and 18 foreign bureaus around the world, three times as many foreign offices as the *Journal* has. Printed in Frankfurt, Germany, the international *Financial Times* leaves for New York on a 4 a.m. flight each day.

Dow Jones executives must be listening.

Closer to home, the nation's largest newspaper chain, the Gannett Company of Rochester, New York, will soon compete with the *Journal* by introducing its own "national" newspaper. Gannett already has more daily newspapers than any other publisher in the country—

eighty-eight located in thirty-seven states and two U.S. territories—as well as the highest total circulation, more than 3.7 million.

A subsidiary of the firm, GANSAT, Gannett Satellite Information Network, is planning a national general-interest newspaper that would be transmitted simultaneously to any or all of Gannett's printing facilities. On June 25, 1981, Gannett distributed prototypes of the paper, *USA Today,* to between 4,000 and 5,000 people. The forty-page working models, each arranged in four sections, make liberal use of bright colors and contain world and national stories, news briefs from various states, a roundup of editorial comments from a number of newspapers, plus sports features and scores. One prototype featured an eight-page "money" section with business stories and stock market listings, while another version had only two pages of financial news. By September, 1982, if all goes according to plan, one of these prototypes will go national.

GANSAT is also considering a strategy to transmit programs by satellite over local cable-television outlets, broadcasting news and stories collected from its newspapers, broadcasting facilities, and the Gannett New Service.

Still another source of competition for Dow Jones is the *New York Times.* Its national edition—a two-section version of the New York edition, printed in Chicago—was launched in August, 1980. In September, 1981, the company announced that it would begin printing the edition at a second location, Lakeland, Florida. This would enable the paper to expand its circulation in the Miami area and permit morning delivery to southeastern states. Publication began on November 2. The page images were transmitted from New York to Lakeland by satellite, and the initial press run was 15,000 copies on weekdays and 35,000 on Sundays.

Now, Number One

Each year about 19.1 billion pages of *The Wall Street Journal* are printed. Their total weight is about 108,000 metric tons, and if all the pages were laid end to end, they would stretch exactly 6,782,700 miles.

The newspaper's strong 1981 performance saw a 3.6 percent increase in circulation, ending the year at 2,000,456. Corporate earnings in 1981 increased 21.1 percent, from $58.8 million to $71,390,000.

Dow Jones & Company currently ranks 414th on the list of *Fortune* magazine's 500 largest U.S. industrial corporations. As the company expands its horizons, *The Wall Street Journal* is becoming less of a mainstay. In 1970, the *Journal* accounted for 94 percent of Dow Jones's net income. Ten years later the figure was 59.4 percent. Today only 5 percent of the company's 4,800 employees work exclusively on the *Journal*. And yet the paper is a remarkable success story.

On January 13, 1980, a *New York Times* headline proclaimed: "Bullish Wall Street Journal Is Largest Daily in U.S." Warren Phillips and his coworkers at the *Journal* took double pleasure in the milestone. Their paper had overtaken the *New York Daily News* to become number one in circulation, and its achievement was being recognized by another rival, the *New York Times*.

In 1982 Dow Jones & Company marked its hundredth anniversary. Satellite transmission, Asian editions, and women in management are only a few of the changes that have taken place since Charles Dow's and Edward Jones's day. The New England Baptist and the Connecticut Yankee would be amazed at most of them. They would also be gratified to know that despite its increased size and scope the company they founded still reflects their original commitment to "The Truth in its Proper Use."

Index

Abelson, Alan, 126, 132-137
  lawsuits concerning, 133-136
Abrams, Bill, 185
Ackell, Joseph, 214-215
Agnew, Spiro, 260, 292-293
Agriculture Department, U.S., 252
"A-heds," 161-162, 218
Allied Chemical, 50
Allied Crude Vegetable Oil Refining Corporation, 104-105
Allis, Sam, 184
Amazon Natural Drug Company, 177-178
American Agronomics Corporation, 133
American Bar Association, 114, 115
American Credit Indemnity Company, 252
American Express Company, 105
American Federation of Labor, 78
American Liberty League, 102
American Motors Corporation, 168-169
American Society of Newspaper Editors, 206
American Stock Exchange, 89, 187, 188
Anderson, John, 141
Anderson, Len, 183
Andrews, Julie, 262
Anreder, Steve, 124
AP (Associated Press), 156, 187, 232, 294
  Dow Jones partnership of, 235-236, 239
AP-Dow Jones Economic Report, 275
AP-Dow Jones News Service, 236, 242, 245, 281
  secret summit scoops of, 275-276
  special services of, 275
Argo Merchant, 148
Armour, Lawrence A., 123
Asian Wall Street Journal, 237-246, 320, 321
  development of, 236-239
  world news coverage by, 242-243
Asian Wall Street Journal Weekly, 244-246, 320, 321
AT&T (American Telephone and Telegraph Company), 22, 50, 206, 273-274
Atlantic Cable, 3
Atlantic Monthly, 306
Atlas Maritime Company, 266-269
Austin, J. Paul, 314

Avery International Corporation, 222
Ayer Award, 147

Bacon, Ken, 311
Badger, Sherwin C., 126
Bagdikian, Ben, 205-207, 309-310
Baker, Bobby, 93
Bancroft, Hugh, 45-60, 120
Bancroft, Jane, 45, 63
Bankers Report, 275
Bank of New York, 89
Barron, Clarence W., 9, 21-44
  background of, 21-22
  Barron's and, 120, 122-123
  "news rules" of, 39
  personal style of, 24-25, 41-44
  purchase of Dow Jones & Company by, 19
Barron's National Business and Financial Weekly, 39, 45-46, 120-137, 225, 262
  contests in, 122, 125
  controversial stories in, 130-133
  Depression era difficulties of, 124
  founding of, 120-121
  Nelson at, 120, 123-124
  Nemeroff suit against, 135-136
  promotion of, 121-123
  SafeCard suit against, 136-137
  Shea as editor of, 125-126
  statistics in, 128-130
  story development in, 130-131
  Telex suit against, 134-135
Bartley, Robert L., 197-213, 287, 299-307
  background of, 197
  editorial slant of, 201-204, 207
  Reagan's economic policies and, 301-307
Bato, 223
Beall, George, 292
Beebe, Lucius, 25
Belasco, Arnold, 211
Bell, Jeffrey, 306
Bergstresser, Charles M., 7, 14, 16, 19
Bettner, Jill, 192
Bleiberg, Bob, 126-137
  background of, 126-127
  editorial opinions of, 127-128

Index